D0075595

Thomas J. Sargent

Rational Expectations and Inflation

Rational Expectations
and Inflation

Rational Expectations and Inflation

Thomas J. Sargent
University of Minnesota

1817

HARPER & ROW, PUBLISHERS, New York
Cambridge, Philadelphia, San Francisco,
London, Mexico City, São Paulo, Singapore, Sydney

Business
HG
229
.S295
1986

To Anne

Sponsoring Editor: John Greenman
Project Editor: Ronni Strell
Cover Design: John Hite
Text Art: Reproduction Drawings Ltd.
Production: Debra L. Forrest
Compositor: The Clarinda Company
Printer and Binder: The Murray Printing Company

Rational Expectations and Inflation

Copyright © 1986 by Harper & Row, Publishers, Inc.

All rights reserved. Printed in the United States of America. No part of
this book may be used or reproduced in any manner whatsoever without
written permission, except in the case of brief quotations embodied in
critical articles and reviews. For information address Harper & Row,
Publishers, Inc., 10 East 53d Street, New York, NY 10022.

Library of Congress Cataloging in Publication Data
Sargent, Thomas J.
    Rational Expectations and inflation.
    1. Inflation (Finance)   2. Rational expectations
(Economic theory)   I. Title.
HG229.S295 1986   332.4'1   85–803
ISBN 0-06-045741-4

85 86 87 88 9 8 7 6 5 4 3 2 1

Contents

Introduction

During the last decade, the idea of rational expectations transformed macroeconomic theory. A simple intuition motivates this idea; namely, that people do not systematically ignore readily available information that could be used to improve their decisions. However, the initial applications of this idea in macroeconomic theory and econometrics have been technically demanding. The highly technical nature of this early work is not surprising, since this work itself grew out of the technical literatures on optimally controlling Keynesian macroeconometric models and on deriving optimal decision rules for the Keynesian categories of consumption, investment, and money demand. One consequence of the highly technical orientation of early work on rational expectations in macroeconomics is that an appreciation has been slow to develop for the relevance of the ideas for the practice of day-to-day macroeconomics. Rational expectations macroeconomics reasons with a new set of concepts and a new language. It is not simply proposing new answers to old questions but a new view about which questions are useful to ask. During the long period of dominance of Keynesian macroeconomic theory, there developed a broad body of practical experience in applying the theory quickly in informal contexts. Such experience created ease of application and communication, which were important ingredients in the practical success of Keynesian economics as an applied theory. One of the (legitimate) reasons for resistance to rational expectations ideas in macroeconomics has been that they are perceived as destroying the old language and tools of applied macroeconomics while providing no workable substitute.

My main reason for writing this book was to try my hand at putting rational expectations macroeconomics to work at an informal, noneconometric level in order to describe and interpret some recent and historical economic events. The events studied mainly involve periods of actual or threatened depreciation in the value of a country's currency and in which a government was interested in preventing that depreciation. To interpret these events, I have used a rational expectations theory of inflation. Besides being a phenomenon of great contemporary interest, the process of inflation has long been thought to be influenced by people's methods of forming expectations about inflation. Thus, the study of inflation provides a natural context for trying to apply rational expectations theories.

Two main ideas run throughout the text. The first is the principle of strategic interdependence, which holds that one person's pattern of behavior depends on the behavior patterns of those forming his environment. When behavior patterns of those forming a person's environment change, the individual can usually profit by adjusting his or her own behavior pattern. This principle, which is at the heart of rational expectations theory, was ignored under standard practice in Keynesian macroeconomics. One of the purposes of this text is to pursue the logical implications of this principle and to apply it repeatedly in interpreting a variety of episodes.

The second idea is that monetary and fiscal policies must be coordinated because the government faces a budget constraint. It follows that there is no "purely monetary" cure for inflation, if *purely monetary* means a policy that can be imposed by the central bank without any assistance from the taxing and spending authorities. This idea will guide our interpretation of the causes of the beginnings and endings of inflationary episodes.

The first chapter, "Rational Expectations and the Reconstruction of Macroeconomics," is an overview that describes some key ideas of rational expectations macroeconomics. This chapter describes in greater detail the role of informal historical studies relative to formal econometric ones. The second chapter, "Reaganomics and Credibility," elaborates the principle of strategic interdependence and applies it to interpret the struggle between monetary and fiscal policy that has occurred in the United States since 1981.

The next two chapters, "The Ends of Four Big Inflations" and "Stopping Moderate Inflations: The Methods of Poincaré and Thatcher," provide interpretations of economic policies and outcomes during several periods when rapid inflation was either occurring or thought to be threatening to occur. The chapter "Some Unpleasant Monetarist Arithmetic," written with Neil Wallace, explores some aspects of the coordination problem facing the monetary and fiscal authority. The unpleasant arithmetic alluded to in the title prevents the central bank from successfully fighting inflation by itself if the fiscal authority persists in running a net-of-interest budget deficit. The analytics of the monetary-fiscal coordination problem that are laid out in this chapter are used extensively in the other chapters.

The final chapter, "Speculations about the Speculation against the Hong Kong Dollar," was written with David Beers and Neil Wallace. It describes some recent events in Hong Kong involving the depreciation of the Hong Kong dollar. We think of the situation as one in which Hong Kong banks, being confronted with a situation in which many of their loans were threatening to go bad, found these bad loans turned into good ones when the central bank acted to depreciate the currency in which the loans and the banks' deposits were denominated. It requires only a little imagination to see the situation in Hong Kong as a microcosm of the international debt crisis. A depreciation of the U.S. dollar via inflation would go a long way toward "making good loans out of bad ones" in the countries now on the verge of technical default.

THOMAS J. SARGENT

chapter 1

Rational Expectations and the Reconstruction of Macroeconomics*

Fans of the National Football League may well have observed the following behavior by the Houston Oilers during the 19-- season. At home against Kansas City, when confronted with a fourth down in its own end of the field, Houston punted 100 percent of the time. The next week, at St. Louis, in the same situation, Houston punted 93 percent of the time. The following week at Oakland, again in that situation, Houston again punted 100 percent of the time, as it did the subsequent week at home against San Diego, and so on and on for the rest of the season. In short, on the basis of the time-series data, Houston has a tendency to punt on fourth downs in its own territory, no matter what team it plays or where.

Having observed this historical record, suppose it is our task to predict how Houston will behave in the future on fourth downs in its own territory. For example, suppose that next week Houston is to play an expansion team at Portland that it has never played before. It seems safe to predict that Houston will punt on fourth downs in its own

---

*This chapter is based on remarks prepared for the September 1980 International Symposium of the Hosei University in Tokyo, Japan.

territory at Portland. This sensible prediction is not based on any understanding of the game of football, but rather on simply extrapolating a past behavior pattern into the future.

In many cases, we would expect this method of prediction to work well. However, for precisely those cases in which predictions are most interesting, the extrapolative method can be expected to break down. For example, suppose that the commissioner of the National Football League announced a rule change, effective next Sunday, that gave a team six downs in which to make a first down. Would we still expect Houston to punt on fourth down? Clearly not; at least no one familiar with the game of football would.

What this example demonstrates is that historical patterns of human behavior often depend on the rules of the game in which people are participating. Since much human behavior is purposeful, it makes sense to expect that it will change to take advantage of changes in the rules. This principle is so familiar to fans of football and other sports that it hardly bears mentioning. However, in the context of economic policy the principle very much deserves mentioning because here it has been routinely ignored—and with some devastating results.[1] Adherents of the theory of rational expectations believe, in fact, that the field of macroeconomics must be reconstructed in order to take account of this principle of human behavior. Their efforts to do that involve basic changes in the ways economists formulate, simulate, and predict with econometric models. They also call for substantial changes in the ways economic policymakers frame their options.[2]

MODELS SHOULD LET BEHAVIOR CHANGE WITH THE RULES OF THE GAME

In order to provide quantitative advice about the effects of alternative economic policies, economists have constructed collections of equations known as *econometric models*.[3] For the most part these models consist of equations that attempt to describe the behavior of economic agents—firms, consumers, and governments—in terms of variables that are assumed to be closely related to their situations. Such equations are often called *decision rules* because they describe the decisions people make about things like consumption rates, investment rates, and portfolios as functions of variables that summarize the information people use to make those decisions. For all of their mathematical sophistication, econometric models amount to statistical devices for organizing and detecting patterns in the past behavior of people's decision making, patterns that can then be used as a basis for predicting their future behavior.

As devices for extrapolating future behavior from the past under a given set of rules of the game, or government policies, these models appear to have performed well.[4] They have not performed well, however, when the rules changed. In formulating advice for policymakers, economists have routinely used these models to predict the consequences of historically unprecedented, hypothetical government interventions that can only be described as changes in the rules of the game. In effect, the models have been manipulated in a way that amounts to assuming that people's patterns of behavior do not depend on those properties of the environment that government interventions would change. The assumption has been that people will act under the new rules just as they have under the old, so that even under new rules, past behavior is still a reliable guide to future behavior. Econometric models used in this way have not been able to predict accurately the consequences of historically unparalleled interventions.[5] To take one recent example, standard Keynesian and monetarist econometric models built in the late 1960s failed to predict the effects on output, employment, and prices that were associated with the unprecedented large deficits and rates of money creation of the 1970s.

Recent research has been directed at building econometric models that take into account that people's behavior patterns will vary systematically with changes in government policies—the rules of the game.[6] Most of this research has been conducted by adherents of the so-called hypothesis of rational expectations. They model people as making decisions in dynamic settings in the face of well-defined constraints. Included among these constraints are laws of motion over time that describe such things as the taxes people must pay and the prices of the goods they buy and sell. The hypothesis of rational expectations is that people understand these laws of motion. The aim of the research is to build models that can predict how people's behavior will change when they are confronted with well-understood changes in ways of administering taxes, government purchases, aspects of monetary policy, and the like.

Example 1: The Investment Decision

A simple example will illustrate both the principle that decision rules depend on the laws of motion that agents face and the extent that standard macroeconomic models have violated this principle. Let k_t be the capital stock of an industry and τ_t be a tax rate on capital. Let τ_t be the first element of z_t, a vector of current and lagged variables, including those that the government considers when it sets the tax rate on capital. We have $\tau_t \equiv e^T z_t$, where e is the unit vector with unity in the first place and zeros elsewhere.[7] Let a firm's optimal accumulation plan require that capital acquisitions obey[8]

$$k_t = \lambda k_{t-1} - \alpha \sum_{j=0}^{\infty} \delta^j E_t \tau_{t+j}$$

$$\alpha > 0,\, 0 < \lambda < 1,\, 0 < \delta < 1 \quad (1.1)$$

where $E_t \tau_{t+j}$ is the tax rate at time t that is expected to prevail at time $t + j$.

Equation 1.1 captures the notion that the demand for capital responds negatively to current and future tax rates. However, equation 1.1 does not become an operational investment schedule or decision rule until we specify how agents' views about the future, $E_t \tau_{t+j}$, are formed. Let us suppose that the actual law of motion for z_t is

$$z_{t+1} = A z_t \quad (1.2)$$

where A is a matrix conformable with z_t.[9] If agents understand this law of motion for z_t, the first element of which is τ_t, then their best forecast of τ_{t+j} is $e^T A^j z_t$. We impose rational expectations by equating agents' expectations $E_t \tau_{t+j}$ to this best forecast. Upon imposing rational expectations, some algebraic manipulation implies the operational investment schedule

$$k_t = \lambda k_{t-1} - \alpha e^T (I - \delta A)^{-1} z_t \quad (1.3)$$

In terms of the list of variables on the right-hand side, equation 1.3 resembles versions of investment schedules that were fit in the heyday of Keynesian macroeconomics in the 1960s. This is not unusual, for the innovation of rational expectations reasoning is much more in the ways equations are interpreted and manipulated to make statements about economic policy than in the look of the equations that are fit. Indeed, the similarity of standard and rational expectations equations suggests what can be shown to be true generally: The rational expectations reconstruction of macroeconomics is not mainly directed at improving the statistical fits of Keynesian or monetarist macroeconomic models over given historical periods and that its success or failure cannot be judged by comparing the R^2's of reconstructed macroeconomic models with those of models constructed and interpreted along earlier lines.

Under the rational expectations assumption, the investment schedule (equation 1.3) and the laws of motion for the tax rate and the variables that help predict it (equation 1.2) have a common set of parameters, namely, those of the matrix A. These parameters appear in the investment schedule because they influence agents' expectations of how future tax rates will affect capital. Futher, notice that all of the variables in z_t appear in the investment schedule, since via equation 1.2 all of these variables help agents forecast future tax rates. (Compare this with the common econometric practice of using only current and lagged values of the tax rate as proxies for expected future tax rates.)

The fact that equations 1.2 and 1.3 share a common set of parameters (the A matrix) reflects the principle that firms' optimal decision rule for accumulating capital, described as a function of current and lagged state and information variables, will depend on the constraints (or laws of motion) that firms face. That is, the firm's pattern of investment behavior will respond systematically to the rules of the game for setting the tax rate τ_t. A widely understood change in the policy for administering the tax rate can be represented as a change in the first row of the A matrix. Any such change in the tax rate regime or policy will thus result in a change in the investment schedule (equation 1.3). The dependence of the coefficients of the investment schedule on the environmental parameters in matrix A is reasonable and readily explicable as a reflection of the principle that agents' rules of behavior change when they encounter changes in the environment in the form of new laws of motion for variables that constrain them.

To illustrate this point, consider two specific tax rate policies. First, consider the policy of a *constant* tax rate $\tau_{t+j} = \tau_t$ for all $j \geq 0$. Then $z_t = \tau_t$, $A = 1$, and the investment schedule is

$$k_t = \lambda k_{t-1} + h_0 \tau_t \tag{1.4}$$

where $h_0 = -\alpha/(1 - \delta)$

Now consider an *on-again, off-again* tax rate policy of the form $\tau_t = -\tau_{t-1}$. In this case $z_t = \tau_t$, $A = -1$, and the investment schedule becomes

$$k_t = \lambda k_{t-1} + h_0 \tau_t \tag{1.5}$$

where now $h_0 = -\alpha/(1 + \delta)$

Here the investment schedule itself changes as the policy for setting the tax rate changes.

Standard econometric practice has not acknowledged that this sort of thing happens. Returning to the more general investment example, the usual econometric practice has been roughly as follows. First, a model is typically specified and estimated of the form

$$k_t = \lambda k_{t-1} + hz_t \tag{1.6}$$

where h is a vector of free parameters of dimension conformable with the vector z_t. Second, holding the parameters h fixed, equation 1.6 is used to predict the implications of alternative paths for the tax rate τ_t. This procedure is equivalent to estimating equation 1.4 from historical data when $\tau_t = \tau_{t-1}$ and then using this same equation to predict the consequences for capital accumulation of instituting an on-again, off-again tax rate policy of the form $\tau_t = -\tau_{t-1}$. Doing this assumes that a single investment schedule of the form of equation 1.6 can be found with a single parameter vector h that will remain fixed regardless of the rules for administering the tax rate.[10]

The fact that equations 1.2 and 1.3 share a common set of parameters implies that the search for such a regime-independent decision schedule is misdirected and bound to fail. This theoretical presumption is backed up by the distressing variety of instances in which estimated econometric models have failed tests for stability of coefficients when new data are added. This problem cannot be overcome by adopting more sophisticated and more general lag distributions for the vector h, as perhaps was hoped in the 1960s.

Example 2: Are Government Deficits Inflationary?

A second example that well illustrates our general principles about the interdependence of the strategic behavior of private agents and the government concerns the inflationary effects of government deficits. We can discuss this matter with the aid of a demand function for base money of the specific form

$$\frac{M_t}{p_t} = \alpha_1 - \alpha_2 E_t \frac{p_{t+1}}{p_t} \qquad \alpha_1 > \alpha_2 > 0 \qquad (1.7)$$

where
M_t = stock of base money at time t
p_t = price level at time t
$E_t(\cdot)$ = value of $(\cdot)$ expected to prevail at time t

Equation 1.7 is a version of the demand schedule for money that Phillip Cagan used to study hyperinflations. It depicts the demand for base money as decreasing with the expected gross rate of inflation, $E_t p_{t+1}/p_t$. A variety of theories imply a demand function for base money with this property.

Equation 1.7 is a difference equation, a solution of which is

$$p_t = \frac{1}{\alpha_1} \sum_{j=0}^{\infty} \left(\frac{\alpha_2}{\alpha_1}\right)^j E_t M_{t+j} \qquad (1.8)$$

which expresses the price level at t as a function of the supply of base money expected to prevail from now into the indefinite future. We shall use equation 1.8 as our theory of the price level.

According to equation 1.8, if government deficits are to influence the price level path, it can only be through their effect on the expected path of base money. However, the government deficit and path of base money are not rigidly linked in any immutable way. The reason is that the government can, at least to a point, borrow by issuing interest-bearing government debt, and so need not necessarily issue base money to cover its deficit. More precisely, we can think of representing the government's budget constraint in the form

$$G_t - T_t = \frac{M_t - M_{t-1}}{p_t} + B_t - (1 + r_{t-1})B_{t-1}$$

$$r_{t-1} \geq 0 \quad (1.9)$$

where G_t = real government expenditures at t

T_t = real taxes net of transfers (except for interest payments on the government debt)

B_t = real value at t of one-period government bonds issued at t, to be paid off at $t + 1$ and to bear interest at the net rate r_t

For simplicity, equation 1.9 assumes that all government interest-bearing debt is one period in maturity. Equation 1.9 must hold for all periods t. Again for simplicity, we shall also think of equations 1.8 and 1.9 as applying to an economy with no growth in population or technical change.

Under the system formed by equations 1.8 and 1.9, the inflationary consequences of government deficits depend sensitively on the government's strategy for servicing the debt that it issues. We consider first a strict Ricardian regime in which government deficits have no effects on the rate of inflation. In this regime, the government always finances its entire deficit or surplus by issuing or retiring interest-bearing government debt. This regime can be characterized by either of the following two equations, which are equivalent in view of equation 1.9:

$$M_t - M_{t-1} = 0 \quad (1.10)$$

$$B_t = E_t \sum_{j=0}^{\infty} R_{tj}^{-1} (T_{t+j+1} - G_{t+j+1}) \quad (1.11)$$

where $R_{tj} = \prod_{i=0}^{j} (1 + r_{t+i})$

Equation 1.10 states that the supply of base money is always constant, while equation 1.11 states that the real value of government debt equals the present value of prospective government surpluses. In this regime a positive value of interest-bearing government debt signals a stream of future government budgets that is in surplus in the present value sense of equation 1.11. Increases in government debt are temporary in a sense made precise in equation 1.11.

In the Ricardian regime, government deficits have no effects on the price path because they are permitted to have no effects on the path of base money. For the path of base money to be unaffected by government deficits, it is necessary that government deficits be temporary and be accompanied by exactly offsetting future government surpluses.

Since the Ricardian regime may seem remote as a description of recent behavior of the U.S. federal government, it is worthwhile to recall that cities and states in the United States are constitutionally forced to operate under a Ricardian rule, since they have no right to issue base money.

There are alternative debt-servicing strategies under which government deficits are inflationary. To take an example at the opposite pole from the Ricardian regime, consider the rule recommended in 1949 by Milton Friedman under which

$$B_t = 0 \quad \text{for all } t \tag{1.12}$$

$$G_t - T_t = \frac{M_t - M_{t-1}}{P_t} \tag{1.13}$$

According to this rule, deficits are always to be financed entirely by issuing additional base money, with interest-bearing government debt never being issued. In this regime, the time path of government deficits affects the time path of the price level in a rigid and immediate way that is described by equations 1.8 and 1.13. Under this regime it is possible for the government budget to be persistently in deficit, within limits imposed by equations 1.13 and 1.7. Deficits need not be temporary.

Bryant and Wallace and Sargent and Wallace have described debt-servicing regimes that are intermediate between Ricardo's and Friedman's. In all versions of these regimes, interest-bearing government debt is issued, but is eventually repaid partly by issuing additional base money. In the regime studied by Sargent and Wallace, the deficit path $G_t - T_t$ is set in such a way, and the demand schedule for interest-bearing government debt is such that eventually the inflation tax must be resorted to, with increases in base money eventually having to be used to finance the budget.

In all regimes of the Bryant-Wallace variety, increases in interest-bearing government debt are typically inflationary, at least eventually because they signal prospective increases in base money. Sooner or later these eventual increases in base money will affect the price level, how soon depending on the coefficients α_1 and α_2 in equations 1.7 and 1.8.

This discussion indicates that the observed correlation between the government deficits and the price level depends on the debt-repayment regime in place when the observations were made. It would be a mistake to estimate the relationship between the deficit and the price path from time-series observations drawn from a period under which a Ricardian regime was in place, and to assert that this same relationship will hold between the deficit and inflation under a regime like the one described by Bryant and Wallace. It would be a mistake because private agents' interpretations of observed deficits, and consequently the impact of observed deficits on the price level, depend on the debt-servicing regime they imagine to be in place. This can thus be viewed as another example of our principle that private agents' rules of behavior depend on their perceptions of the rules of the game they are playing.

GENERAL IMPLICATIONS OF THE EXAMPLES

These two examples illustrate the general presumption that the systematic behavior of private agents and the random behavior of market outcomes both will change whenever agents' constraints change, as when government policy or other parts of the environment change. To make reliable statements about policy interventions, we need dynamic models and econometric procedures that are consistent with this general presumption. Foremost, we need a new and stricter definition of the class of parameters that can be regarded as *structural*. The body of doctrine associated with the simultaneous equations model in econometrics properly directs the attention of the researcher beyond reduced-form parameters to the parameters of structural equations that are meant to describe those aspects of people's behavior that remain constant across a range of hypothetical environments. Although such structural parameters are needed to analyze an interesting class of policy interventions, most often included among them have been parameters of equations describing the rules of choice for private agents.

Consumption functions, investment schedules, and demand functions for assets are all examples of such rules of choice. In dynamic settings, regarding the parameters of these rules of choice as structural or invariant under policy interventions violates the principle that optimal decision rules depend on the environment in which agents believe they are operating.

If parameters of decision rules cannot be regarded as structural or invariant under policy interventions, deeper objects that can must be sought. The best that can be hoped for is that parameters characterizing private agents' preferences and technologies will not change when changes in economic policy change the environment. If dynamic econometric models were formulated explicitly in terms of the parameters of preferences, technologies, and constraints, in principle they could be used to predict the effects on observed behavior of changes in policy rules. In terms of our investment example with equations 1.2 and 1.3, the idea would be to estimate the free parameters of the model $(\lambda, \alpha, \delta, A)$. With these estimates, economists could predict how the investment schedule would change if different A's occurred.[11]

NEW ECONOMETRIC METHODS

Private Agents' Strategies Reflect Government's Choice of Rules of the Game

A major research effort is currently under way by economists to develop theoretical and econometric methods capable of isolating parameters that are structural in the above sense, that is, parameters that are invariant under government interventions in the form of changes in the rules of the game. This is a very ambitious undertaking, one that is in many ways more difficult and ambitious than was the impressive effort of the Cowles Commission in the late 1940s that created the econometric methods that made Keynesian econometric models possible: For what is required is a theoretical and statistical framework that permits the economist to estimate how private agents' decision rules or strategies depend on the decision rules or strategies used by the government. Any successful version of this research effort will embody the principle that the parameters of private agents' decision rules are not among the free parameters of the model, but are themselves functions of (among other things) parameters describing the rules used by the government. Achieving success in this endeavor requires that many new methods and results be achieved in technical aspects of econometrics and dynamic economic theory.

Lucas and Sargent have formalized the ideas behind this research effort in the following way. They let h denote a collection of decision rules of private agents. Each element of h is itself a function that maps some private agent's information about his state at a particular point in time into his decision at that point in time. Consumption, investment, and demand functions for money are all examples of elements of h. Lucas and Sargent let f denote a collection of elements that forms the "environment" facing private agents. Some elements of f represent rules of the game or decision rules selected by the government, which map the government's information at some date into its decisions at that date. For example, included among f might be decision rules for fiscal and monetary policy variables. The fundamental principle that we are concerned with can be summarized as stating that the elements of h are partly functions of f. Lucas and Sargent represent this mapping formally by

$$h = T(f) \qquad (1.14)$$

The mapping T represents "cross-equation restrictions," since each element of h and of f is itself a decision rule or equation determining the choice of some variable under an agent's control.

The new econometric methods have been aimed principally at utilizing time series of observations on an economy that was operating for some period under a *single* set of government rules or strategies.[12] The idea is to impose sufficient structure on the observations (i.e., sufficient structure on the mapping T in equation 1.14) that by observing the decisions h of private agents and f for the government, we can isolate the free parameters of agents' preferences and constraints that determine T and that will enable us to predict how private agents' decision rules h would change if the government were to adopt some new and perhaps historically unprecedented rules f. The theoretical models that enable one to hope to carry off this task are characterized by "cross-equation restrictions," across equations for the decision rules of private agents and the decision rules of the government. These restrictions summarize the dependence of private agents' strategies on the government's strategies. To understand the economic process, in the sense of being able to predict the consequences of changes in the rules of the game set by the government, is to understand these restrictions. The hope is that by utilizing these restrictions, observations on an economy operating under a single set of rules can be interpreted and used to make predictions about how the economy would behave under brand new rules. Possessing the ability to do this is a sine qua non for scientific and quantitative evaluation of alternative government rules.

Impressive technical progress is being made in this research endeavor, and there are grounds for being reasonably optimistic that economists will eventually be able to deliver econometric methods that are useful for predicting the effects of changes in government policy rules. However, it is wise to keep in mind what an ambitious task this is. It requires several leaps of faith in economic theory to hope that this line of research will realize all of its aims, although the success of this research line will eventually have to be judged not in absolute terms but vis-à-vis alternative lines of research designed to achieve the same objectives.

Though they are being developed rapidly, the new methods described above are still in their infancy, and as yet capable of handling only relatively small and simple dynamic systems. We now have several interesting empirical applications of these methods, which demonstrate their feasibility. But we are still some way from a model suitable for analyzing many interesting questions of macroeconomic policy. This is one reason that it is useful to pursue alternative styles of analysis that try to reflect the basic principle that private agents' behavior depends on the rules of the game set by the government. This brings us to economic history.

HISTORICAL AND CROSS-COUNTRY ANALYSIS

History provides a number of examples of economies that have apparently operated for more or less extended periods of time under alternative rules of the game or government strategies for selecting fiscal, monetary, and regulatory actions. By studying records of these economies, one can hope to find direct evidence of the dependence of private agents' decision rules h on those aspects of the environment f selected by the policy authorities. These historical records amount to distinct pairs of observations $h_1, f_1; h_2, f_2; \cdots ; h_n, f_n$ that can be viewed as observations at different points of the mapping T given by equation 1.14. In a concrete sense such a collection of cross-regime observations permits direct observations on at least parts of the T mapping.

These are the evident advantages of the historical or cross-country analysis. There are also evident disadvantages. The observations on different h_i, f_i pairs usually come in the form of observations from distant times and/or places. For this reason, the data are often so fragmentary and questionable in quality that they are incapable of supporting the kind of formal time-series econometric analysis described above. Less formal methods of analysis must be used for such data. To the extent that these less formal methods require more judgment, discretion, and cleverness from the analyst, they are in a sense less reproducible and automatic than are the formal methods. The weaving of plausible heuristic stories this style of analysis involves is one of the things that the formal time-series methods developed by rational expectations analysts and their econometric predecessors sought to avoid. Furthermore, it is often an arguable matter to identify alternative countries or historical periods as operating under distinct government policy regimes or rules of the game f.

Despite these genuine disadvantages of the historical and cross-country method of study, it is my belief that such studies are well worth the effort. The hope of getting some direct peeks at distinct observations, however fragmentary and noisy, on the $h = T(f)$ mapping easily justifies appreciable efforts in this direction. It is this hope that motivated the three historical chapters that comprise the heart of this book. Besides, the practical success of the rational expectations approach to macroeconomics perhaps ultimately depends on whether it can become a routine device that can be used to think about macroeconomic problems informally and on the backs of envelopes.

These chapters represent attempts to put the theory into practice in such an informal context.

IMPLICATIONS FOR POLICYMAKERS

These ideas have implications not only for theoretical and econometric practices but also for the ways in which policymakers and their advisers think about the choices confronting them. In particular, the rational expectations approach directs attention away from particular isolated actions and toward choices among feasible rules of the game, or repeated strategies for choosing policy variables. While Keynesian and monetarist macroeconomic models have been used to try to analyze what the effects of isolated actions would be, it is now clear that the answers they have given have necessarily been bad, if only because such questions are ill-posed.

In terms of our investment example, by selecting different values for the first row of A, we can analyze the effects on current and subsequent investment of switching from one well-understood policy for setting the tax rate to another—that is, we can analyze the effects of different *strategies* for setting the tax rate. However, we cannot analyze the effects on current and subsequent investment of alternative *actions* consisting of different possible settings for the tax rate τ_t at a particular point in time $t = \bar{t}$. For in order to make predictions, we must specify agents' views about the law of motion A, and this is not done when we simply consider actions consisting of alternative settings for τ_t at one isolated point in time. This idea is so widely accepted as to be uncontroversial among decision theorists (and football fans); but even today practicing macroeconomists often ignore it.

To take a concrete example, in the United States there was recently interest in analyzing what would happen to the rate of domestic extraction of oil and gas if the tax on profits of oil producers increased a lot on a particular date. Would supply go up or down if the tax were raised to X percent on July 1? The only scientifically respectable answer to this question is "I don't know." Such a rise in the oil-profits tax rate could be interpreted as reflecting one of a variety of different tax strategies (A matrices), each with different implications for current and prospective extraction of oil.

For example, suppose that oil companies had reason to believe that the increase in the tax is temporary and will be repealed after the election. In that case, they would respond by decreasing their rate of supply now and increasing it later, thus reallocating their sales to periods in which their shareholders get a larger share of profits and the government a smaller share. Yet suppose that oil companies believed that the increase in the tax rate on July 1 is only the beginning and that further increases will follow. In that case the response to the tax rate increase would be the reverse: to increase supply now and decrease it later in order to benefit companies' shareholders. This example illustrates that people's views about the government's strategy for setting the tax rate are decisive in determining their responses to any given actions and that the effects of actions cannot be reliably evaluated in isolation from the policy rule or strategy of which they are an element.

A completely analogous version of this example can easily be constructed for our deficit example around the question: "Are large current government deficits accompanied by tight monetary policy actions inflationary?" This question is also ill-posed because it fails to specify the debt repayment strategy to be used by the government. The way in which current deficits are correlated with inflation depends sensitively on what debt repayment regime is in place.

What policymakers (and econometricians) should recognize, then, is that societies face a meaningful set of choices about alternative economic policy regimes. For example, the proper question is not about the size of tax cut to impose now in response to a recession but about the proper strategy for repeatedly adjusting tax rates in response to the state of the economy, year in and year out. Strategic questions of this nature abound in fiscal, monetary, regulatory, and labor market matters. Private agents face the problem of determining the government regime under which they are operating, and they often devote considerable resources to doing so. Whether governments realize it or not, they do make decisions about these regimes. They would be wise to face these decisions deliberately rather than ignore them and pretend to be able to make good decisions by taking one seemingly unrelated action after another.

NOTES

1. Charles Whiteman and Ian Bain are responsible for impressing upon me the many parallels between football and macroeconomics. This example is admittedly one that will strike true football fans as excessively crude. More delicate examples of actual changes in rules abound, such as the effects on the game of moving the goalposts in the NFL back ten yards in 1974, of the rule change in 1974 that a missed field goal outside the 20-yard line resulted in the ball being turned over to the other team at the original line of scrimmage, or the rule change in 1974 forbidding defensive backs from hitting receivers after they had moved five yards downfield from the line of scrimmage.
2. This is the message of Lucas [3].
3. Lucas and Sargent [4] provide a brief explanation of econometric models and their uses in macroeconomics.
4. This evidence is cited by Litterman [2] and his references.
5. Sims [7] and Lucas [3] describe why econometric models can perform well in extrapolating the future from the past, assuming no changes in rules of the game, while performing poorly in predicting the consequences of changes in the rules.
6. For an example of such research and extensive lists of further references, see Hansen and Sargent [1] and Lucas and Sargent [5].
7. Here T denotes matrix transposition.
8. The investment schedule (equation 1.1) can be derived from the following dynamic model of a firm. A firm chooses sequences of capital to maximize

$$E_0 \sum_{t=0}^{\infty} \beta^t \left[f_1 k_t - \frac{f_2}{2} k_t^2 - f_3 k_t \tau_t - \frac{d}{2} (k_t - k_{t-1})^2 \right]$$

where $f_1, f_2, f_3, d > 0; 0 > \beta > 1$; and E_0 is the mathematical expectation operator conditioned on information known at time 0. The maximization is subject to k_{t-1}, τ_t being known at the time t. Maximization problems of this kind are analyzed in Sargent [6]. The parameters λ, α, and δ can be shown to be functions of f_1, f_2, f_3, and d.
9. The eigenvalues of A are assumed to be less than δ^{-1} in absolute value.
10. This is analogous to assuming that Houston's propensity to punt on fourth down does not depend on the number of downs per series determined by the NFL rules.

11. As claimed in note 8, the parameters λ, α, δ can be shown to be functions of the parameters f_1, f_2, f_3, d of the present value function being maximized in the equation.

12. If sufficient data are available, these same econometric methods can be readily modified to pooling observations on h_i, f_i from several regimes $i = 1, \cdots, n$ in order to estimate T. The reader of Hansen and Sargent [1] can immediately see how samples of data drawn from different h_i, f_i can be pooled using either the maximum likelihood or method of moments estimator.

REFERENCES

1. Hansen, Lars P., and Thomas J. Sargent. 1980. Formulating and estimating dynamic linear rational expectations models. *Journal of Economic Dynamics and Control* 2 (February):7–46.
2. Litterman, Robert B. 1979. Techniques of forecasting using vector autoregressions. Working Paper 115, Federal Reserve Bank of Minneapolis.
3. Lucas, Robert E., Jr. 1976. Econometric policy evaluation: A critique. In *The Phillips Curve and Labor Markets,* ed. by K. Brunner and A. H. Meltzer. Carnegie-Rochester Conference Series on Public Policy 1:19–46. Amsterdam: North-Holland.
4. Lucas, Robert E., Jr., and Thomas J. Sargent. 1979. After Keynesian macroeconomics. Federal Reserve Bank of Minneapolis *Quarterly Review* 3 (Spring):1–16.
5. _____, eds. 1981. *Rational Expectations and Econometric Practice*. Minneapolis: University of Minnesota Press.
6. Sargent, Thomas J. 1979. *Macroeconomic Theory*. New York: Academic Press.
7. Sims, Christopher A. 1980. Macroeconomics and reality. *Econometrica* 48 (January):1–48.

chapter *2*

Reaganomics and Credibility

> HOWARD: Dandy, the Vikings had the momentum throughout the first half. Let's see if the momentum stays with the Vikes into the second half. Otherwise, it's going to be a long night for the Bears.
>
> DANDY DON: Yes, Howard. It'll also be interesting to see if the Bears continue to be confused by the new formation that Bud Grant has installed for this game. We haven't seen the Vikings throw play-action passes as much as they have this evening, and this has surprised the Bears. If the Bears can figure out the Vikes' new strategy and adjust to it, it will be a new ball game.
>
> MONDAY NIGHT FOOTBALL

An offensive football team is a collection of individuals with a common objective: to score a touchdown. This objective is attained by the cooperation of eleven players, each of whom is ultimately in control of his own actions. The effectiveness of any one player's actions depends intricately on the actions of his teammates. If the quarterback decides to throw the ball 30 yards downfield to the right side on a count of three, it is necessary for success that a receiver run a pass pattern that will place him in a position to catch the ball. If the quarterback calls a "keeper" and runs around the end, it is important that the end not run a pass pattern but that he block. Thus, the quarterback and the end, and all the other players, face a problem of coordination. It will not do to simply announce vague objectives in the huddle, such as "Let's score a touchdown." Instead, somehow each player must reach a precise understanding of what each of his colleagues is planning to do on the next play and of the "contingency plans" that each player will use as the play develops or breaks down. All football teams (except apparently one that I root for) accomplish this coordination task by giving one player, either the quarterback or a player just sent in by the coach, the authority to direct the actions of all the others by calling the play. A football team is an example of a system for which complete decentralization or "laissez faire" is not a good idea.

The example from football contains important lessons about making macroeconomic policy. Within a single country, the authorities who are charged with responsibility for making monetary and fiscal policy are very much in the position of the end and the quarterback, for their activities must be coordinated, one way or the other, and their objectives are presumably identical. In the world as a whole, the monetary and fiscal authorities of different countries have to somehow coordinate their policies, since one country's choices of monetary and fiscal strategies influence the options open to the others so long as there is some freedom to exchange goods and make loans across borders. However, despite the interrelated consequences of their actions upon a common system, fiscal and monetary authorities from different countries sometimes have differing and even opposing goals. (Sometimes the goals may even seem so opposed that the proper analogy is not to a quarterback and an end but to two opposing football teams—say the Cowboys and the Redskins.) Presumably, the example of the quarterback and the end rings truest for the coordination of monetary and fiscal policy within one country, for the assumption that the authorities share common objectives is better here than in the international case.

This chapter views the monetary and fiscal authorities of a single country as a "team" and judges their patterns of behavior against standards absorbed from the sports pages. This view provides a broad framework for summarizing classic doctrines and controversies in government finance, and also serves as a basis for criticizing the way in which monetary and fiscal policies have been coordinated de facto in the United States over the last several years.

I shall begin with a few formal definitions of concepts that will help to clarify the analogy between the quarterback-end problem and the monetary-fiscal problem.

DYNAMIC GAMES

A *game* consists of a collection of players and a set of rules specifying rewards and penalties. A *dynamic game* is one that requires time to complete and whose current score depends on past actions of the various players. In life, most games are dynamic.

Each player in a game is supposed to have a goal or objective that depends on the rewards and penalties specified in the rules of the game. This goal may be idiosyncratic (such as personal glory or personal profit) or altruistic (such as the success of one's team or country). A *team game* is one in which two or more players have a common objective. Football and soccer are team games. So, perhaps, is the game of managing a country's monetary and fiscal affairs, at least if those in charge have in mind a common objective.

Each player in a dynamic game tries to achieve his objective by choosing a *strategy*. A strategy is defined as a rule that describes how a player's actions during the game depend on the information he receives during the course of the game. Another term for a player's strategy is *contingency plan*. This term evokes the notion that each action taken by a player ought to depend on the situation as it is understood when that action is executed. A strategy relates a player's actions over time into a sensible pattern. Since time elapses during a dynamic game, whether a single action (or *move*) is a good one cannot be judged in isolation from past and subsequently planned moves.

In general, each player chooses his strategy given his perception of the strategies of other players and given his perception of the influence that his own choice of strategy has on the strategies chosen by other players. If player A correctly believes that he influences the choice of player B's strategy, then player A is said to be *dominant* relative to player B. To complete a description of a dynamic game, it is necessary to specify a structure of dominance across the players in the game. An *equilibrium* or *solution* of a dynamic game is a structure of dominance and a collection of strategies of all the players in the game that maximizes their respective objective functions, subject to each player's perception of the strategies of all the remaining players. Evidently, a solution of a dynamic game requires that all players' perceptions of the structure of dominance be consistent and that their chosen strategies be mutually feasible, in the sense of being consistent with the physical technologies in place and with the strategies being employed by the other players (or *agents*).

Alternative structures of dominance give rise to different ways of playing a game, or really different games. For example, in a *Nash equilibrium,* each agent in the game takes the strategies of the other agents as given and beyond his influence. Nash players interact in this way despite the fact that each player's choice of strategy influences the strategies chosen by all the other players. In a "Stackelberg" or *dominant-player* equilibrium, one player takes into account the influence that his choice of strategy has on the strategies of the remaining players; the remaining players act as followers and ignore the influence of their strategies on the dominant player's strategy. Usually, the dominant player is imagined to be large and powerful and the followers are imagined to be individually weak, numerous, and dispersed. If there is a small number of powerful players (say, two), then possibilities exist for a struggle between them for dominance. It can happen that each of two players wants to be dominant and wants the other player to act as a follower. If both sides try to implement their desired strategies, an impasse, or a state of *Stackelberg warfare,* exists. Stackelberg warfare is not an equilibrium or a solution of the game, because the wishes and perceptions on which the two players are acting are not mutually consistent. Situations of Stackelberg warfare are pathologies and represent attempts to implement disorderly and infeasible coordination schemes. Below, I shall assert that recent American monetary and fiscal policy has been in a state of Stackelberg warfare.

A fundamental and general principle that emerges from the study of dynamic games is that agents' strategies are interdependent. Interdependence of strategies generally holds regardless of the structure of dominance, though the exact forms of dependence will hinge on it. In football, the principle of strategic interdependence is reflected in the need for a quarterback and an end to coordinate their strategies. It is also reflected in the coordination problem facing monetary and fiscal authorities.

The reader who is familiar with the game of football will be able to recognize how the categories defined above apply to football. From the viewpoint of a single football team, football is a dynamic team game in which each player's optimal strategy depends on the optimal strategies of the other players as well as on the strategy being used by the opposing team and the rules set by the league. The optimal strategy for a given team depends on the rules of the game and on the strategies chosen by the opposing team. Since my main purpose is to analyze the macroeconomy and not the National Football League, I will not pursue the analysis of football as a dynamic game any further here. Instead, I shall now describe aspects of the economy of a single country as a dynamic game.

AN ECONOMY AS A DYNAMIC GAME

The economy or game is imagined to consist of three players: the public, the monetary authority, and the fiscal authority. The public consists of people, who are organized into households, agencies of the government, and corporations and who are the ultimate beneficiaries of all economic activity. The public makes decisions about consumption, investment, and private employment and pays the taxes imposed on it by the fiscal authority. The public also sets the terms on which it will accumulate government debts of various forms. The fiscal authority makes decisions about public expenditures and about the rates at which taxes are to be collected from the public. By making these decisions, the fiscal authority determines the rate of government deficit—the amount by which government expenditures exceed tax collections.[1] The deficit is financed by the issuing of government debt, either in the interest-bearing form of government bonds or in the noninterest-bearing form of currency and bank reserves (often called "high-powered money"). The decision about the composition of the debt as between bonds of various maturities and currency or high-powered money is, at each point in time, under the control of the monetary authority. The monetary authority exercises this control through its authority to engage in open-market exchanges of one kind of public debt for another. Thus, while the fiscal authority influences the rate of addition to the public debt, the monetary authority determines its composition. *Debt management* is a term that is aptly used to describe what the monetary authority does.[2]

Macroeconomic analysis of the rational expectations variety aims to study the interactions of these three classes of agents as a dynamic team game. Abstracting from distributional effects across members of the public (according to a long tradition in macroeconomics), the monetary and fiscal authorities are imagined to share common objectives with the public and with each other. These common objectives make it a team situation. The aspect that all three players are making decisions that affect the future state of the system makes it a dynamic game. Thus, the public chooses investment rates in physical and human capital and the terms on which it is willing to accumulate various amounts and types of government debt; the fiscal authority determines the current and the prospective state of total government indebtedness; and the monetary authority determines the composition of the debt.

I now put this structure of ideas to work by using it to analyze a classic issue of government finance that is important today: the inflationary consequences of government deficits and of alternative ways of financing them.

Government expenditures can be financed by alternative combinations of levying taxes, borrowing in interest-bearing form, and printing high-powered money. The consequences for the price level path of alternative methods of financing a given stream of government expenditures can differ, and in ways that depend on how the strategies of the public and of the fiscal and monetary authorities are imagined to interact. To discuss these consequences, we need models of the decision strategies of each of our three groups of agents and of their interactions. We can describe some of the major issues with the aid of simple strategic models for each of our players.

In the tradition of Keynes, the public is assumed to be willing to hold interest-bearing government debt on the same terms on which it holds private evidences of indebtedness. This means that public borrowing is assumed to pay the same interest rate as private borrowing and that the total amount of government and private borrowing must be consistent with the public's limited capacity to accumulate wealth. Let us assume that all interest-bearing government debt is one period in maturity, and let us denote the one-period real pretax net rate of return on private securities between t and $t + 1$ as $r(t)$. We assume that $r(t)$ is an exogenous sequence and that $r(t)$ is greater than 0. For simplicity, we assume an economy that is not growing over time. We also abstract from uncertainty.

The public's willingness to accumulate real interest-bearing government debt, $B(t)$, is assumed to be limited. In particular, we assume that $B(t)$ is constrained by

$$B(t) \leq \overline{B} \qquad (2.1)$$

Equation 2.1 asserts that, like all private borrowers, the government is faced with an upper bound on the amount of debt that it can place. One upper bound on $B(t)$ is total wealth in a country. When all savings of a country have been absorbed in government debt, no more government debt can be placed. In practice, the actual upper bound $\overline{B}$ is far lower than the total wealth. In August 1982, $B(t)$ in Mexico appeared to have hit $\overline{B}$. In France, between 1924 and 1926, $B(t)$ appeared to have been close to $\overline{B}$, precipitating a continuing financial crisis and the "waltz of the portfolios" of the finance ministers of France.

The public's willingness to accumulate base money is assumed to be described by a demand function of the specific form

$$\frac{M(t)}{p(t)} = a(1) - a(2)E_t\left[\frac{p(t + 1)}{p(t)}\right] \qquad a(1) > a(2) \geq 0 \quad (2.2)$$

where $M(t)$ is the stock of base money at time t, $p(t)$ is the price level at time t, and $E_t[\cdot]$ is the value of $[\cdot]$ expected to prevail by the public as of time t.

Equation 2.2 is a version of the demand function for money that Cagan [2] used to study hyperinflation. It depicts the demand for real base money as a decreasing function of the expected gross rate of inflation $E_t[p(t + 1)/p(t)]$. A variety of theories imply a demand function for base money of this form. There is also ample empirical evidence that is consistent with the inverse dependence between real balances $M(t)/p(t)$ and expected inflation $E_t[p(t + 1)/p(t)]$ that is posited by equation 2.2. For example, in the year before August 1946, the price level in Hungary increased by a factor of about 4×10^{24}. It is reasonable to expect that people had caught on to the extraordinarily rapid ongoing inflation, so that $E_t[p(t + 1)/p(t)]$ was large by the middle of 1946. In August 1946 the real value of high-powered money $M(t)/p(t)$ in Hungary, measured in 1946 U.S. dollars, was less than \$25,000.

The system that emerges from writing down the version of equation 2.2 that is appropriate for dates $t, t + 1, t + 2, \ldots$ can be solved to express $p(t)$ solely in terms of expected future values of $M(t)$:

$$p(t) = \frac{1}{a(1)}\sum_{j=0}^{\infty}\left(\frac{a(2)}{a(1)}\right)^{j} E_tM(t + j) \qquad (2.3)$$

Equation 2.3 expresses the price level at t as a function of the supply of base money expected to prevail from now into the indefinite future. The logic underlying this equation is simple: Equation 2.2 implies that the price level at t varies directly with the money supply at t and with the price level expected to prevail at $t + 1$. Equation 2.2 also implies that the price level at $t + 1$ varies directly with the money supply at $t + 1$ and with the price level expected to prevail at $t + 2$, and so on. Upon the elimination of future expected price levels from this infinite sequence of relationships, equation 2.3 emerges. Notice that in the special case of $a(2) = 0$, equation 2.3 becomes a simple version of the quantity theory of money, stating that the price level at t is proportional to the supply of high-powered money at t.

Equation 2.3 shows how the price level at t is determined by the interaction of the public's preference for holding high-powered money, which is reflected in the parameters $a(1)$ and $a(2)$, with the expected path of high-powered money now and into the indefinite future. According to equation 2.3, if government deficits are to influence the price level, it can only be through their effects on the expected path of high-powered money. In this sense, equation 2.3 embodies the monetarist presumption that inflation is always a monetary phenomenon.

The government deficit and the level and rate of change of the stock of base money are not related in any necessary way at a particular point in time. The reason is that the government can (at least up to a point) borrow by issuing interest-bearing debt, and so need not issue base money to cover its deficit. More precisely, we can think of representing the government's budget constraint in the form[4]

$$G(t) - T(t) = \frac{M(t) - M(t - 1)}{p(t)} \\ + B(t) - [1 + r(t - 1)]B(t - 1) \tag{2.4}$$

where $G(t)$ is real government expenditures at t, $T(t)$ is real tax collections net of transfers (except for interest payments on the government debt), and $B(t)$ is the real value at t of one-period bonds issued at t, to be paid off at $t + 1$ and to bear interest at net real rate $r(t)$. Equation 2.4 asserts that the real government deficit at t, $G(t) - T(t)$, can be financed by a combination of printing new high-powered money in the amount $M(t) - M(t - 1)$, which raises $[M(t) - M(t - 1)]/p(t)$ in real resources, and borrowing in interest-bearing form $B(t)$ in excess of the principle and interest on the debt that is maturing, $[1 + r(t - 1)]B(t - 1)$. Equation 2.4 must hold for all t. For simplicity, equation 2.4 assumes that all government interest-bearing debt is one period in maturity. It is important to point out that the formulation of equation 2.4 assumes in effect that government debt is indexed and constitutes a sure claim on given amounts of future goods. Either the debt is regarded as explicitly indexed or else the bonds are nominal ones, with the nominal rate of interest imagined to adjust by the subsequently realized rate of inflation so that they turn out to bear real rate $r(t)$ in equilibrium. In a rational expectations model in which there is no objective uncertainty—the kind of model we have in mind here—these two interpretations are equivalent. In either one of these interpretations, the government is imagined to honor its commitments to repay interest-bearing debt at the real interest rate that was anticipated at the time the debt was contracted. In reality, when part of the outstanding government debt is nominal, the government has the option of "defaulting" on part of it by acting so as to inflate at a higher rate than had been expected when the debt was contracted. In the subsequent presentation I shall begin by assuming that the government always abstains from defaulting on any of its interest-bearing debt.

Imagine that there is a fiscal authority that selects a time stream of $G(t)$ and $T(t)$. A consequence of the fiscal authority's choice is a stream of government deficits net of interest payments, $G(t) - T(t)$. There is also a monetary authority that determines the composition of the government debt in the hands of the public through open-market operations. The monetary authority's open-market operations at time t are subject to a constraint, which is derived by simply rearranging equation 2.4:

$$M(t) + p(t)B(t) = M(t - 1) + [1 + r(t - 1)]p(t)B(t - 1) \\ + p(t)[G(t) - T(t)]$$

The monetary authority is free to choose $M(t)$ and $p(t)B(t)$ subject to the constraint that they add up to the total on the right-hand side of the preceding equation. In other words, at a point in time the monetary authority can exchange base money for bonds of equal value.

ARE GOVERNMENT DEFICITS INFLATIONARY?

Under the system formed by equations 2.3 and 2.4, the inflationary consequences of a government deficit at time t depend sensitively on the government's strategy for servicing the debt that it issues. This dependence can be illustrated by considering two polar regimes for servicing the debt and for coordinating monetary and fiscal policy.

Consider first a strict Ricardian regime in which government deficits have no effects on the rate of inflation. In this regime, the government always finances its entire deficit or surplus by issuing or retiring interest-bearing debt. Additional base money is never issued to finance a deficit. This regime can be characterized by either of the following two equations, which are equivalent in view of equations 2.4 and 2.1:

$$M(t) - M(t - 1) = 0 \quad \text{for all } t \tag{2.5}$$

$$B(t) = E_t \sum_{j=0}^{\infty} R_{tj}^{-1}[T(t + j + 1) - G(t + j + 1)] \quad \text{for all } t \quad (2.6)$$

where

$$R_{tj} = \prod_{i=0}^{j} [1 + r(t + i)]$$

Equation 2.5 states that the supply of base money is always a constant; equation 2.6 states that the real value of interest-bearing government debt at t equals the present value of prospective government surpluses. In this regime a positive value of interest-bearing government debt signals a stream of future government budgets that is in surplus in the present value sense of equation 2.6. Increases in government debt are necessarily temporary, in a sense made precise by equation 2.6.[5]

In the Ricardian regime, government deficits have no effects on the price path because they are permitted to have no effects on the path of base money. For the path of base money to be unaffected by government deficits, it is necessary that the government deficits be temporary and be expected to be accompanied by offsetting future government surpluses. In the Ricardian regime, the government behaves like a firm with respect to financing its deficit. To finance a given deficit, the government competes for funds from lenders on an equal footing with private borrowers. To attract funds, the government must offer lenders a prospective stream of net revenues sufficient to support the value that it presently proposes to borrow. The government's stream of net revenues is $T(t) - G(t)$. The present value of this stream forms the "backing" for the government's borrowing, just as the present value of a stream of prospective net revenues from a new machine might form the backing for a private loan. Furthermore, like any private borrower, the government can borrow in interest-bearing form only a limited amount determined by the maximum present value of the prospective government surpluses that the economy can support. This is the limit $\overline{B}$ embodied in equation 2.1.

The Ricardian regime may seem remote as a description of recent behavior of the U.S. government and some major U.S. trading partners. It is worthwhile to recall that states and cities in the United States are constitutionally required to operate under a Ricardian rule, since they have no right to issue base money. In the nineteenth century the Ricardian rule was followed, with temporary lapses, by Great Britain, the United States, and the more advanced European countries. (It is no coincidence that the economically advanced countries all adopted such a rule and that they all abandoned it at about the same time, during and after World War I. There are irresistible forces impelling countries that trade with each other to coordinate their monetary and fiscal policies. These forces often cause countries to run similar fiscal policies. A country had to follow a Ricardian rule, or something close to it, in order to adhere to the international gold standard.)

Alternatives to the Ricardian debt-servicing regime exist under which government deficits are inflationary. To take an example at the opposite pole from the Ricardian regime, let us consider a rule that was followed for a while during the great revolutions in France and Russia, was used during each of the great European hyperinflations of the twentieth century, and was advocated in one version by Milton Friedman in 1948. This rule can be characterized by either of the two following equations:

$$B(t) = 0 \quad \text{for all } t \tag{2.7}$$

$$G(t) - T(t) = \frac{M(t) - M(t-1)}{p(t)} \quad \text{for all } t \tag{2.8}$$

In view of the government budget constraint (equation 2.4), these two equations are equivalent characterizations of a rule in which the entire deficit is always immediately financed by the printing of additional base money. Interest-bearing debt is never issued. In this regime, the time path of government deficits affects the time path of both base money and the price level in a rigid and immediate way that is described by equation 2.8 and by our theory of the price level, equation 2.3. Under this debt-servicing regime, it is possible for the government budget to be persistently in deficit, within limits imposed by equation 2.8 and by the demand function for base money (equation 2.2) or its implied theory of the price level (equation 2.3). Deficits need not be temporary.

In this regime, the government finances a current deficit not by a promise to run surpluses in the future, as in the Ricardian regime, but instead by levying an immediate "inflation tax" on the present holders of base money. Whereas the Ricardian regime involves a commitment ultimately to abstain from any resort to an inflation tax, the polar alternative [4] involves a promise that any government deficit will be immediately and fully monetized. I shall return later to the question of why Milton Friedman, who has never been an advocate of monetary regimes leading to rampant inflation, would at one time have advocated full monetization of government deficits—the regime that has accompanied the worst inflations in history.

It is possible to imagine deficit-financing regimes that are intermediate between Ricardo's and Friedman's. Bryant and Wallace [1] and Sargent and Wallace [10] have described such regimes. In all versions of these regimes, interest-bearing government debt is issued, but it is eventually repaid at least partly by the issuing of additional base money. In the regime studied by Sargent and Wallace, the deficit path involves such a persistent stream of large deficits that eventually the inflation tax must be resorted to; increases in base money have to be used to finance the budget.

In all these intermediate deficit-financing regimes of the Bryant-Wallace variety, increases in interest-bearing government debt are typically inflationary, at least eventually, because they signal eventual increases in base money. Sooner or later, these prospective increases in base money will increase the price level; how soon depends on the coefficients $a(1)$ and $a(2)$ in equation 2.2. According to equation 2.3, the closer $a(2)/a(1)$ is to unity, the bigger is the effect of a given future increase in base money on the price level today. This is true because, according to equation 2.2, the larger $a(2)$ is relative to $a(1)$, the more sensitive the current price level is to the expected future price level and therefore also to expected future values of base money.

The preceding discussion indicates that the observed correlation between government deficits and the price level depends on the debt-repayment regime that was in place when the observations were generated. On the one hand, under a Ricardian regime, deficits and the price level would be uncorrelated, because government deficits would not cause movements in the stock of base money. On the other hand, under Friedman's regime, deficits would be highly correlated with the price level. It would therefore be a mistake to estimate the relationship between the deficit and the price path from time-series observations drawn from a period under which a Ricardian regime was in place and to assert that this same relationship will hold between the deficit and inflation under a regime like that described by Friedman or Bryant and Wallace. It would be a mistake because private agents' interpretations of observed deficits, and consequently the impact of observed deficits on the price level, depend on the debt-servicing regime that they imagine to be in place.

The Ricardian regime, Friedman's 1948 regime, and the intermediate Bryant-Wallace regimes each involve solutions of one kind or another to the problem of coordinating the actions of the monetary and fiscal authorities. The government budget constraint (equation 2.4) implies that coordination is necessary, for a monetary authority, by virtue of its control over the division of government debt in the hands of the public between interest-bearing debt and base money, controls the flow of revenues from the inflation tax that can be used to cover current and future deficits. In principle, the monetary authority has the power to force the system into the Ricardian regime by simply refusing to monetize any interest-bearing government debt. The fiscal authority would thereby be compelled to place its debt with private lenders, presumably by competing on an equal footing with other borrowers.

Under each of the debt-servicing regimes described so far, interest-bearing government debt has been assumed in effect to be indexed. As mentioned earlier, either the debt is regarded as explicitly indexed, or else the rationality of the public's price level expectations and the fact that the government is imagined to adhere to policies or entire time paths of $G(t) - T(t, M(t))$, and $B(t)$ mean that a system with nominal government debt behaves just like a system with indexed government bonds.[6]

Since we want to apply the results of our reasoning to recent U.S. experience in which government borrowing is in nominal terms, it is important to stress the aspect of the preceding regimes that government plans are adhered to. Though in some of the above regimes the government may resort to an inflation tax, it is known in advance that the government plans to do so. There is no element of fraud or deception in the inflation generated under such regimes.

However, when all or part of the government interest-bearing debt is in nominal form, at each point in time the government appears to have the option of defaulting on part of the debt by inflating at a rate greater than had initially been expected. In the context of the rational expectations assumption that we are working with here, inflation at a greater rate than had initially been expected by the public is brought about when the government departs from an initial plan for $G(t) - T(t, M(t)$, and $B(t)$ that was thought by the public to be in place and embarks on a plan implying a higher price level for the present period than had originally been anticipated. Resorting to this option is a form of default because it gives holders of interest-bearing government debt and base money different real rates of return than they initially had bargained for on the basis of the originally planned time paths of $G(t) - T(t)$, $M(t)$, and $B(t)$. This default option can be represented by reformulating the government budget constraint (equation 2.4) in terms of the nominal interest rate on government interest-bearing debt. Let $r_n(t)$ be the nominal interest rate on one-period debt from period t to $t + 1$. Then the real rate of interest $r(t - 1)$ is related to $r_n(t - 1)$ as follows:

$$1 + r(t - 1) = [1 + r_n(t - 1)]\frac{p(t - 1)}{p(t)}$$

This equation states that, with a previously fixed nominal rate of interest, the realized real rate of interest between $t - 1$ and t is lower the higher is the price level at t. We can use the above equation to write the government budget constraint as

$$G(t) - T(t) = \frac{M(t) - M(t - 1)}{p(t)} + B(t)$$
$$- B(t - 1)[1 + r_n(t - 1)]\frac{p(t - 1)}{p(t)} \quad (2.9)$$

This equation shows how generating a higher price level than had previously been expected helps to finance current deficit and to diminish the need to sell new government debt.

There are serious questions about whether, and under what circumstances, a government should resort to the option of defaulting that is present when part of the debt is in nominal terms. There is also a serious question of the scope that a government actually has for repeatedly resorting to the default option.[7] Presumably, a government that once reneges on its plans for $G(t) - T(t)$, $M(t)$, and $B(t)$ is less likely to be trusted the next time. The public can be expected to evaluate subsequent government plans and announcements against the background of the government's reputation for executing previous plans. Prospective lenders to a government and holders of its base money thus have some latitude to punish a government with a history of defaulting on its plans.

REAGANOMICS AND CREDIBILITY

I have argued that the government budget constraint requires that monetary and fiscal policies be coordinated and that a variety of coherent and default-free schemes for coordinating them can be imagined, the Ricardian regime and Friedman's 1948 regime being polar examples. I have also indicated that when some of the government debt is in nominal form (and remember that base money itself is in such a nominal form) there lurks the possibility of defaulting on part of the debt by reneging on the original plan for time paths of monetary and fiscal variables. I shall now use these ideas as a basis for criticizing the program for coordinating monetary and fiscal policy that was implicit during the first year and a half or so of the first Reagan administration.

The Reagan administration came into power encouraging a policy for the monetary authority that would be appropriate for the Ricardian regime but advocating plans for taxes and expenditures that could be feasible only, if at all, under some version of a Bryant-Wallace regime. The administration initially supported a commitment to a monetarist policy of $M(t) - M(t - 1) = 0$ forever. Simultaneously, however, in conjunction with the Congress, the administration adopted tax and expenditure plans that implied large positive values of $G(t) - T(t)$ into the indefinite future. As we have seen above, such monetary and fiscal policies are incompatible; it is simply not feasible to carry out both of them.

My colleague Neil Wallace has described the scheme for coordinating monetary and fiscal policies that was being utilized at the inception of the Reagan administration as coordination via resort to a "game of chicken." The monetary authority had promised to stick to a tight-money policy of $M(t) - M(t - 1) = 0$ for all future t's, come hell or high water, but meanwhile the fiscal authority had set in place tax and expenditure plans that implied large values of $G(t) - T(t)$ into the indefinite future. On the one hand, if the monetary authority could successfully stick to its guns and forever refuse to monetize any government debt, then eventually the arithmetic of the government's budget constraint would compel the fiscal authority to back down and to swing its budget into balance. On the other hand, if the fiscal authority were to stick to its guns and simply refuse to reduce the stream of $G(t) - T(t)$, then eventually the arithmetic of the government budget constraint would compel the monetary authority to monetize large parts of the deficit. All that is clear is that in this situation, one of the two parties to the conflict eventually has to give in. (The party to capitulate is called a "chicken.")

This situation can be likened to one in which the quarterback of a football team (the fiscal authority) announces that he is going to run the ball and wants the tight end to block, while simultaneously the tight end (the monetary authority) announces that he wants to catch a pass and will run a pass route on the next play. The quarterback and the tight end point out to one another that the other had better capitulate or else the next play will go badly. About the only thing that is certain about this situation is that it cannot long endure.

Coordinating monetary and fiscal policies by use of such a game of chicken necessarily confronts private agents with uncertainty about subsequent taxes, rates of inflation, and rates of interest on government securities. Unlike uncertainty about the weather or about the success of a new technology or machine, the uncertainty injected into the economy over the outcome of a struggle between monetary and fiscal policies, such as I have described, is entirely avoidable and unnecessary. Private agents are forced to form opinions about when and how the conflict between government agencies will be resolved. Some of the observed market reactions to that situation can be interpreted in terms of the preponderance of public opinion about how the conflict would eventually be resolved. For example, the high long-term nominal interest rates that prevailed in 1981 and 1982 can be interpreted as reflecting the market's guess that large deficits would persist and eventually be monetized in large part, leading to high inflation rates in the future. In addition, the very injection of substantial extraneous uncertainty is capable of triggering contractions in output and expansions of unemployment due to the additional sheer confusion faced by agents.

In this interpretation Reaganomics was not credible because it was not feasible. It was simply not feasible simultaneously to carry out both the fiscal and the monetary aspects of Reaganomics. Therefore, to rational observers, Reaganomics was incredible. This was paradoxical because, more than in any other recent administration, spokesmen for the Reagan administration initially placed substantial stress on "announcement effects" and the immediate benefits that would flow from adhering to a credible long-run strategy.

However, there may be another, more favorable interpretation of Reaganomics that involves a more complicated game of chicken against the background of the government budget constraint. This game of chicken involves not two but three players. Imagine that a first player sets a path for $T(t)$, a second player sets a path for $G(t)$, and a third player (via open-market operations) sets a path for $M(t) - M(t - 1)$. Suppose that the first and third players wish to reduce the size of the government, as measured by the stream of $G(t)$. Although these two players do not directly control $G(t)$, by acting together they can bring pressure upon it; for if the entire path of $T(t)$ is somehow reduced and if the monetary authority maintains a policy of setting $M(t) - M(t - 1) = 0$ for all future t's, then the arithmetic of equation 2.4 and the implied need to finance current deficits by promising to run future surpluses will cause the second player to capitulate and to reduce $G(t)$.

Though oversimplified, this three-player game captures the motivation of some advocates of the Reagan administration's policies. The administration can be viewed as having implemented a strategy of moving quickly to reduce taxes before announcing or planning concrete expenditure reductions, while simultaneously encouraging tight monetary policy, and then opposing rescinding tax decreases in order to balance the large deficits that threatened to develop in the future. Viewed in this way, this game of chicken, fought against the backdrop of the arithmetic of equation 2.4, is a struggle over how large the government of the United States is to be. The particular strategy for reducing the size of the government that I have described is attractive, even for one who wants a smaller government, only if one is relatively confident that the uncertainties injected into monetary and fiscal arrangements by fighting the struggle in this way will not have an unduly adverse effect on the performance of national output and employment.

CONCLUSION

There are a variety of methods of coordinating monetary and fiscal policies that are superior to Wallace's game of chicken. For example, a case can be made that either the Ricardian regime or Friedman's 1948 regime dominates the game of chicken. The game of chicken that I have described amounts to a struggle for dominance between the fiscal and monetary authorities, in which each player promises to stick to a strategy that is feasible only if the other player acts as a follower. (Such a situation, in which each player seems to behave like a leader, is the case of Stackelberg warfare referred to above.) Under the Ricardian regime, the monetary authority in effect dominates the fiscal authority insofar as decisions about the present value of government deficit are concerned. Under Friedman's 1948 regime, it is the fiscal authority that dominates the monetary authority insofar as decisions about the rate of growth of base money are concerned. Each of these polar regimes has a well-defined structure of dominance, and each has relatively straightforward implications for the paths of government interest-bearing debt and base money, to which the public can be imagined to adjust readily. Furthermore, each of the polar regimes entails a relatively clear assignment of responsibility for inflation, insofar as government policy influences the rate of inflation. As I have portrayed the structure of the economy and characterized the conduct of policy under the Ricardian regime, inflation can emerge only if there occur changes in the preferences of the public, in the structure of legal regulations, or perhaps in the conduct of foreign governments that supply substitutes for base money and government debt—each of which would be reflected in a change in our parameters $a(1)$ and $a(2)$. Under Friedman's 1948 scheme, government deficits have direct and immediate inflationary consequences that everyone can see.

How is the question of coordination of monetary and fiscal policies to be resolved? Current legislation in the United States leaves the method of resolution open, so that in practice it is resolved by the successive interactions of a succession of personalities and administrations within our fiscal and monetary institutions. It can be argued that superior outcomes would be achieved if the responsibilities of the monetary and fiscal authorities were to be legislatively or constitutionally restricted so as to determine in advance which institutions are to lead and which are to follow.

NOTES

1. Technically, this is the government deficit net of interest payments.
2. Since its decisions about the composition of the debt influence the interest payments that the government must make, the monetary authority helps determine the government deficit gross of interest payments and thereby the rate at which total government debt changes.
3. When $a(2) = 0$, equation 2.2 becomes a simple version of the quantity theory of money.
4. Another way to write equation 2.4 is

$$G(t) - T(t) + r(t - 1)B(t - 1)$$
$$= \frac{M(t) - M(t - 1)}{p(t)} + B(t) - B(t - 1)$$

   The term $G(t) - T(t) + r(t - 1)B(t - 1)$ is often called the government deficit gross of interest payments, while $G(t) - T(t)$ is termed the government deficit net of interest payments. The monetary authority is assumed to control the ratio of $B(t)$ to $M(t)$ at each point in time. It thereby influences the subsequent rate of growth of total government indebtedness by influencing the interest expenses $r(t - 1)B(t - 1)$ that appear in equation 2.4.
5. One way to implement the regime given by equations 2.5 and 2.6 is simply to adjust current taxes $T(t)$ by an amount equal to any variations in interest payments $r(t - 1)B(t - 1)$ that are associated with variations in past government expenditures or taxes. This policy amounts always to levying current taxes sufficient to service the interest payments that are currently due. This is the way McCallum [8] proceeds in one of his experiments.
6. This is one of the findings of the theoretical literature on indexed government bonds: that, under general circumstances, they make no difference to a rational expectations equilibrium. See Liviatan [7] or Peled [9].
7. These questions are raised and discussed by Kydland and Prescott [6] and Calvo [3].

REFERENCES

1. Bryant, John, and Neil Wallace. 1980. A suggestion for further simplifying the theory of money. Staff Report 62, Federal Reserve Bank of Minneapolis.
2. Cagan, Phillip. 1956. The monetary dynamics of hyperinflation. In M. Friedman, ed., *Studies in the Quantity Theory of Money*. Chicago: University of Chicago Press.
3. Calvo, Guillermo. 1978. On the time consistency of optimal policy in a monetary economy. *Econometrica* 46 (November):1411–1428.
4. Friedman, Milton. 1948. A monetary and fiscal framework for economic stability. *American Economic Review* 38 (June):245–264.
5. Friedman, Milton. 1960. *A Program for Monetary Stability*. New York: Fordham University Press.
6. Kydland, Finn E., and Edward C. Prescott. 1977. Rules rather than discretion: The inconsistency of optimal plans. *Journal of Political Economy* 85 (June):473–491.
7. Liviatan, Nissan. 1983. On equilibrium wage indexation and neutrality of indexation policy. In P. Aspe-Armella, R. Dornbusch, and M. Obstfeld, eds., *Financial Policies and the World Capital Market: The Problem of Latin American Countries*. Chicago: University of Chicago Press.
8. McCallum, Bennett T. 1984. Are bond-financed deficits inflationary? A Ricardian analysis. *Journal of Political Economy* 92 (February):123–135.
9. Peled, Dan. 1980. Government index bonds—do they improve matters? Ph.D. diss., University of Minnesota.
10. Sargent, Thomas J., and Neil Wallace. 1981. Some unpleasant monetarist arithmetic. Federal Reserve Bank of Minneapolis *Quarterly Review* 5 (Fall):1–17.

chapter 3

The Ends of
Four Big Inflations

INTRODUCTION

Since the middle 1960s, many Western economies have experienced persistent and growing rates of inflation. Some prominent economists and statesmen have been convinced that this inflation has a stubborn, self-sustaining momentum and that either it simply is not susceptible to cure by conventional measures of monetary and fiscal restraint or, in terms of the consequent widespread and sustained unemployment, the cost of eradicating inflation by monetary and fiscal measures would be prohibitively high. It is often claimed that there is an underlying rate of inflation that responds slowly, if at all, to restrictive monetary and fiscal measures.[1] Evidently, this underlying rate of inflation is the rate of inflation that firms and workers have come to expect will prevail in the future. There is momentum in this process because firms and workers supposedly form their expectations by extrapolating past rates of inflation into the future. If this is true, the years from the middle 1960s to the early 1980s left firms and workers with a legacy of high expected rates of inflation that promise to respond only slowly, if at all, to restrictive monetary and fiscal policy actions. According to this view, restrictive monetary and fiscal actions in the first instance cause substantial reductions in output and employment but have little, if any, effects in reducing the rate of inflation. For the economy of the United States, a widely cited estimate is that for every one per-

40

centage point reduction in the annual inflation rate accomplished by restrictive monetary and fiscal measures, $220 billion of annual GNP would be lost. For the $2500 billion U.S. economy, the cost of achieving zero percent inflation would be great, indeed, according to this estimate.

An alternative "rational expectations" view denies that there is any inherent momentum in the present process of inflation.[2] This view maintains that firms and workers have now come to expect high rates of inflation in the future and that they strike inflationary bargains in light of these expectations.[3] However, it is held that people expect high rates of inflation in the future precisely because the government's current and prospective monetary and fiscal policies warrant those expectations. Further, the current rate of inflation and people's expectations about future rates of inflation may well seem to respond slowly to isolated *actions* of restrictive monetary and fiscal policy that are viewed as temporary departures from what is perceived as a long-term government *policy* involving high average rates of government deficits and monetary expansion in the future. Thus inflation only *seems* to have a momentum of its own; it is actually the long-term government policy of persistently running large deficits and creating money at high rates that imparts the momentum to the inflation rate. An implication of this view is that inflation can be stopped much more quickly than advocates of the "momentum" view have indicated and that their estimates of the length of time and the costs of stopping inflation in terms of foregone output ($220 billion of GNP for one percentage point in the inflation rate) are erroneous. This is not to say that it would be easy to eradicate inflation. On the contrary, it would require far more than a few temporary restrictive fiscal and monetary actions. It would require a change in the policy *regime*: There must be an abrupt change in the continuing government *policy*, or *strategy*, for setting deficits now and in the future that is sufficiently binding as to be widely believed. Economists do not now possess reliable, empirically tried and true models that can enable them to predict precisely how rapidly and with what disruption in terms of lost output and employment such a regime change will work its effects. How costly such a move would be in terms of foregone output and how long it would be in taking effect would depend partly on how resolute and evident the government's commitment was.

This chapter describes several dramatic historical experiences that I believe to be consistent with the "rational expectations" view but that seem difficult to reconcile with the "momentum" model of inflation. The idea is to stand back from our current predicament and to examine the measures that successfully brought drastic inflations under control in several European countries in the 1920s. I shall describe and interpret events in Austria, Hungary, Germany, and Poland, countries which experienced a dramatic "hyperinflation" in which, after the passage of several months, price indexes assumed astronomical proportions. The basic data to be studied are the price indexes in Figures 3.1–3.4. These data are recorded in a logarithmic scale, so that they will fit on a page. For all four countries, and especially Germany, the rise in the price level was spectacular. The graphs also reveal that in each case inflation stopped abruptly rather than gradually. I shall also briefly describe events in Czechoslovakia, a country surrounded by neighbors experiencing hyperinflations, but which successfully achieved a stable currency itself. My reason for studying these episodes is that they are laboratories for the study of regime

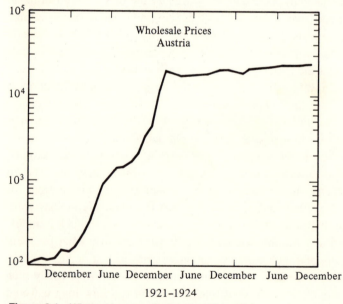

Figure 3.1   Wholesale prices in Austria 1921–1924.

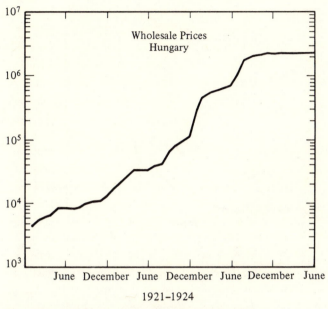

Figure 3.2 Wholesale prices in Hungary 1921–1924

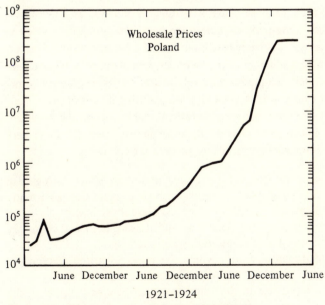

Figure 3.3 Wholesale prices in Poland 1921–1924.

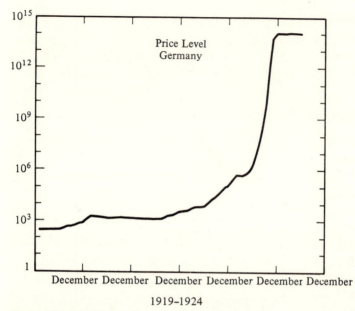

Figure 3.4 Wholesale prices in Germany 1919–1924.

changes. Within each of Austria, Hungary, Poland, and Germany, there occurred a dramatic change in the fiscal policy regime, which in each instance was associated with the end of a hyperinflation. Further, though it shared some problems with its four neighbors, Czechoslovakia deliberately adopted a relatively restrictive fiscal policy regime, with the avowed aim of maintaining the value of its currency.

While there are many differences in details among the Austrian, Hungarian, Polish, and German hyperinflations, there are some very important common features. These include the following:

1. The nature of the fiscal policy regime in effect during each of the hyperinflations. Each of the four countries persistently ran enormous budget deficits on current account.
2. The nature of the deliberate and drastic fiscal and monetary measures taken to end the hyperinflations.
3. The immediacy with which the price level and foreign exchanges suddenly stabilized.[4]
4. The rapid rise in the "high-powered" money supply in the months and years after the rapid inflation had ended.

I shall assemble and interpret the facts in the light of a view about the forces that give money value and about the way the international monetary system worked in the 1920s. Before interpreting the historical facts, I now turn to a brief description of this view.

THE GOLD STANDARD

After World War I, the United States was on the gold standard. The U.S. government stood ready to convert a dollar into a specified amount of gold on demand. To understate things, immediately after the war, Hungary, Austria, Poland, and Germany were not on the gold standard. In practice, their currencies were largely "fiat," or unbacked. The governments of these countries resorted to the printing of new unbacked money to finance government deficits.[5] This was done on such a scale that it led to a depreciation of the currencies of spectacular proportions. In the end, the German mark stabilized at 1 trillion (10^{12}) paper marks to the prewar gold mark, the Polish mark at 1.8 million paper marks to the gold zloty, the Austrian crown at 14,400 paper crowns to the prewar Austro-Hungarian crown, and the Hungarian krone at 14,500 paper crowns to the prewar Austro-Hungarian crown [13, p. 101].

This chapter focuses on the deliberate changes in policy that Hungary, Austria, Poland, and Germany made to end their hyperinflations, and the deliberate choice of policy that Czechoslovakia made to avoid inflation in the first place. The hyperinflations were each ended by restoring or virtually restoring convertibility to the dollar or equivalently to gold. For this reason it is good to keep in mind the nature of the restrictions that adherence to the gold standard imposed on a government. Under the gold standard, a government issued demand notes and longer-term debt it promised to convert into gold under certain specified conditions, that is, on demand, for notes. Presumably, people were willing to hold these claims at full value if the government's promise to pay were judged to be good. The government's promise to pay was "backed" only partially by its holding of gold reserves. More important in practice, since usually a government did not hold 100 percent reserves of gold, a government's notes and debts were backed by the commitment of the government to levy taxes in sufficient amounts, given its expenditures, to make good on its debt. In effect, the notes were backed by the government's pursuit of an appropriate budget policy. During the 1920s, John Maynard Keynes emphasized that the size of a government's gold reserve was not the determinant of whether it could successfully maintain convertibility with gold: Its fiscal policy was.[6] According to this view, what mattered was not the current government deficit but the present value of current and prospective future government deficits. The government was like a firm whose prospective receipts were its future tax collections. The value of the government's debt was, to a first approximation, equal to the present value of current and future government surpluses. So under a gold standard, a government must honor its debts and could not engage in inflationary finance. In order to assign a value to the government's debt, it was necessary to have a view about the fiscal policy regime in effect, that is, the rule determining the government deficit as a function of the state of the economy now and in the future. The public's perception of the fiscal regime influenced the value of government debt through private agents' expectations about the present value of the revenue streams backing that debt.[7] It will be worthwhile to keep this view of the gold standard in mind as we turn to review the events surrounding the ends of the four hyperinflations.[8]

However, it will be useful first to expand a little more generally on the distinction between the effects of isolated *actions* taken within the context of a given general strategy, on the one hand, and the effects of choosing among alternative general strategies or rules for repeatedly taking actions, on the other. The latter choice I refer to as a choice of regime. The values of government expenditures and tax rates for one particular quarter are examples of actions, while the rules, implicit or explicit, for repeatedly selecting government expenditures and tax rates as functions of the state of the economy are examples of regimes. Recent work in dynamic macroeconomics has discovered the following general principle: Whenever there is a change in the government strategy or regime, private economic agents can be expected to change their strategies or rules for choosing consumption rates, investment rates, portfolios, and so on.[9] The reason is that private agents' behavior is selfish, or at least purposeful, so that when the government switches its strategy, private agents usually find it in their best interests to change theirs. One by-product of this principle is that most of the empirical relations captured in standard econometric models cannot be expected to remain constant across contemplated changes in government policy regimes. For this reason predictions made under the assumption that such relations will remain constant across regime changes ought not to be believed. The estimate that a 1 percent reduction in inflation would cost $220 billion GNP annually is one example of such a faulty predicton. When an important change in regime occurs, dynamic macroeconomics would predict that the entire pattern of correlations among variables will change in quantitatively important ways.

While the distinction between isolated actions and strategy regimes is clear in principle, it is an admittedly delicate task to interpret whether particular historical episodes reflect isolated actions within the same old rules of the game or whether they reflect a new set of rules or government strategies.[10] All that we have to go on are the recorded actions actually taken, together with the pronouncements of public officials, laws, legislative votes, and sometimes constitutional provisions. Out of this material we are to fashion a view about the government strategy being used. Common sense suggests and technical econometric considerations confirm the difficulties in making such interpretations in general. Having said this, I believe that the examples discussed below are about as close to being laboratories for studying regime changes as history has provided.

AUSTRIA

At the end of World War I, the Austro-Hungarian empire dissolved into a number of successor states, of which Austria was one. From having been the center of an empire of 625,000 square kilometers and 50 million inhabitants, Austria was reduced to a mere 80,000 square kilometers and 6.5 million inhabitants. Having suffered food scarcities during the war that were produced by an effective Allied blockade, Austria found itself confronted with new national borders and trade barriers that cut it off from the food sources formerly within its empire. Further, the government of Austria reabsorbed a large number of Austrian imperial bureaucrats who were no longer welcome in the

Table 3.1   AUSTRIAN BUDGETS, 1919–1922
In Millions of Paper Crowns

	Receipts	Expen- ditures	Deficit	Percentage of expenditures covered by new issues of paper money
1 January–30 June 1919	1,339	4,043	2,704	67
1 July 1919–30 June 1920	6,295	16,873	10,578	63
1 July 1920–30 June 1921	29,483	70,601	41,118	58
1 January–31 December 1922	209,763	347,533	137,770	40

Source: Pasvolsky [25, p. 102].

other successor states. Austrians also faced a large-scale unemployment problem stemming from the need to reconvert the economy to
peaceful activities and to adjust to the new national borders. If this
were not enough, as a loser of the war Austria owed the Reparation
Commission sums that for a long time were uncertain in amount but
were presumed eventually to be substantial. The Reparation Commission, in effect, held a blanket mortgage against the assets and revenues
of the Austrian government.

Austria responded to these pressing problems by making large
expenditures in the form of food relief and payments to the unemployed. In addition, the state railroads and monopolies ran deficits, as
taxes and prices were kept relatively low. The government did not
collect enough taxes to cover expenditures and so ran very substantial
deficits during the years 1919 to 1922 (see Table 3.1). As Table 3.1
shows, in these years the deficit was typically over 50 percent of the
total government expenditures. The government financed these deficits
by selling treasury bills to the Austrian section of the Austro-Hungarian bank. The result was a very rapid increase in the volume of "high-
powered" money, defined as the notes and demand deposit obligations
of the central bank (see Table 3.2). As the figures in Table 3.2 indicate, between March 1919 and August 1922 the total note circulation
in Austria[11] of the Austro-Hungarian bank increased by a factor of
288. This expansion of central bank notes stemmed mainly from the
bank's policy of discounting treasury bills. However, it also resulted

Table 3.2 TOTAL NOTE CIRCULATION OF AUSTRIAN CROWNS
In Thousands of Crowns

Year	Month	Value	Year	Month	Value
1919	January	—	1922	May	397,829,313
	February	—		June	549,915,678
	March	4,687,056		July	786,225,601
	April	5,577,851		August	1,353,403,632
	May	5,960,003		September	2,277,677,738
	June	7,397,692		October	2,970,916,607
	July	8,391,405		November	3,417,786,498
	August	9,241,135		December	4,080,177,238
	September	9,781,112	1923	January	4,110,551,163
	October	10,819,310		February	4,207,991,722
	November	11,193,670		March	4,459,117,216
	December	12,134,474		April	4,577,382,333
1920	January	13,266,878		May	4,837,042,081
	February	14,292,809		June	5,432,619,312
	March	15,457,749		July	5,684,133,721
	April	15,523,832		August	5,894,786,367
	May	15,793,805		September	6,225,109,352
	June	16,971,344		October	6,607,839,105
	July	18,721,495		November	6,577,616,341
	August	20,050,281		December	7,125,755,190
	September	22,271,686	1924	January	6,735,109,000
	October	25,120,385		February	7,364,441,000
	November	28,072,331		March	7,144,901,000
	December	30,645,658		April	7,135,471,000
1921	January	34,525,634		May	7,552,620,000
	February	38,352,648		June	7,774,958,000
	March	41,067,299		July	7,995,647,000
	April	45,036,723		August	5,894,786,367
	May	45,583,194		September	7,998,509,000
	June	49,685,140		October	8,213,003,000
	July	54,107,281		November	8,070,021,000
	August	58,533,766		December	8,387,767,000
	September	70,170,798	1925	January	7,902,217,000
1922	January	227,015,925		February	7,957,242,000
	February	259,931,138		March	7,897,792,000
	March	304,063,642		April	7,976,420,000
	April	346,697,776			

Source: Young [36, vol. 2, p. 292].

partly from the central bank's practice of making loans and discounts to private agents at nominal interest rates of between 6 and 9 percent per annum, rates that by any standard were far too low in view of the inflation rate, which averaged 10,000 percent per annum from January 1921 to August 1922 (Table 3.3).[12]

In response to these government actions and what seemed like prospects for their indefinite continuation, the Austrian crown depreciated internationally and domestic prices rose rapidly (see Tables 3.3 and 3.4). While between January 1921 and August 1922 the note circulation of the central bank increased by a factor of 39, the retail price index increased by a factor of 110 (see Tables 3.3 and 3.4) so that the real value of the note circulation diminished during the currency depreciation.[13] The "flight from the crown" occurred as people chose to hold less of their wealth in the form of the rapidly depreciating crown, attempting instead to hold foreign currencies or real assets.[14] From the viewpoint of financing its deficit, the government of Austria had an interest in resisting the flight from the crown because this had the effect of diminishing the resources that the government could command by printing money. Therefore, the government established a system of exchange controls administered by an agency called the Devisenzentrale. The essential function of this agency was to increase the amount of Austrian crowns held by Austrians, which it accomplished by adopting measures making it difficult or illegal for Austrians to hold foreign currencies and other substitutes for Austrian crowns.[15] Despite these regulations, it is certain that Austrian citizens were holding large amounts of foreign currencies during 1921 and 1922.

Table 3.4 reveals that the Austrian crown abruptly stabilized in August 1922, while Table 3.3 indicates that prices abruptly stabilized a month later. This occurred despite the fact that the central bank's note circulation continued to increase rapidly, as Table 3.1 indicates. Furthermore, there occurred no change in currency units or "currency reform," at least not for another year and a half.

The depreciation of the Austrian crown was suddenly stopped by the intervention of the Council of the League of Nations and the resulting binding commitment of the government of Austria to reorder Austrian fiscal and monetary strategies dramatically. After Austria's increasingly desperate pleas to the Allied governments for interna-

Table 3.3 AUSTRIAN RETAIL PRICES, 1921–1924

		Retail price index, 52 commodities
1921	January	100
	February	114
	March	122
	April	116
	May	121
	June	150
	July	143
	August	167
	September	215
	October	333
	November	566
	December	942
1922	January	1,142
	February	1,428
	March	1,457
	April	1,619
	May	2,028
	June	3,421
	July	4,830
	August	11,046
	September	20,090
	October	18,567
	November	17,681
	December	17,409
1923	January	17,526
	February	17,851
	March	18,205
	April	19,428
	May	20,450
	June	20,482
	July	19,368
	August	18,511
	September	20,955
	October	21,166
	November	21,479
	December	21,849
1924	January	22,941
	February	23,336
	March	23,336
	April	23,361
	May	23,797
	June	24,267

Source: Young [36, vol. 2, p. 293].

Table 3.4   EXCHANGE RATES, AUSTRIAN CROWNS PER U.S. DOLLAR, IN NEW YORK MARKET

	1919	1920	1921	1922	1923	1924
January	17.09	271.43	654.00	7,375.00	71,500.00	70,760.00
February	20.72	250.00	722.50	6,350.00	71,150.00	70,760.00
March	25.85	206.66	676.00	7,487.50	71,000.00	70,760.00
April	26.03	200.00	661.00	7,937.50	70,850.00	70,760.00
May	24.75	155.83	604.00	11,100.00	70,800.00	70,760.00
June	29.63	145.00	720.00	18,900.00	70,800.00	70,760.00
July	37.24	165.00	957.00	42,350.00	70,760.00	70,760.00
August	42.50	237.14	1,081.50	77,300.00	70,760.00	70,760.00
September	68.50	255.00	2,520.00	74,210.00	70,760.00	70,760.00
October	99.50	358.33	4,355.00	73,550.00	70,760.00	70,760.00
November	130.00	493.66	8,520.00	71,400.00	70,760.00	70,760.00
December	155.00	659.40	5,275.00	70,925.00	70,760.00	70,760.00

Source: Young [36, vol. 2, p. 294].

tional aid had repeatedly been rejected or only partially fulfilled, in late August 1922 the Council of the League of Nations undertook to enter into serious negotiations to reconstruct the financial system of Austria. These negotiations led to the signing of three protocols on 2 October 1922 that successfully guided the financial reconstruction of Austria. It is remarkable that even before the precise details of the protocols were publicly announced, the fact of the serious deliberations of the council brought relief to the situation. This can be seen in Tables 3.3 and 3.4, and was described by Pasvolsky as follows:

> The moment the Council of the League decided to take up in earnest the question of Austrian reconstruction, there was immediately a widespread conviction that the solution of the problem was at hand. This conviction communicated itself first of all to that delicately adjusted mechanism, the international exchange market. Nearly two weeks before Chancellor Seipel officially laid the Austrian question before the Council of the League, on August 25, the foreign exchange rate ceased to soar and began to decline, the internal price level following suit three weeks later. The printing presses in Austria were still grinding out new currency; the various ministries were still dispersing this new currency through the country by means of continuing budgetary deficits. Yet the rate of exchange was slowly declining. The crisis was checked [25, p. 116].

The first protocol was a declaration signed by Great Britain, France, Italy, Czechoslovakia, and Austria that reaffirmed the political independence and sovereignty of Austria.[16] The second protocol provided conditions for an international loan of 650 million gold crowns to Austria. The third protocol was signed by Austria alone and laid out a plan for reconstruction of its fiscal and monetary affairs. The Austrian government promised to establish a new independent central bank, to cease running large deficits, and to bind itself not to finance deficits with advances of notes from the central bank. Further, the government of Austria agreed to accept in Austria a commissioner general, appointed by the Council of the League, who was to be responsible for monitoring the fulfillment of Austria's commitments. The government of Austria also agreed to furnish security to back the reconstruction loan. At the same time it was understood that the Reparation Commission would give up or modify its claim on the resources of the government of Austria.

The government of Austria and the League both moved swiftly to execute the plan outlined in the protocols. In legislation of 14 November 1922, the Austrian National Bank was formed to replace the old Austrian section of the Austro-Hungarian bank; it was to take over the assets and functions of the Devisenzentrale. The new bank began operations on 1 January 1923 and was specifically forbidden from lending to the government except on the security of an equal amount of gold and foreign assets. The bank was also required to cover its note issues with certain minimal proportions of gold, foreign earning assets, and commercial bills. Further, once the government's debt to the bank had been reduced to 30 million gold crowns, the bank was obligated to resume convertibility into gold.

The government moved to balance its budget by taking concrete steps in several directions. Expenditures were reduced by discharging thousands of government employees. Under the reconstruction scheme, the government promised gradually to discharge a total of 100,000 state employees. Deficits in government enterprises were reduced by raising prices of government-sold goods and services. New taxes and more efficient means of collecting tax and custom revenues were instituted. The results of these measures can be seen by comparing the figures in Table 3.5 with those in Table 3.1. Within two years the government was able to balance the budget.

Table 3.5 THE AUSTRIAN BUDGET, 1923–1925
In Millions of Schillings

Item	Closed accounts		
	1923	1924	1925
Total revenue	697.4	900.6	908.5
Current expenditures	779.6	810.0	741.4
Deficit (−) or surplus (+)	− 82.2	+ 90.6	+ 167.1
Capital expenditures	76.0	103.6	90.6
Total balance	− 158.2	− 13.0	+ 76.5

Source: Pasvolsky [25, p. 127].
Note: 1 schilling = 10,000 paper crowns.

The stabilization of the Austrian crown was not achieved via a currency reform. At the end of 1924 a new unit of currency was introduced, the schilling, equal to 10,000 paper crowns. The introduction of this new unit of currency occurred long after the exchange rate had been stabilized and was surely an incidental measure.[17]

Table 3.2 reveals that from August 1922, when the exchange rate suddenly stabilized, to December 1924, the circulating notes of the Austrian central bank increased by a factor of over 6. The phenomenon of the achievement of price stability in the face of a sixfold increase in the stock of "high-powered" money was widely regarded by contemporaries as violating the quantity theory of money, and so it seems to do. However, these observations are not at all paradoxical when interpreted in the light of a view that distinguishes sharply between unbacked, or "outside," money, on the one hand, and backed, or "inside," money, on the other hand. In particular, the balance sheet of the central bank and the nature of its open-market operations changed dramatically after the carrying out of the League's protocols, with the consequence that the proper interpretation of the figures on the total note obligations of the central bank changed substantially. Before the protocols, the liabilities of the central bank were backed mainly by government treasury bills; that is, they were not backed at all, since treasury bills signified no commitment to raise revenues through future tax collections. After the execution of the protocols, the liabilities of the central bank became backed by gold, foreign assets, and commercial paper, and ultimately by the power of the government to collect taxes. At the margin, central bank liabilities were backed 100 percent by gold, foreign assets, and commercial paper as notes and the deposits were created through open-market operations in those assets (see Table 3.6). The value of the crown was backed by the commitment of the government to run a fiscal policy compatible with maintaining the convertibility of its liabilities into dollars. Given such a fiscal regime, to a first approximation, the intermediating activities of the central bank did not affect the value of the crown so long as the assets purchased by the bank were sufficiently valuable. Thus the sixfold increase in the liabilities of the central bank after the protocols ought not to be regarded as inflationary. The willingness of Austrians to convert hoards of foreign exchange into crowns, which is reflected in Table 3.6, is not surprising since the stabilization of the crown made it a much more desirable asset to hold relative to foreign exchange.[18]

The available figures on unemployment indicate that the stabilization of the crown was attended by a substantial increase in the unemployment rate, though unemployment had begun to climb well before stabilization was achieved (see Table 3.7). The number of recipients of state unemployment benefits gradually climbed from a low of 8,700 in December 1921 to 83,000 in December 1922. It climbed to 167,000 by March 1923, and then receded to 76,000 in November 1923 [25, p. 161]. How much of this unemployment was due to the achievement of currency stabilization and how much was due to the real dislocations affecting the Austrian economy cannot be determined. However, it is true that currency stabilization was achieved in Austria very suddenly, and with a cost in increased unemployment and foregone output that was minor compared with the $220 billion GNP that some current analysts estimate would be lost in the United States per one percentage point inflation reduction.

HUNGARY

Like its old partner in the Hapsburg monarchy, Hungary emerged from World War I as a country much reduced in land, population, and power. It retained only 25 percent of its territory (down from 325,000

Table 3.6 AUSTRIAN NATIONAL BANK BALANCE SHEET
End of Month, in Millions of Crowns

	Gold	Foreign exchange and currency	Loans and discounts	Treasury bills	Notes in circulation	Deposits
1923:						
January	49,304	1,058,244	731,046	2,556,848	4,110,551	279,092
February	83,438	1,029,134	728,884	2,552,682	4,207,992	178,752
March	86,097	1,336,385	821,397	2,550,159	4,459,117	329,109
April	73,270	1,439,999	741,858	2,550,159	4,577,382	226,273
May	73,391	1,682,209	875,942	2,550,159	4,837,042	343,339
June	73,391	2,532,316	730,848	2,547,212	5,432,619	362,237
July	73,391	2,947,216	658,966	2,539,777	5,684,134	535,121
August	73,391	3,050,085	647,936	2,538,719	5,894,786	413,383
September	73,391	3,126,599	863,317	2,537,661	6,225,109	373,673
October	62,117	3,356,232	1,069,340	2,536,604	6,607,839	414,882
November	62,117	3,504,652	1,094,620	2,535,547	6,577,616	617,321
December	83,177	3,832,132	1,325,380	2,534,490	7,125,755	649,424
1924:						
January	91,274	3,811,148	1,253,110	2,533,434	6,735,109	536,982
February	105,536	3,921,594	1,737,334	2,532,379	7,364,441	558,800
March	106,663	3,953,872	1,733,400	2,295,428	7,144,901	752,814
April	107,059	3,669,333	2,131,984	2,294,471	7,315,471	696,141
May	107,443	3,344,337	2,660,449	2,259,839	7,554,620	641,001
June	107,762	3,178,339	3,092,470	2,237,794	7,774,958	741,400
July	108,342	3,254,477	3,304,876	2,231,173	7,995,647	896,032
August	108,256	3,453,177	3,226,962	2,219,459	8,002,142	997,677
September	108,950	3,724,916	2,852,688	2,210,527	7,998,509	890,537
October	109,327	4,032,485	2,379,700	2,202,106	8,213,003	502,579
November	110,643	4,312,355	1,945,627	2,196,181	8,072,021	484,750
December	110,890	4,770,548	1,881,593	2,178,185	8,387,767	533,450
1925:						
January	111,314	3,337,911	1,545,295	2,172,491	7,902,217	438,390
February	111,474	3,310,032	1,285,158	2,150,151	7,957,242	315,771
March	111,649	3,202,802	1,047,719	2,107,949	7,897,792	295,498
April	112,168	3,474,672	1,059,069	2,088,777	7,976,420	236,957

Source: Young [36, vol. 2, p. 291].

**Table 3.7 NUMBER OF AUSTRIAN UNEMPLOYED
IN RECEIPT OF RELIEF**
In Thousands

Beginning of	1922	1923	1924	1925	1926
January	17	117	98	154	208
April	42	153	107	176	202
July	33	93	64	118	151
October	38	79	78	119	148

Source: League of Nations [14, p. 87].

square kilometers to 92,000) and only 37 percent of its population
(down from 21 million to about 8 million). Its financial and economic
life was disrupted by the newly drawn national borders separating it
from peoples and economic institutions formerly within the domain of
the Hapsburg monarchy.

At the end of the war, Hungary experienced political turmoil as
the Hapsburg King Charles was replaced by the government of Prince
Karolyi. In March 1919, the Karolyi government was overthrown by
the Bolsheviks under Bela Kun. The regime of Bela Kun lasted only
four months, as Rumania invaded Hungary, occupied it for a few
weeks, and then withdrew. A new repressive right-wing regime under
Admiral Horthy then took power. The "white terror" against leftists
carried out by supporters of Horthy took even more lives than the "red
terror" that had occurred under Bela Kun.

At the end of the war, the currency of Hungary consisted of the
notes of the Austro-Hungarian bank. By the provisions of the peace
treaties of Trianon and St. Germain, the successor states to the Austro-
Hungarian empire were required to stamp the notes of the Austro-
Hungarian bank that were held by their residents, in effect, thereby
recognizing those notes as debts of the respective new states. Before
Hungary executed this provision of the Treaty of Trianon, the currency
situation grew more complicated, for the Bolshevik regime had access
to the plates for printing one- and two-crown Austro-Hungarian bank
notes, and it used them to print more notes. The Bolshevik government also issued new so-called white notes. Each of these Bolshevik-
issued currencies was honored by the subsequent government.

Table 3.8   HUNGARIAN BUDGET ESTIMATES, 1920–1924
In Millions of Paper Crowns

	Revenue	Expenditures	Deficit	Percentage of expenditures covered by issues of paper money
1920–21	10,520	20,210	9,690	47.9
1921–22	20,296	26,764	6,468	24.1
1922–23	152,802	193,455	40,653	21.0
1923–24	2,168,140	3,307,099	1,138,959	34.4

Source: Pasvolsky [24, p. 299].

The Austro-Hungarian bank was liquidated at the end of 1919, and it was replaced by an Austrian section and a Hungarian section. The functions of the Hungarian section of the old bank were assumed in August 1921 by a State Note Institute, which was under the control of the minister of finance. In August 1921, the Note Institute issued its own notes, the Hungarian krone, in exchange for Hungarian stamped notes of the Austro-Hungarian bank and several other classes of notes, including those that had been issued by the Bolshevik regime.

As a loser of the war, Hungary owed reparations according to the Treaty of Trianon. The Reparation Commission had a lien on the resources of the government of Hungary. However, neither the total amount owed nor a schedule of payments was fixed for many years after the war. This circumstance alone created serious obstacles in terms of achieving a stable value for Hungary's currency and other debts, since the unclear reparations obligations made uncertain the nature of the resources that backed those debts.

From 1919 until 1924 the government of Hungary ran substantial budget deficits. The government's budget estimates in Table 3.8 are reported by Pasvolsky substantially to understate the size of the deficits [25, p. 298]. These deficits were financed by borrowing from the State Note Institute and were a major cause of a rapid increase in the note and deposit liabilities of the institute. An additional cause of the increase in liabilities of the institute was the increasing volume of loans and discounts that it made to private agents (see Table 3.9). These loans were made at a very low interest rate, in view of the rapid rate of price appreciation, and to a large extent amounted to simple gifts from the Note Institute to those lucky enough to receive loans on such generous terms. These private loans accounted for a much larger increase in high-powered money in the Hungarian than in the other three hyperinflations we shall study.

As Table 3.10 shows, the Hungarian krone depreciated rapidly on foreign exchange markets, and domestic prices rose rapidly. Between January 1922 and April 1924, the price index increased by a factor of 263. In the same period, the total notes and deposit liabilities of the Note Institute increased by a factor of 85, so that the real value of its liabilities decreased substantially. As in the case of Austria, this decrease was symptomatic of a "flight from the krone," as residents of Hungary attempted to economize on their holdings of krones and instead to hold assets denominated in more stable currencies. As in the case of Austria, the government of Hungary resisted this trend by establishing in August 1922 a Hungarian Devisenzentrale within the State Note Institute.

Table 3.10 indicates that in March 1924, the rise in prices and the depreciation of the krone internationally both abruptly halted. The stabilization occurred in the face of continued expansion in the liabilities of the central bank, which increased by a factor of 3.15 between March 1924 and January 1925 (see Table 3.9). This pattern parallels what occurred in Austria and has a similar explanation.

As in Austria, the financial reconstruction of Hungary was accomplished with the intervention of the League of Nations. Together with the Reparation Commission and the government of Hungary, the League devised a plan that reduced and clarified the reparations commitment of Hungary, arranged for an international loan that would help finance government expenditures, and committed Hungary to establish a balanced budget and a central bank legally bound to refuse any government demand for unbacked credit. On 21 February 1924, the Reparation Commission agreed to give up its lien on Hungary's resources so that these could be used to secure a recon-

Table 3.9 BALANCE SHEET OF HUNGARIAN CENTRAL BANK OR STATE NOTE INSTITUTE

Millions of Kronen

	Gold coin and bullion	Silver coin	Foreign currency and exchange	Bills Discounted
1921:				
January	—	—	—	10,924
February	—	—	—	13,202
March	—	—	—	12,862
April	—	—	—	12,178
May	—	—	—	11,847
June	—	—	—	11,693
July	—	—	—	11,787
August	4	1	—	17,799
September	5	1	—	20,994
October	12	1	—	22,403
November	12	1	—	23,650
December	12	1	—	23,859
1922:				
January	13	1	—	24,195
February	13	1	—	23,952
March	13	1	—	24,574
April	13	1	—	25,120
May	13	1	—	25,326
June	13	1	—	25,445
July	13	1	—	28,783
August	13	1	—	37,617
September	14	1	—	46,963
October	14	1	—	51,631
November	15	1	—	49,246
December	16	1	—	50,702
1923:				
January	14	1	—	54,516
February	23	1	—	58,358
March	23	1	—	71,284
April	23	1	—	83,800
May	23	1	—	93,396

Advances on securities	Advances to treasury	Notes in circulation	Current accounts and deposits
195	—	15,206	3,851
162	—	15,571	5,531
160	—	15,650	5,246
110	—	13,114	6,802
111	—	13,686	5,760
108	—	18,096	1,162
107	—	15,799	3,532
1,199	—	17,326	2,975
1,194	—	20,845	2,407
1,185	900	23,643	2,154
1,176	1,000	24,742	2,353
1,158	900	25,175	2,240
1,147	1,300	25,680	2,488
1,504	1,900	26,758	2,354
1,565	3,000	29,327	2,224
1,565	4,100	30,580	2,901
1,560	5,500	31,930	3,289
1,556	6,900	33,600	3,741
1,546	7,200	38,357	3,929
1,773	7,600	46,242	5,417
1,848	8,900	58,458	5,929
1,728	12,000	70,005	5,189
1,861	12,500	72,016	6,408
2,016	16,500	75,887	4,761
2,007	20,000	73,717	5,888
2,013	24,000	75,135	6,600
2,584	29,000	82,205	11,152
2,817	37,000	100,101	9,793
1,763	47,200	119,285	10,609

(Continued)

61

Table 3.9 BALANCE SHEET OF HUNGARIAN CENTRAL BANK OR STATE NOTE INSTITUTE *(Continued)*

	Gold coin and bullion	Silver coin	Foreign currency and exchange	Bills discounted
June	23	1	—	120,608
July	22	1	—	165,927
August	22	1	—	273,605
September	22	1	—	380,454
October	23	1	—	494,501
November	23	1	—	531,403
December	23	1	—	582,117
1924:				
January	24	1	—	654,294
February	23	1	—	746,471
March	24	1	—	802,756
April	24	1	—	1,125,898
May	24	1	—	1,420,385
June[a]	246,947	9,823	681,268	1,192,517
July	441,832	13,545	1,110,926	1,257,597
August	449,945	13,558	1,382,885	1,438,454
September	540,425	13,560	1,385,880	1,756,636
October	503,377	13,301	1,658,674	1,872,385
November	508,411	13,301	1,816,102	1,984,540
December	532,842	13,299	1,933,356	1,976,888
1925:				
January	509,848	12,373	1,967,314	1,848,620
February	596,334	12,374	1,989,096	1,676,594
March	669,107	12,374	1,984,006	1,514,532
April	653,534	12,136	2,081,998	1,485,898

Source: Young [36, vol. 2, p. 321].

Note: Figures prior to June 1924 are those of the State Note Institute. The Hungarian National Bank opened 24 June 1924 and took over the affairs of the institute.

[a]After this date gold and silver holdings are shown in terms of paper crowns. Other changes were also made in the presentation of accounts after the opening of the new Hungarian National Bank in June.

struction loan. A variety of Western nations also agreed to give up their liens on Hungary so that the new loan could be floated.

Advances on securities	Advances to treasury	Notes in circulation	Current accounts and deposits
2,490	59,700	154,996	12,742
1,762	79,700	226,285	21,977
1,789	143,000	399,487	23,629
1,776	243,000	588,810	60,246
1,663	269,000	744,926	60,176
1,047	306,000	853,989	74,970
935	401,000	931,337	84,791
9,346	526,000	1,084,677	105,481
34,023	699,000	1,278,437	164,838
4,598	824,000	1,606,875	253,935
12,456	944,000	2,098,091	308,121
13,437	1,054,000	2,486,257	527,137
17,566	1,980,000	2,893,719	1,135,710
—	1,980,000	3,277,943	1,424,578
—	1,978,130	3,659,757	1,473,231
—	1,977,306	4,115,925	1,416,400
—	1,976,455	4,635,090	1,465,356
—	1,975,631	4,442,644	1,929,754
—	1,974,781	4,513,990	2,069,468
—	1,973,930	4,449,650	2,138,629
—	1,973,163	4,237,985	2,542,262
—	1,969,809	4,270,096	2,552,762
—	1,968,987	4,526,216	2,470,507

The League's reconstruction plan was embodied in two protocols. The first was signed by Great Britain, France, Italy, Czechoslovakia, Rumania, and Hungary and guaranteed the "political independence, territorial integrity, and sovereignty of Hungary." The second protocol outlined the terms of the reconstruction plan and committed

Table 3.10 HUNGARIAN PRICE AND EXCHANGE RATE

	Hungarian index of prices[a]	Cents per crown in New York
1921:		
July	4,200	0.3323
August	5,400	0.2629
September	6,250	0,1944
October	6,750	0.1432
November	8,300	0.1078
December	8,250	0.1512
1922:		
January	8,100	0.1525
February	8,500	0.1497
March	9,900	0.1256
April	10,750	0.1258
May	11,000	0.1261
June	12,900	0.1079
July	17,400	0.0760
August	21,400	0.0595
September	26,600	0.0423
October	32,900	0.0402
November	32,600	0.0413
December	33,400	0.0430
1923:		
January	38,500	0.0392
February	41,800	0.0395
March	66,000	0.0289
April	83,500	0.0217
May	94,000	0.0191
June	144,500	0.0140
July	286,000	0.0097
August	462,500	0.0056
September	554,000	0.0055
October	587,000	0.0054
November	635,000	0.0054
December	714,000	0.0052

(Continued)

Table 3.10   HUNGARIAN PRICE AND EXCHANGE RATE *(Continued)*

	Hungarian index of prices[a]	Cents per crown in New York
1924:		
January	1,026,000	0.0039
February	1,839,100	0.0033
March	2,076,700	0.0015
April	2,134,600	0.0014
May	2,269,600	0.0012
June	2,207,800	0.0011
July	2,294,500	0.0012
August	2,242,000	0.0013
September	2,236,600	0.0013
October	2,285,200	0.0013
November	2,309,500	0.0013
December	2,346,600	0.0013
1925:		
January	2,307,500	0.0014
February	2,218,700	0.0014
March	2,117,800	0.0014

Source: Young [36, vol. 2, p. 323].

[a]From July 1921 through November 1923, the index numbers represent retail prices and are based on 60 commodities with July 1914 = 100. From December 1923 through March 1925, the figures are based on wholesale prices computed by the Hungarian Central Statistical Office. They refer to the prices of 52 commodities on the last day of the month with 1913 = 100.

Hungary to balance its budget and form a central bank truly independent of the Finance Ministry. The government was also obligated to accept in Hungary a commissioner general, responsible to the League, to monitor and supervise the government's fulfillment of its commitment to fiscal and monetary reform.

A reconstruction loan of 250 million gold krones was successfully placed abroad in July 1924. The loan was secured by receipts from customs duties and sugar taxes and revenues from the salt and tobacco monopolies. The purpose of the loan was to give

Table 3.11   HUNGARIAN BUDGET, 1924–1925
In Millions of Crowns

Period	Preliminary treasury accounts			Reconstruction scheme		
	Receipts	Expen- ditures	Surplus (+) or deficit (−)	Receipts	Expen- ditures	Surplus (+) or deficit (−)
Jul.–Dec. 1924	208.0	205.9	+2.1	143.8	186.3	−42.5
Jan.–Jun. 1925	245.1	216.9	+28.2	150.0	207.6	−57.6
Fiscal year 1924–25	453.1	422.8	+30.3	293.8	393.9	−100.1

Source: Pasvolsky [25, p. 322].

the government a concrete means of converting future promises to tax into current resources while avoiding the need to place its debt domestically.

By a law of 26 April 1924, the Hungarian National Bank was established, and it began operations on 24 June. The bank assumed the assets and liabilities of the State Note Institute and took over the functions of the foreign exchange control office, the Devisenzentrale. The bank was prohibited from making any additional loans or advances to the government, except upon full security of gold or foreign bills. The bank was also required to hold gold reserves of certain specified percentages behind its liabilities.

The government of Hungary also tried to establish a balanced budget. Both by cutting expenditures and raising tax collections, the government was successful in moving quickly to a balanced budget (see Table 3.11). Indeed, the proceeds of the reconstruction loan were used perceptibly more slowly than had been anticipated in the reconstruction plan.

As Table 3.9 confirms, the stabilization of the krone was accompanied by a substantial *increase* in the total liabilities of the central bank. But as with Austria, the drastic shift in the fiscal policy regime that occasioned the stabilization also changed the appropriate interpretation of these figures. As Table 3.9 indicates and as the regulations

Table 3.12   **NUMBER OF UNEMPLOYED IN HUNGARY**[a]
In Thousands of Workers

End of	1924	1925	1926
January	—	37	28
February	—	37	29
March	—	37	29
April	22	36	26
May	23	30	28
June	25	34	26
July	31	32	
August	30	27	
September	20	25	
October	30	23	
November	31	26	
December	33	27	

Source: League of Nations [15, p. 50].
[a]Figures relate only to members of Union of Socialist Workers.

governing the bank required, after the League's intervention the note and deposit liabilities of the central bank became backed, 100 percent at the margin, by holdings of gold, foreign exchange, and commercial paper. In effect, the central bank's liabilities represented "fiat money" before the League's plan was in effect; after that plan was in effect, they represented more or less backed claims on British sterling,[19] the foreign currency to which Hungary pegged its exchange as a condition for British participation in the reconstruction loan.

Figures on unemployment in Hungary are reported in Table 3.12, and unfortunately begin only immediately after the price stabilization had already occurred. All that can be inferred from these figures is that immediately after the stabilization, unemployment was not any higher than it was one or two years later. This is consistent either with the hypothesis that the stabilization process had little adverse effect on unemployment or with the hypothesis that the adverse effect was so long-lasting that no recovery occurred within the time span of the figures recorded. The former hypothesis seems more plausible to me.

Table 3.13 POLISH RECEIPTS AND EXPENDITURES
In Thousands of Zloty

	1921	1922	1923	1924	1925
Receipts:					
Administration	261,676	467,979	—	—	1,491,743
State Enterprises	11,413	14,556	—	—	133,530
Monopolies	72,222	47,893	—	—	356,611
Total	345,311	530,428	426,000	1,703,000	1,981,884
Expenditures:					
Administration	765,263	734,310	—	—	1,830,231
State Enterprises	115,589	145,003	—	—	106,343
Monopolies	—	—	—	—	45,019
Total	880,852	879,313	1,119,800	1,629,000	1,981,593
Deficit	535,541	348,885	692,000	—	—
Surplus	—	—	—	74,000	251

Source: Young [36, vol. 2, p. 183].
Note: Conversion from marks to zloty was made on the following basis: 1921, 1 zloty = 303.75 marks. First quarter 1922, 1 zloty = 513.52 marks; second quarter, 691.49 marks; third quarter, 1,024.97 marks; and fourth quarter, 1,933.87 marks.

POLAND

The new nation of Poland came into existence at the end of World War I and was formed from territories formerly belonging to Germany, Austro-Hungary, and Russia. At the time of its formation, Poland possessed a varied currency consisting of Russian rubles, crowns of the Austro-Hungarian bank, German marks, and Polish marks issued by the Polish State Loan Bank, which had been established by Germany to control the currency in the part of Poland occupied by Germany during the war. For Poland, the armistice of 1918 did not bring peace, a costly war with Soviet Russia being waged until the fall of 1920. Poland was devastated by the fighting and by Germany's practice of stripping it of its machinery and materials during World War I.[20]

The new government of Poland ran very large deficits up to 1924 (see Table 3.13). These deficits were financed by government borrowing from the Polish State Loan Bank, which the new government had taken over from the Germans. From January 1922 to December 1923, the outstanding notes of the Polish State Loan Bank increased by a factor of 523 (Table 3.14). Over the same period, the price index increased by a factor of 2402 while the dollar exchange rate decreased by a factor of 1397 (see Tables 3.15 and 3.16). As in the other inflations we have studied, the real value of the note circulation decreased as people engaged in a "flight from the mark." Extensive government exchange controls were imposed to resist this trend.

Tables 3.14 and 3.15 indicate that the rapid inflation and exchange depreciation both suddenly stopped in January 1924. Unlike the cases of Austria and Hungary, in Poland the initial stabilization was achieved without foreign loans or intervention, although later in 1927, after currency depreciation threatened to renew, a substantial foreign loan was arranged [13, p. 111]. But in terms of the substantial fiscal and monetary regime changes that accompanied the end of the inflation, there is much similarity to the Austrian and Hungarian experiences. The two interrelated changes were a dramatic move toward a balanced government budget and the establishment of an independent central bank that was prohibited from making additional unsecured loans to the government. In January 1924, the minister of finance was granted broad powers to effect monetary and fiscal reform. The minister immediately initiated the establishment of the Bank of Poland, which was to assume the functions of the Polish State Loan Bank. The eventual goal was to restore convertibility with gold. The bank was required to hold a 30 percent reserve behind its notes, to consist of gold and foreign paper assets denominated in stable currencies. Beyond this reserve, the bank's notes had to be secured by private bills of exchange and silver. A maximum credit to the government of 50 million zlotys was permitted. The government also moved swiftly to balance the budget (see Table 3.13).

In January 1924, a new currency unit became effective, the gold zloty, worth 1.8 million paper marks. The zloty was equal in gold content to 19.29 cents.

Table 3.14 reveals that from January 1924 to December 1924, the note circulation of the central bank increased by a factor of 3.2, in the face of relative stability of the price level and the exchange rate (see Tables 3.15 and 3.16). This phenomenon matches what occurred

Table 3.14 BALANCE SHEET OF BANK OF POLAND, 1918–1925
End of Month Figures

Month	Gold[a]	Silver[a] (including base coin)	Balances with foreign banks
Polish State Loan Bank Figures (Prior to May 1924) in Millions of Marks			
1918:			
October	—	—	—
November	—	—	—
December	—	—	—
1919:			
January	—	—	—
February	—	—	—
March	3.7	4.2	3.9
April	3.7	4.4	9.4
May	3.7	8.9	5.8
June	4.9	14.8	14.6
July	5.7	20.1	13.3
August	6.1	20.5	20.3
September	6.3	21.6	69.8
October	6.5	24.3	91.0
November	6.6	24.6	151.6
December	6.6	25.5	344.6
1920:			
January	6.6	25.5	244.1
February	6.8	25.9	565.7
March	6.8	25.9	685.4
April	6.8	25.9	685.5
May	6.8	25.9	565.7
June	6.8	25.9	894.7
July	6.8	25.9	1,130.9
August	9.0	33.8	1,273.4
September	9.1	34.1	174.9
October	9.5	34.4	236.7
November	10.1	35.4	203.8
December	12.4	37.6	80.7
December	12.4	37.6	80.7

| Discounts | Advances | | Note circulation |
	Commercial	Government	
Polish State Loan Bank Figures (Prior to May 1924) in Millions of Marks			
7.0	180.8	—	880.2
7.0	184.0	13.9	930.5
6.4	183.7	117.8	1,023.8
5.0	194.7	209.9	1,098.1
4.2	196.4	315.0	1,160.0
3.5	189.7	400.0	1,223.2
2.5	192.8	575.0	1,346.0
1.8	193.2	925.0	1,548.3
1.3	185.9	1,125.0	1,784.6
1.1	193.9	1,925.0	2,087.9
0.7	107.4	2,525.0	2,466.6
0.1	218.9	3,225.0	2,964.7
0.3	242.4	4,375.0	3,723.6
3.4	270.2	5,375.0	4,236.2
3.9	243.8	6,825.0	5,316.3
3.7	278.5	8,275.0	6,719.9
6.4	303.0	10,775.0	8,300.3
8.2	319.1	14,775.0	10,690.6
14.8	316.7	19,375.0	16,027.9
47.2	320.9	22,375.0	17,934.7
161.4	488.2	27,625.0	21,730.1
325.9	9,847.5	33,375.0	26,311.4
465.8	1,466.1	40,625.0	31,085.8
333.9	1,862.9	40,625.0	33,203.5
259.1	2,527.0	46,925.0	38,456.8
396.0	3,278.4	49,625.0	43,236.2
611.6	3,999.2	59,625.0	43,236.2
611.6	3,999.2	59,625.0	49,361.5

(Continued)

71

Table 3.14   BALANCE SHEET OF BANK OF POLAND, 1918–1925
(Continued)

Month	Gold[a]	Silver[a] (including base coin)	Balances with foreign banks
1921:			
January	12.7	39.2	205.8
February	12.8	39.2	476.0
March	13.1	39.8	908.5
April	13.4	40.3	870.7
May	13.5	40.1	536.5
June	14.3	41.1	493.6
July	19.1	41.5	601.3
August	19.2	42.0	368.7
September	19.4	42.5	1,217.5
October	20.2	42.9	2,341.3
November	22.6	43.5	7,040.1
December	24.9	43.9	12,707.9
1922:			
January	26.3	44.2	13,614.2
February	28.3	44.4	14,207.7
March	29.0	44.7	1,156.4
April	29.5	45.2	7,388.0
May	30.1	45.3	23,073.4
June	30.9	45.3	20,521.4
July	31.5	45.4	21,741.0
August	31.6	45.4	51,747.2
September	32.4	45.4	67,384.1
October	33.5	45.4	64,060.9
November	33.8	45.4	78,959.0
December	41.0	45.4	48,580.4
1923:			
January	41.1	44.1	34,721.8
February	41.4	44.1	71,883.7
March	41.7	44.2	29,868.7
April	41.9	44.2	50,851.9
May	41.9	44.3	43,900.7

Discounts	Advances		Note circulation
	Commercial	Government	
1,040.2	4,100.2	65,625.0	55,079.5
955.1	4,143.5	8,777,125.0	62,560.4
781.0	4,745.7	93,625.0	74,087.4
927.0	4,994.4	106,625.0	86,755.3
1,395.2	4,979.0	117,625.0	94,575.8
1,557.3	5,306.5	130,625.0	102,697.3
2,504.2	6,291.5	140,625.0	115,242.3
3,885.4	7,776.9	158,000.0	133,734.2
6,237.3	9,878.6	178,000.0	152,792.1
9,529.5	12,022.3	198,500.0	182,777.3
14,347.2	15,144.3	214,000.0	207,029.0
15,324.4	19,300.0	221,000.0	229,537.6
15,951.6	21,776.9	227,350.0	239,615.3
19,555.0	22,327.7	230,600.0	247,209.5
25,451.1	25,473.3	232,100.0	250,665.5
28,688.8	29,063.7	220,000.0	260,553.8
34,555.0	26,067.0	217,000.0	276,001.1
46,629.8	24,499.5	235,000.0	300,101.1
47,661.2	24,054.4	260,000.0	335,426.6
56,366.6	21,079.9	285,000.0	385,787.5
64,093.0	22,239.4	342,000.0	463,706.0
81,781.9	26,576.5	453,500.0	579,972.7
107,320.1	41,278.1	519,500.0	661,092.4
133,400.8	47,904.1	675,600.0	793,437.5
174,950.1	51,899.9	799,500.0	909,160.3
219,610.7	61,037.1	1,085,000.0	1,177,300.8
274,657.8	85,323.2	1,752,000.0	1,841,205.6
304,725.4	156,815.4	2,161,500.0	2,332,396.8
449,440.7	217,162.3	2,377,000.0	2,733,794.1

(Continued)

Table 3.14 BALANCE SHEET OF BANK OF POLAND, 1918–1925
(Continued)

Month	Gold[a]	Silver[a] (including base coin)	Balances with foreign banks
June	43.9	39.8	276,506.3
July	46.9	34.8	384,375.1
August	48.0	32.9	340,354.4
September	53.2	20.7	857,084.5
October	54.2	19.1	1,510,794.3
November	54.3	19.5	6,499,791.5
December	54.9	19.6	57,499,741.7
1924:			
January	66.2	19.8	91,533,085.2
February	66.7	19.8	172,626,128.8
March	68.0	20.3	220,658,210.7
April	55.7	21.2	277,340,925.7

After Conversion of State Loan Bank into Bank of Poland, Figures in Gold Zlotys; No Ciphers Omitted; 1 Zloty = 19.3 Cents

May	11,684,963[b]		214,191,336
June	83,392,914[b]		256,972,386
July	93,683,430[b]		272,137,898
August	98,288,324[b]		266,390,583
September	99,900,015[b]		233,646,562
October	100,686,634	16,521,223	241,894,738
November	102,809,285	21,951,828	247,034,974
December	103,362,870	27,543,698	269,045,551
1925:			
January	104,249,258	27,658,749	242,115,258
February	107,032,735	27,481,871	206,317,320
March	116,619,825	28,158,597	259,392,902
April	117,428,697	28,358,000	216,114,621

Source: Young [36, vol. 2, p. 348].
[a]Gold at par; silver coin at face value.
[b]Gold and silver.

| Discounts | Advances | | Note circulation |
	Commercial	Government	
627,339.5	310,862.7	2,996,500.0	3,566,649.1
758,112.8	390,850.9	4,190,500.0	4,478,709.0
1,372,150.9	637,268.2	6,473,000.0	6,871,776.5
2,077,128.6	670,019.6	10,265,500.0	11,197,737.8
3,540,434.4	1,836,712.7	19,080,500.0	23,080,402.2
8,467,033.7	3,951,781.9	42,854,000.0	53,217,494.6
20,588,037.9	28,065,396.8	111,332,000.0	125,371,955.3
43,916,802.8	54,181,445.2	238,200,000.0	313,659,830.0
67,216,289.7	83,829,440.5	291,700,000.0	528,913,418.7
138,649,934.8	81,231,988.5	291,700,000.0	596,244,205.6
199,248,956.4	60,589,081.0	291,700,000.0	570,697,550.5

After Conversion of State Loan Bank into Bank of Poland, Figures in Gold Zlotys; No Ciphers Omitted; 1 Zloty = 19.3 Cents

126,522,906	1,801,936	—	244,977,010
138,862,243	5,826,971	—	334,405,730
166,713,469	8,236,693	—	394,262,550
199,710,736	8,224,610	—	430,263,045
233,788,177	9,230,850	—	460,383,770
245,054,984	12,374,342	—	503,701,830
249,560,999	12,371,166	—	497,600,470
256,954,853	23,897,766	—	550,873,960
270,423,615	23,468,829	—	553,174,980
286,229,180	28,467,930	18,222,212	549,637,420
306,562,690	25,477,638	· 403,354	563,171,945
294,632,508	27,319,944	35,977,630	567,178,830

Table 3.15 POLISH INDEX NUMBERS OF WHOLESALE PRICES, 1921–1925

Year	Month	Wholesale price index[a]	Year	Month	Wholesale price index[a]
1921	January	25,139	1923	April	1,058,920
	February	31,827		May	1,125,350
	March	32,882		June	1,881,410
	April	31,710		July	3,069,970
	May	32,639		August	5,294,680
	June	35,392		September	7,302,200
	July	45,654		October	27,380,680
	August	53,100		November	67,943,700
	September	60,203		December	142,300,700
	October	65,539	1924	January	242,167,700
	November	58,583		February	248,429,600
	December	57,046		March	245,277,900
1922	January	59,231		April	242,321,800
	February	63,445		May	
	March	73,465		June	
	April	75,106		July	
	May	78,634		August	
	June	87,694		September	
	July	101,587		October	
	August	135,786		November	
	September	152,365		December	
	October	201,326	1925	January	
	November	275,647		February	
	December	346,353		March	
1923	January	544,690		April	
	February	859,110		May	
	March	988,500			

Source: Young [36, vol. 2, p. 349].
[a]1914 = 100.

in Austria and Hungary and has a similar explanation. As Table 3.14 reveals, the increased note circulation during this period was effectively backed 100 percent by gold, foreign exchange, and private paper.

The available figures on unemployment are summarized in Table 3.17. The stabilization of the price level in January 1924 is accompanied by an abrupt rise in the number of unemployed. Another rise

Table 3.16 POLISH EXCHANGE RATES, 1919–1925

Year	Month	Cents per Polish mark	Year	Month	Cents per Polish mark
1919	July	6.88	1922	September	0.0127
	August	5.63		October	0.0095
	September	3.88		November	0.0065
	October	3.08		December	0.0057
	November	1.88	1923	January	0.0043
	December	1.29		February	0.0025
1920	January	0.70		March	0.0024
	February	0.68		April	0.0023
	March	0.67		May	0.0021
	April	0.60		June	0.0013
	May	0.51		July	0.0007
	June	0.59		August	0.0004
	July	0.61		September	0.00035
	August	0.47		October	0.0001113
	September	0.45		November	0.0000502
	October	0.37		December	0.0000234
	November	0.26	1924	January	0.0000116
	December	0.16		February	0.0000109
1921	January	0.145		March	0.0000113
	February	0.130		April	0.0000114
	March	0.132		May	—

Year	Month		Year	Month	Cents per zloty
1921	April	0.130		June	10.29
	May	0.124		July	19.25
	June	0.082		August	19.23
	July	0.0516		September	19.22
	August	0.0489		October	19.22
	September	0.0256		November	19.21
	October	0.0212		December	19.20
	November	0.0290	1925	January	19.18
	December	0.0313		February	19.18
1922	January	0.0327		March	19.18
	February	0.0286		April	19.18
	March	0.0236		May	19.18
	April	0.0262		June	19.18
	May	0.0249			
	June	0.0237			
	July	0.0185			
	August	0.0135			

Source: Young [36, vol. 2, p. 350].

Table 3.17   POLISH UNEMPLOYED

1921:		1923:	
January	74,000	January	81,184
February	90,000	February	106,729
March	80,000	March	114,576
April	88,000	April	112,755
May	130,000	May	93,731
June	115,000	June	76,397
July	95,000	July	64,563
August	65,000	August	56,515
September	70,000	September	—
October	78,000	October	—
November	120,000	November	—
December	173,000	December	67,581
1922:		1924:	
January	221,444	January	100,580
February	206,442	February	110,737
March	170,125	March	112,583
April	148,625	April	109,000
May	128,916	May	84,000
June	98,581	June	97,870
July	85,240	July	149,097
August	69,692	August	159,820
September	68,000	September	155,245
October	61,000	October	147,065
November	62,000	November	150,180
December	75,000	December	159,060

Source: Statistiches Jahrbuch für das Deutsche Reich [33].

occurs in July of 1924. While the figures indicate substantial unemployment in late 1924, unemployment is not an order of magnitude worse than before the stabilization, and certainly not anywhere nearly as bad as would be predicted by application of the same method of analysis that was used to fabricate the prediction for the contemporary United States that each percentage point reduction in inflation would require a reduction of $220 billion in real GNP.

The Polish zloty depreciated internationally from late 1925 onward but stabilized in autumn of 1926 at around 72 percent of its level of January 1924. At the same time, the domestic price level stabilized at about 50 percent above its level of January 1924. The threatened renewal of inflation has been attributed to the government's premature relaxation of exchange controls and the tendency of the central bank to make private loans at insufficient interest rates [13, p. 108].

GERMANY

After World War I, Germany owed staggering reparations to the Allied countries. This fact dominated Germany's public finance from 1919 until 1923 and was a most important force for hyperinflation.

At the conclusion of the war, Germany experienced a political revolution and established a republican government. The early postwar governments were dominated by moderate Socialists, who for a variety of reasons reached accommodations with centers of military and industrial power of the prewar regime [26, pp. 146–50]. These accommodations in effect undermined the willingness and capability of the government to meet its admittedly staggering revenue needs through explicit taxation.

Of the four episodes that we have studied, Germany's hyperinflation was the most spectacular, as the figures on wholesale prices and exchange rates in Tables 3.18 and 3.19 reveal. The inflation became most severe after the military occupation of the Ruhr by the French in January 1923. The German government was determined to fight the French occupation by a policy of passive resistance, making direct payments to striking workers that were financed by discounting treasury bills with the Reichsbank.

Table 3.20 estimates the budget of Germany for 1920 to 1923 [7, pp. 40–41]. The table reveals that except for 1923, the budget would not have been badly out of balance except for the massive reparations payments made. The disruption caused to Germany's finances by the reparations situation is surely understated by the reparations figures given in Table 3.20. For one thing, considerably larger sums were initially expected of Germany than it ever was eventually able to pay. For another thing, the extent of Germany's total obligation and the required schedule of payments was for a long time uncertain and under negotiation. From the viewpoint that the value of a state's currency and other debt depends intimately on the fiscal policy it intends

Table 3.18   GERMAN WHOLESALE PRICES, 1914–1924

Year	Month	Price Index	Year	Month	Price Index
1914	January	96		April	163
	February	96		May	163
	March	96		June	165
	April	95		July	172
	May	97		August	203
	June	99		September	199
	July	99		October	201
	August	109		November	203
	September	111		December	203
	October	118	1918	January	204
	November	123		February	198
	December	125		March	198
1915	January	126		April	204
	February	133		May	203
	March	139		June	209
	April	142		July	208
	May	139		August	235
	June	139		September	230
	July	150		October	234
	August	146		November	234
	September	145		December	245
	October	147	1919	January	262
	November	147		February	270
	December	148		March	274
1916	January	150		April	286
	February	151		May	297
	March	148		June	308
	April	149		July	339
	May	151		August	422
	June	152		September	493
	July	161		October	562
	August	159		November	678
	September	154		December	803
	October	153	1920	January	1,260
	November	151		February	1,690
	December	151		March	1,710
1917	January	156		April	1,570
	February	158		May	1,510
	March	159		June	1,380

(Continued)

Table 3.18   GERMAN WHOLESALE PRICES, 1914–1924 *(Continued)*

Year	Month	Price Index	Year	Month	Price Index
	July	1,370		October	56,600
	August	1,450		November	115,100
	September	1,500		December	147,480
	October	1,470	1923	January	278,500
	November	1,510		February	588,500
	December	1,440		March	488,800
1921	January	1,440		April	521,200
	February	1,380		May	817,000
	March	1,340		June	1,938,500
	April	1,330		July	7,478,700
	May	1,310		August	94,404,100
	June	1,370		September	2,394,889,300
	July	1,430		October	709,480,000,000
	August	1,920		November	72,570,000,000,000
	September	2,070		December	126,160,000,000,000
	October	2,460	1924	January	117,320,000,000,000
	November	3,420		February	116,170,000,000,000
	December	3,490		March	120,670,000,000,000
1922	January	3,670		April	124,050,000,000,000
	February	4,100		May	122,460,000,000,000
	March	5,430		June	115,900,000,000,000
	April	6,360		July	115[a]
	May	6,460		August	120[a]
	June	7,030		September	127[a]
	July	10,160		October	131[a]
	August	19,200		November	129[a]
	September	28,700		December	131[a]

Source: Young [36, vol. 1, p. 503].
[a]On basis of prices in reichsmarks. [1 reichsmark = 1 trillion (10^{12}) former marks.]

to run, the uncertainty about the reparations owed by the German government necessarily cast a long shadow over its prospects for a stable currency.

As Table 3.21 reveals, the note circulation of the Reichsbank increased dramatically from 1921 to 1923, especially in the several months before November 1923. As pointed out by Young [36], at the end of October 1923, over 99 percent of outstanding Reichsbank notes

Table 3.19 GERMAN EXCHANGE RATES, 1914–1925

Year	Month	Cents per mark	Year	Month	Cents per mark
1920	January	1.69	1922	August	0.10
	February	1.05		September	0.07
	March	1.26		October	0.03
	April	1.67		November	0.01
	May	2.19		December	0.01
	June	2.56	1923	January	0.007
	July	2.53		February	0.004
	August	2.10		March	0.005
	September	1.72		April	0.004
	October	1.48		May	0.002
	November	1.32		June	0.001
	December	1.37		July	0.000,3
1921	January	1.60		August	0.000,033,9
	February	1.64		September	0.000,001,88
	March	1.60		October	0.000,000,068
	April	1.57		November	0.000,000,000,043
	May	1.63		December	0.000,000,000,022,7
	June	1.44	1924	January	22.6
	July	1.30		February	21.8
	August	1.19		March	22.0
	September	0.96		April	22.0
	October	0.68		May	22.3
	November	0.39		June	23.4
	December	0.53		July	23.9
1922	January	0.52		August	23.8
	February	0.48		September	23.8
	March	0.36		October	23.8
	April	0.35		November	23.8
	May	0.34		December	23.8
	June	0.32	1925[a]	January	23.8
	July	0.20			

Source: Young [36, vol. 1, p. 532].

[a]Cents per rentenmark and (after October 1924) per reichsmark. 1 rentenmark is equivalent to 1 reichsmark or 1 billion former paper marks. The reichsmark is the equivalent of the gold mark worth 23.82 cents.

had been placed in circulation within the previous 30 days.[21] Table 3.21 reveals the extent to which the Reichsbank note circulation was backed by discounted treasury bills. During 1923, the Reichsbank also began discounting large volumes of commercial bills. Since these loans were made at nominal rates of interest far below the rate of inflation, they amounted virtually to government transfer payments to the recipients of the loans.

Especially during the great inflation of 1923, a force came into play that was also present in the other hyperinflations we have studied. Given the method of assessing taxes in nominal terms, lags between the time when taxes were levied and the time when they were collected led to reduced revenues as the government evidently repeatedly underestimated the prospective rate of inflation and as the rapid inflation gave people a large incentive to delay paying their taxes. This effect probably partially accounts for the reduced tax revenues collected during the first nine months of 1923. The French occupation of the Ruhr also helps explain it.

In response to the inflationary public finance and despite the efforts of the government to impose exchange controls, there occurred a "flight from the German mark" in which the real value of reichsmark notes decreased dramatically. The figures in Table 3.18 indicate that between January 1922 and July 1923, wholesale prices increased by a factor of 2038 while Reichsbank notes increased by a factor of 378. Between January 1922 and August 1923, wholesale prices increased by a factor of 25,723 while Reichsbank notes circulating increased by a factor of 5748. The fact that prices increased proportionately many times more than did the Reichsbank note circulation is symptomatic of the efforts of Germans to economize on their holdings of rapidly depreciating German marks. Toward the end of the hyperinflation, Germans made every effort to avoid holding marks and held large quantities of foreign exchange for purposes of conducting transaction. By October 1923, it has been roughly estimated, the real value of foreign currencies circulating in Germany was at least equal to and perhaps several times the real value of Reichsbank notes circulating.[22]

The figures in Tables 3.18 and 3.19 show that prices suddenly stopped rising and the mark stopped depreciating in late November 1923. The event of stabilization was attended by a "monetary reform," in which on 15 October 1923 a new currency unit called the rentenmark was declared equivalent to 1 trillion (10^{12}) paper marks. While great psychological significance has sometimes been assigned

**Table 3.20   REAL GERMAN REVENUES AND EXPENDITURES,
CALCULATED ON THE BASIS
OF THE COST-OF-LIVING INDEX**
In Millions of Gold Marks

	Revenue			
	Taxes	**Sundries**	**Deficit covered by loan transactions**	**Total**
1920–21	4,090.8	132.9	7,041.9	11,265.6
1921–22	5,235.7	100.5	6,627.4	11,963.6
1922–23	3,529.1	51.4	6,384.5	9,965.0
1923–24 (first 9 months)	1,496.1	180.6	11,836.5	13,513.2

Source: Young [36, vol. 2, p. 393].

to this unit change, it is difficult to attribute any substantial effects to what was in itself only a cosmetic measure.[23] The substantive aspect of the decree of 15 October was the establishing of a Rentenbank to take over the note issue functions of the Reichsbank. The decree put binding limits upon both the total volume of rentenmarks that could be issued, 3.2 billion marks, and the maximum amount that could be issued to the government, 1.2 billion marks. This limitation on the amount of credit that could be extended to the government was announced at a time when the government was financing virtually 100 percent of its expenditures by means of note issue [36, vol. 1, p. 421]. In December 1923, the management of the Rentenbank was tested by the government and effectively made clear its intent to meet its obligation to limit government borrowing to within the amount decreed.

Simultaneously and abruptly three things happened: additional government borrowing from the central bank stopped, the government budget swung into balance, and inflation stopped. Table 3.22 shows the dramatic progress toward a balanced budget that was made in the months after the Rentenbank decree.

The government moved to balance the budget by taking a series of deliberate, permanent actions to raise taxes and eliminate expendi-

Expenditures					
Repayment of floating debt	Interest on floating debt	Subsidies to railroads	Execution of Versailles treaty	Sundries	Total
821.7	—	—	—	—	11,265.6
1,039.5	811.6	1,114.4	5,110.6	5,738.4	11,963.4
81.0	344.4	1,685.5	3,600.0	4,254.1	9,965.0
—	931.0	3,725.0	—	—	13,513.2

tures. Young reports that "by the personnel decree of October 27, 1923, the number of government employees was cut by 25 percent; all temporary employees were to be discharged; all above the age of 65 years were to be retired. An additional 10 percent of the civil servants were to be discharged by January 1924. The railways, overstaffed as a result of post-war demobilization, discharged 120,000 men during 1923 and 60,000 more during 1924. The postal administration reduced its staff by 65,000 men; the Reichsbank itself which had increased the number of its employees from 13,316 at the close of 1922 to 22,909 at the close of 1923, began the discharge of its superfluous force in December, as soon as the effects of stabilization became manifest" [36, vol. 1, p. 422].

Substantially aiding the fiscal situation, Germany also obtained relief from her reparation obligations. Reparations payments were temporarily suspended, and the Dawes plan assigned Germany a much more manageable schedule of payments.

Table 3.21 documents a pattern that we have seen in the three other hyperinflations: The substantial growth of central bank note and demand deposit liabilities in the months *after* the currency was stabilized. As in the other cases that we have studied, the best explanation

Table 3.21   BALANCE SHEET OF GERMAN REICHSBANK, 1921–1924

	Discounted bills	
	Treasury bills	Commercial bills
1921:		
January	50,594,540	2,742,406
February	53,690,412	2,760,927
March	64,533,894	2,268,745
April	58,841,630	2,052,099
May	62,953,604	1,809,936
June	79,607,790	1,565,406
July	79,981,967	1,135,529
August	84,043,891	1,002,497
September	98,442,137	1,142,218
October	98,704,768	881,474
November	114,023,417	1,445,667
December	132,380,906	1,061,754
1922:		
January	126,160,402	1,592,416
February	134,251,808	1,856,936
March	146,531,247	2,151,677
April	155,617,524	2,403,044
May	167,793,922	3,376,599
June	186,125,747	4,751,748
July	207,858,232	8,122,066
August	249,765,773	21,704,341
September	349,169,650	50,234,414
October	477,201,494	101,155,267
November	672,222,197	246,948,596
December	1,184,464,359	422,235,296
1923:		
January	1,609,081,121	697,216,424
February	2,947,363,994	1,829,341,080
March	4,552,011,661	2,372,101,757
April	6,224,899,348	2,986,116,724
May	8,021,904,840	4,014,693,720
June	18,338[b]	6,914,198,630
July	53,752[b]	18,314[b]

Total discounted treasury and commercial bills	Advances	Securities
53,336,946	8,881	147,126
56,451,339	11,522	185,788
66,802,639	2,805	217,044
60,803,729	9,238	225,777
64,763,540	16,624	258,664
81,172,196	6,079	282,716
81,117,496	10,686	283,381
85,046,388	7,704	258,319
99,564,355	3,289	277,977
99,586,242	47,775	282,179
115,469,084	90,370	247,699
133,392,660	8,476	195,912
127,752,818	20,548	198,725
136,108,744	62,305	215,362
148,682,924	20,688	205,936
158,020,568	134,314	229,242
171,170,521	54,361	199,314
190,877,495	58,994	307,564
215,980,298	141,276	313,488
271,470,114	172,966	241,162
400,004,064	61,516	416,193
578,356,761	624,368	502,348
919,170,793	51,425,030[a]	381,068
1,606,699,655	773,974	469,972
2,306,297,545	95,316,552	483,318
4,776,705,074	27,422,282	1,209,935
6,924,113,418	2,132,906	1,690,011
9,211,016,072	20,466,948	1,207,105
12,036,598,560	61,030,322	697,611
25,252,198,630	188,548,574	344,819
72,066[b]	2,553,177,597	1,422,291

(Continued)

87

Table 3.21 BALANCE SHEET OF GERMAN REICHSBANK, 1921–1924
(Continued)

	Discounted bills	
	Treasury bills	Commercial bills
August	987,219[b]	164,644[b]
September	45,216,224[b]	3,660,094[b]
October	6,578,650,939[b]	1,058,129,855[b]
15 November	189,801,468,187[b]	39,529,577,254[b]
30 November	96,874,330,250[b]	347,301,037,776[b]
December	c	322,724,948,986[b]
1924:[d]		
January	—	—
February	—	—
March	—	—
April	—	—
May	—	—
June	—	—
July	—	—
August	—	—
September	—	—
15 October[e]	—	—
31 October	—	—
November	—	—
December	—	—

		Demand deposits
	Notes in circulation	Public
1921:		
January	66,620,804	4,055,904
February	67,426,959	7,291,052
March	69,417,228	15,206,381
April	70,839,725	11,595,618
May	71,838,866	3,548,492
June	75,321,095	5,647,805

Total discounted treasury and commercial bills	Advances	Securities
1,151,863[b]	25,261[b]	15,539,853
48,876,318[b]	98,522[b]	1,801,579,570
7,636,780,794[b]	41,787,532[b]	9,536,953[2]
229,331,045,441[b]	535,714,637[b]	8,901,495[2]
444,175,368,026[b]	7,742,665,263[b]	336,495,629[2]
322,724,948,986[b]	268,325,819,530[b]	65,791,385[2]
755,866	336,520	12
1,165,649	306,618	25
1,767,443	143,102	533
1,916,969	156,362	91,984
1,954,930	128,597	80,011
1,897,959	108,789	76,378
1,798,097	62,489	76,509
1,860,843	59,983	76,331
2,169,684	54,424	78,305
2,153,943	15,947	77,517
2,339,616	33,443	77,699
2,290,166	18,628	77,808
2,064,094	16,960	77,999

Demand Deposits		
Other	Total demand deposits	Due to the Rentenbank
11,778,060	15,833,964	
10,066,036	17,357,088	
12,836,292	28,042,673	
9,260,271	20,855,889	
10,545,201	14,093,693	
14,744,903	20,392,708	

(Continued)

Table 3.21 BALANCE SHEET OF GERMAN REICHSBANK, 1921–1924
(Continued)

| | Demand Deposits | |
| | | |
	Notes in circulation	Public
July	77,390,853	4,810,026
August	80,072,721	4,850,843
September	86,384,286	4,618,087
October	91,527,679	5,239,628
November	100,943,632	5,144,615
December	113,639,464	7,591,343
1922:		
January	115,375,766	5,286,950
February	120,026,387	5,806,922
March	130,671,352	7,743,735
April	140,420,057	7,577,862
May	151,949,179	7,711,279
June	169,211,792	10,125,837
July	189,794,722	9,197,727
August	238,147,160	13,708,213
September	316,869,799	30,034,309
October	469,456,818	34,270,926
November	754,086,109	50,353,945
December	1,280,094,831	153,190,991
1923:		
January	1,984,496,469	157,058,537
February	3,512,787,777	253,915,266
March	5,517,919,651	368,550,293
April	6,545,984,355	454,403,079
May	8,563,749,470	652,575,366
June	17,291[b]	1,648,114,327
July	43,595[b]	3,779,235,298
August	663,200[b]	206,168[b]
September	28,228,815[b]	8,186,467[b]
October	2,496,822,909[b]	606,660,673[b]
15 November	92,844,720,743[b]	72,457,230,513[b]
30 November	400,267,640,302[b]	120,478,936,906[b]
December	496,507,424,772[b]	303,114,560,004[b]

| | Demand Deposits | |
Other	Total demand deposits	Due to the Rentenbank
11,014,130	15,824,156	
8,798,756	13,649,599	
15,362,208	19,980,295	
13,063,035	18,302,663	
20,168,499[b]	25,313,114	
25,314,330	32,905,673	
18,125,502	23,421,452	
20,719,150	26,526,072	
25,614,597	33,358,332	
24,038,306	31,616,168	
25,416,711	33,127,990	
27,047,908	37,173,745	
30,778,489	39,976,216	
42,416,241	56,124,454	
79,978,068	110,012,377	
106,508,333	140,779,259	
190,615,514	240,969,459	
377,335,296	530,526,287	
605,205,692	763,264,229	
1,329,065,770	1,582,981,036	
1,903,533,291	2,272,083,584	
3,399,871,714	3,854,274,793	
4,410,494,865	5,063,070,231	
8,304,602,339	9,952,716,666	
24,078[b]	27,857[b]	
384,912[b]	591,080[b]	
8,781,150[b]	16,966,617[b]	
3,261,424,030[b]	3,868,085,703[b]	
57,095,366,904[b]	129,552,597,417[b]	
253,497,803,653[b]	373,976,740,559[b]	
244,906,637,001[b]	548,024,197,005[b]	

(Continued)

Table 3.21 BALANCE SHEET OF GERMAN REICHSBANK, 1921–1924 (Continued)

| | Demand Deposits | |
	Notes in circulation	Public
1924:[d]		
January	483,675	492,985
February	587,875	367,551
March	689,864	352,360
April	776,949	474,411
May	926,874	545,252
June	1,097,309	493,043
July	1,211,038	452,597
August	1,391,895	264,064
September	1,520,511	307,515
15 October[e]	1,396,748	—
31 October	1,780,930	—
November	1,863,200	—
December	1,941,440	—

Source: Young [36, vol. 1, pp. 528—29].

Note: End of month figures, in thousands of current marks; from January 1924 in thousands of rentenmarks or reichsmarks. 1 rentenmark is equivalent to 1 reichsmark or 1 trillion (10^{12}) former paper marks. The reichsmark is the equivalent of the gold mark worth 23.82 cents.

[a]The large increase of advances at the close of November 1922 occurred because the Reichsbank had to take over temporarily the financing of food supplies from the loan bureaus (Darlehuskassen), as the latter were unable to extend the needed accommodation, their oustanding notes having reached the maximum amount permitted by law.

[b]In billions.

[c]A decree of 15 November 1923 discontinued the discounting of treasury bills by the Reichsbank.

[d]See note above.

[e]Date of first statement of reorganized Reichsbank.

for this is that at the margin the postinflation increase in notes was no longer backed by government debt. Instead, in the German case, it was largely backed by discounted commercial bills. The nature of the system of promises and claims behind the central bank's liabilities

| | Demand deposits | |
Other	Total demand deposits	Due to the Rentenbank
281,320	281,305	200,000
282,958	650,509	400,000
352,334	704,694	800,000
330,561	804,972	800,000
259,203	804,455	800,000
280,884	773,927	800,000
290,390	742,987	800,000
297,791	561,855	800,000
362,581	670,096	800,000
—	828,511	800,000
—	708,728	800,000
—	703,938	684,664
—	820,865	456,508

changed when after the Rentenbank decree the central bank no longer offered additional credit to the government. So once again the interpretation of the time series on central bank notes and deposits must undergo a very substantial change.

By all available measures, the stabilization of the German mark was accompanied by increases in output and employment and decreases in unemployment [7, Chapter 12]. While 1924 was not a good year for German business, it was much better than 1923. Table 3.23 is representative of the figures assembled by Graham, and shows that 1924 suffers in comparison with 1922 but that 1925 was a good year. In these figures one cannot find much convincing evidence of a favorable trade-off between inflation and output, since the year of spectacular inflation, 1923, was a very bad year for employment and physical production. Certainly a large part of the poor performance of 1923

Table 3.22 **ORDINARY REVENUES AND EXPENDITURES OF THE GERMAN FEDERAL GOVERNMENT**
From Wirtschift and Statistik, Issued by the Statistisches Reichsamt, in Millions of Gold Marks

	Ordinary revenue		Ordinary expenditures	Excess of revenue (+) or expenditure (−)
	Total	**Of which taxes yielded**		
1923:				
November	68.1	63.2	—	—
December	333.9	312.3	668.7	−334.8
1924:				
January	520.6	503.5	396.5	+124.1
February	445.0	418.0	462.8	−17.8
March	632.4	595.3	498.6	133.8
April	579.5	523.8	523.5	+56.0
May	566.7	518.7	459.1	+107.6
June	529.7	472.3	504.5	+25.2
July	622.2	583.1	535.1	+86.9
August	618.2	592.0	597.6	+20.6
September	665.6	609.2	581.6	+84.0
October	714.3	686.7	693.0	+21.3

Source: Young [36, vol. 1, p. 422].

was due to the French occupation of the Ruhr and the policy of passive resistance.

Despite the evident absence of a "Phillips curve" trade-off between inflation and real output in the figures in Tables 3.18 and 3.23, there is ample evidence that the German inflation was far from "neutral" and that there were important "real effects." Graham [7] gives evidence that the inflation and the associated reduction in real rates of return to high-powered money and other government debt were accompanied by real overinvestment in many kinds of capital goods.[24] There is little doubt that the "irrational" structure of capital characterizing Germany after stabilization led to subsequent problems of adjustment in labor and other markets.

Table 3.23   INDEX OF PHYSICAL VOLUME
OF PRODUCTION PER CAPITA
IN GERMANY

Year	Index of production	Year	Index of production
1920	61	1924	77
1921	77	1925	90
1922	86	1926	86
1923	54	1927	111

Source: Graham [7, p. 287].

CZECHOSLOVAKIA

After World War I, the new nation of Czechoslovakia was formed out of territories formerly belonging to Austria and Hungary. Under the leadership of a distinguished minister of finance, Dr. Alois Rasin, immediately after the war Czechoslovakia adopted the conservative fiscal and monetary policies its neighbors adopted only after their currencies had depreciated radically. As a result, Czechoslovakia avoided the hyperinflation experienced by its neighbors.

Under Rasin's leadership, Czechoslovakia early on showed that it was serious about attaining a stable currency. Even before the peace treaties required it, Czechoslovakia stamped the Austro-Hungarian notes then circulating within its border with the Czechoslovakian stamp, thereby recognizing them as its own debt. There was considerable drama associated with this event, as the National Assembly passed the plans for stamping in secret sessions on 25 February 1919. From 26 February to 9 March, the frontiers of the country were unexpectedly closed and foreign mail service was closed. Only Austro-Hungarian notes circulating within the country could be presented for stamping. As part of the stamping process, the government retained part of the notes in the form of a forced loan.[25] About 8 billion crowns were stamped.

A banking office in the Ministry of Finance took over the affairs of the old Austro-Hungarian bank. Czechoslovakia moved quickly to

Table 3.24 **CZECHOSLOVAKIA, RECEIPTS, AND EXPENDITURES, 1919–1925**
Exclusive of Expenditures for Capital Improvements Covered by Loans

	1919		1920		1921	
	Estimated	Actual	Estimated	Actual	Estimated	Actual
Revenue						
Ordinary	2,614	—	7,950	—	15,923	—
Extraordinary	1,096	—	2,477	—	1,376	—
Total	3,710	—	10,427	13,455	17,299	21,894
Expenditure						
Ordinary	2,610	—	7,175	—	10,672	—
Extraordinary	6,005	—	8,103	—	7,354	—
Total	8,615	7,450	15,278	13,931	18,026	18,558
Deficit	4,905	—	4,851	476	727	—
Surplus	—	—	—	—	—	3,336

Source: Young [36, vol. 2, p. 71].

limit by statute the total government note circulation and to prevent inflationary government finance. A law of 10 April 1919 strictly limited the fiduciary or unbacked note circulation of the banking office to about 7 billion crowns. This law was obeyed, and forced the government to finance its expenditures by levying taxes or else issuing debt, which, because of the statutory restriction on government note issues, were interpreted as promises to tax in the future.

From 1920 on, Czechoslovakia ran only modest deficits on current account (see Table 3.24). Among other taxes, Czechoslovakia imposed a progressive capital levy on property, which raised a cumulative amount of about 11 billion crowns by 1925. It also imposed an increment tax on the increased wealth individuals had obtained during the war.

Table 3.25 shows the note and deposit liabilities of the banking office. The government's abstention from inflationary finance shows up in these figures.

1922		1923		1924		1925	
Estimated	Actual	Estimated	Actual	Estimated	Actual	Estimated	Actual
17,291	—	17,961	—	15,987	—	—	—
1,593	—	851	—	404	—	—	—
18,884	17,733	18,812	15,664	16,391	—	15,702	—
13,289	—	13,605	—	12,200	—	—	—
6,524	—	5,773	—	4,703	—	—	—
19,813	18,663	19,378	16,540	16,993	—	15,974	—
929	930	565	876	603	—	272	—
—	—	—	—	—	—	—	—

Table 3.26 shows the path of exchange rates and how, after declining until November 1921, the Czechoslovakian crown rapidly gained to about 3 United States cents.

Table 3.27 shows the price levels. From 1922 to 1923, Czechoslovakia actually experienced a deflation. Indeed, Rasin's initial plan had been to restore the Czechoslovakian crown to the prewar gold par value of the old Austro-Hungarian crown. Following Rasin's assassination, this plan was abandoned and the crown was stabilized at about 2.96 cents.

CONCLUSION

The essential measures that ended hyperinflation in Germany, Austria, Hungary, and Poland were, first, the creation of an independent central bank that was legally committed to refuse the government's demand for additional unsecured credit and, second, a simultaneous al-

Table 3.25 **NOTE ISSUE OF BANKING OFFICE OF CZECHOSLOVAKIA, 1919–1924**

In Thousands of Czech Crowns

Year	Month	State notes in circulation	Year	Month	State notes in circulation
1919	April	—	1922	May	9,717,750
	May	—		June	9,838,205
	June	—		July	9,916,077
	July	161,106		August	10,171,383
	August	664,997		September	10,196,880
	September	1,443,570		October	10,139,366
	October	2,512,199		November	9,996,550
	November	3,513,405		December	10,064,049
	December	4,723,303	1923	January	9,222,434
1920	January	5,574,688		February	8,947,988
	February	6,462,825		March	9,157,407
	March	7,216,438		April	9,567,369
	April	7,216,438		May	9,327,676
	May	8,268,695		June	9,375,991
	June	9,729,233		July	9,448,086
	July	9,267,874		August	9,218,475
	August	9,814,920		September	9,311,378
	September	10,310,228		October	9,278,999
	October	10,920,514		November	9,250,688
	November	10,946,653		December	9,598,903
	December	11,288,512	1924	January	8,820,093
1921	January	10,888,319		February	8,506,467
	February	10,914,786		March	8,280,390
	March	10,921,956		April	8,198,653
	April	10,928,560		May	9,078,418
	May	10,851,403		June	8,081,106
	June	11,167,515		July	8,090,034
	July	11,134,327		August	9,139,792
	August	11,455,175		September	8,222,658
	September	11,570,881		October	8,585,847
	October	12,327,159		November	8,500,942
	November	11,871,647		December	8,810,357
	December	12,129,573	1925	January	7,916,540
1922	January	11,230,065		February	7,727,880
	February	10,743,958		March	7,680,867
	March	10,323,069		April	7,525,934
	April	10,075,757			

Source: Young [36, vol. 2, pp. 305–6].

Table 3.26   CZECHOSLOVAKIAN EXCHANGE RATES, 1919–1924

Year	Month	Cents per crown	Year	Month	Cents per crown
1919	January	—	1922	April	1.960
	February	—		May	1.921
	March	—		June	1.924
	April	6.135		July	2.185
	May	—		August	2.902
	June	—		September	3.231
	July	5.625		October	3.285
	August	4.575		November	3.176
	September	4.575		December	3.097
	October	3.100	1923	January	2.856
	November	1.950		February	2.958
	December	1.900		March	2.969
1920	January	1.425		April	2.978
	February	.975		May	2.979
	March	1.275		June	2.993
	April	1.530		July	2.997
	May	2.195		August	2.934
	June	2.335		September	2.995
	July	2.195		October	2.971
	August	1.810		November	2.906
	September	1.535		December	2.925
	October	1.245	1924	January	2.898
	November	1.165		February	2.902
	December	1.190		March	2.902
1921	January	1.300		April	2.957
	February	1.290		May	2.939
	March	1.307		June	2.936
	April	1.365		July	2.953
	May	1.460		August	2.979
	June	1.420		September	2.993
	July	1.312		October	2.981
	August	1.225		November	2.989
	September	1.160		December	3.018
	October	1.049	1925	January	3.00
	November	1.038		February	2.96
	December	1.249		March	2.97
1922	January	1.732		April	2.96
	February	1.855		May	2.96
	March	1.733		June	2.96

Source: Young [36, vol. 2, p. 307].

Table 3.27   CZECHOSLOVAKIAN WHOLESALE PRICES, 1922–1924

Year	Month	Wholesale price index	Year	Month	Wholesale price index
1922	January	1675	1923	October	973
	February	1520		November	965
	March	1552		December	984
	April	1491	1924	January	974
	May	1471		February	999
	June	1471		March	1021
	July	1464		April	1008
	August	1386		May	1015
	September	1155		June	981
	October	1059		July	953
	November	1017		August	986
	December	999		September	982
1923	January	1003		October	999
	February	1019		November	1013
	March	1028		December	1024
	April	1031	1925	January	1045
	May	1030		February	1048
	June	1001		March	1034
	July	968		April	1019
	August	958		May	1006
	September	957			

Source: Young [36, vol. 2, p. 307].
Note: July 1914 = 100.

teration in the fiscal policy regime.[26] These measures were interrelated and coordinated. They had the effect of binding the government to place its debt with private parties and foreign governments that would value that debt according to whether it was backed by sufficiently large prospective taxes relative to public expenditures. In each case we have studied, once it became widely understood that the government would not rely on the central bank for its finances, the inflation terminated and the exchanges stabilized. We have further seen that it was not simply the increasing quantity of central bank notes that caused the hyperinflation, since in each case the note circulation continued to grow rapidly after the exchange rate and price level had been stabilized. Rather, it was the growth of fiat currency that was unbacked, or backed only by government bills, which there never was a prospect to retire through taxation.

The changes that ended the hyperinflations were not isolated restrictive actions within a given set of rules of the game or general policy. Earlier attempts to stabilize the exchanges in Hungary under Hegedus [25, pp. 304–7], and also in Germany, failed precisely because they did not change the rules of the game under which fiscal policy had to be conducted.[27]

In discussing this subject with various people, I have encountered the view that the events described here are so extreme and bizarre that they do not bear on the subject of inflation in the contemporary United States. On the contrary, it is precisely because the events were so extreme that they are relevant. The four incidents we have studied are akin to laboratory experiments in which the elemental forces that cause and can be used to stop inflation are easiest to spot. I believe that these incidents are full of lessons about our own, less dramatic predicament with inflation, if only we interpret them correctly.

NOTES

1. "Most economists believe that the underlying inflation rate—roughly defined as wage costs less productivity gains—now stands at 9 to 10 percent, and that only a long period of restraint can reduce that rate significantly" (*Newsweek,* 19 May 1980, p. 59).
2. Paul Samuelson has aptly summarized the rational expectations view: "I should report that there is a new school, the so-called 'rational expectationists.' They are optimistic that inflation can be wiped out with little pain if only the government makes *credible* its determination to do so. But neither history nor reason tempt one to bet their way" (*Newsweek,* 28 April 1980). The second sentence of this quote is probably as shrewd a summary of the rational expectations view as can be made in a single sentence. However, it is difficult to agree with the third sentence: As for "reason," no one denies that logically coherent and well-reasoned models underlie the claims of the "rational expectationists"; as for history, the evidence summarized in this chapter is surely relevant.
3. There is actually no such thing as a "rational expectations school" in the sense of a collection of economists with an agreed-upon model of the economy and view about optimal monetary and fiscal policy. In fact, among economists who use the assumption of rational expectations there

is wide disagreement about these matters. What characterizes adherents to the notion of rational expectations is their intention to build models by assuming that private agents understand the dynamic environment in which they operate approximately as well as do government policymakers. Adherence to this notion leaves ample room for substantial diversity about the many other details of a model. For some examples of rational expectations models with diverse implications, see Lucas [21], Barro [2], Wallace [35], Townsend [34], and Sargent and Wallace [31]. Despite their diversity, it is true that all of these models impel us to think about optimal government policy in substantially different ways than were standard in macroeconomics before the advent of the doctrine of rational expectations in the early 1970s.

4. Bresciani-Turroni wrote: "Whoever studies the recent economic history of Europe is struck by a most surprising fact: the rapid monetary restoration of some countries where for several years paper money had continually depreciated. In some cases the stabilization of the exchange was not obtained by a continuous effort, prolonged over a period of years, whose effects would show themselves slowly in the progressive economic and financial restoration of the country, as occurred before the War in several well-known cases of monetary reform. Instead, the passing from a period of tempestuous depreciation of the currency to an almost complete stability of the exchange was very sudden" [3, p. 334]. Compare these remarks with the opinion of Samuelson cited in note 2 above.

5. The notes were "backed" mainly by treasury bills that, in those times, could not be expected to be paid off by levying taxes, but only by printing more notes or treasury bills.

6. Keynes wrote: "It is not lack of gold but the absence of other internal adjustments which prevents the leading European countries from returning to a pre-war gold standard. Most of them have plenty of gold for the purpose as soon as the other conditions favorable to the restoration of a gold standard have returned" (Keynes [11, p. 132]). Writing about Germany in 1923, Keynes said: "The government cannot introduce a sound money, because, in the absence of other revenue, the printing of an unsound money is the only way by which it can live" (Keynes [10, p. 67]).

7. This view can be expressed more precisely by referring to the technical literature of optimum economic growth. I am recommending that a good first model of the gold standard or other commodity money is a real equilibrium growth model in which a government issues debt, makes expenditures, and collects taxes. Examples of these models were studied by Arrow and Kurz [1]. In such models government debt is valued according to the same economic considerations that give private debt value, namely, the prospective net revenue stream of the institution issuing the debt. A real equilibrium growth model of this kind can also be used to provide a formal rationalization of my claim below that open-market operations in

private securities, foreign exchange, and gold should have no effect on the price level, i.e., the value of government demand debt.

8. It is relatively straightforward to produce a variety of workable theoretical models of a commodity money or gold standard, along the lines of note 7. It is considerably more difficult to produce a model of a fiat money, which is costless to produce, inconvertible, and of no utility except in exchange. Kareken and Wallace [9], Wallace [35], and Townsend [34] describe some of the ramifications of this observation. The workable models of fiat money that we do have—for example, those of Townsend [34] and Wallace [35]—immediately raise the question of whether voluntarily held fiat money can continue to be valued at all in the face of substantial budget deficits of the order of magnitude studied in this chapter. Such models lead one to assign an important role to government restrictions, particularly on foreign exchange transactions, in maintaining a valued, if involuntarily held, fiat money. Keynes [10] and Nichols [24] also emphasized the role of such restrictions.

9. The sweeping implications of this principle for standard ways of formulating and using econometric models were first described by Lucas [19]. The principle itself has emerged in a variety of contexts involving economic dynamics. For some examples, see Lucas [20] and Sargent and Wallace [30].

10. Sargent and Wallace [32] describe a sense in which it might be difficult to imagine that a regime change can occur. As they discovered, thinking about regime changes in the context of rational expectations models soon leads one to issues of free will.

11. The Treaty of St. Germain, signed in September of 1919, required the successor states of the Austro-Hungarian empire to stamp their share of the notes of the Austro-Hungarian bank. The stamp converted those notes to the currency, i.e. debt, of the new states. The Austrian section of the old Austro-Hungarian bank functioned as the central bank of Austria for several years after the war.

12. Needless to say, the central bank encountered a strong demand for loans at this rate and had to ration credit.

13. At the time, some commentators argued that since the real value of currency had decreased and so in a sense currency was scarce, the increased note issue of the central bank was not the prime cause of the inflation. Some even argued that money was "tight" and that the central bank was valiantly struggling to meet the shortage of currency by adding printing presses and employees. This argument is now widely regarded as fallacious by macroeconomists. Disturbingly, however, one hears the very same argument in the contemporary United States.

14. "In Vienna, during the period of collapse, mushroom exchange banks sprang up at every street corner, where you could change your krone into Zurich francs within a few minutes of receiving them, and so avoid the

risk of loss during the time it would take you to reach your usual bank. It became a reasonable criticism to allege that a prudent man at a cafe ordering a bock of beer should order a second bock at the same time, even at the expense of drinking it tepid, lest the price should rise meanwhile'' (Keynes [10, p. 51]).

15. See Young [36, vol. 2, p. 16]. That a government might want to adopt such measures if it were using inflationary finance was pointed out by Nichols [24].

16. The content of this protocol is highly sensible when it is remembered that the value of a state's currency and other debt, at least under the gold standard, is determined by its ability to back that debt with an appropriate fiscal policy. In this respect its situation is no different from that of a firm. In 1922 there was widespread concern within and without Austria that its sovereignty was at risk. (See the desperate note delivered by the Austrian minister to the Supreme Council of the Allied governments quoted by Pasvolsky [25, p. 115]). The first protocol aimed to clarify the extent to which Austria remained a political and economic entity capable of backing its debts. A similar protocol was signed at the inception of Hungary's financial reconstruction.

17. It should be noted that for two years the new bank vigorously exercised its authority to control transactions in foreign currency. Only after March 1925 were restrictions on trading foreign exchange removed.

18. This explanation is consistent with the argument advanced by Fama [6]. There is an alternative explanation of these observations that neglects the distinction between inside and outside money, and that interprets the observations in terms of a demand function for the total quantity of "money." For instance, Cagan [4] posited the demand schedule for money to take the form

$$M_t - P_t = \alpha(E_t P_{t+1} - P_t) \qquad \alpha < 0 \qquad (1)$$

where P_t is the logarithm of the price level, M_t is the logarithm of the money supply, and $E_t P_{t+1}$ is people's expectation of the log of price next period. There is always a problem in defining an empirical counterpart to M_t, but it is often taken to be the note and deposit liabilities of the central bank or "high-powered" money. The money demand schedule or "portfolio balance" schedule incorporates the idea that people want to hold less wealth in the form of real balances the faster the currency is expected to depreciate. Equation (1) can be solved to give an expression for the equilibrium price level of the form

$$P_t = \frac{1}{1 - \alpha} \sum_{i=0}^{\infty} \left(\frac{\alpha}{\alpha - 1} \right)^i E_t M_{t+i} \qquad (2)$$

where $E_t M_{t+i}$ is what at time t people expect the money supply to be at time $t + i$.

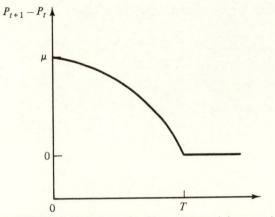

Figure 3.N.1 Inflation path with an expected decrease in money supply growth from μ to 0 to time T.

Consider the following two experiments. First, suppose that the government engages in a policy, *which everyone knows in advance,* of making the money supply grow at the constant high rate $\mu > 0$ from time 0 to time $T - 1$, and then at the rate zero from time T onward. In this case the inflation rate would follow the path depicted in Figure 3.N.1.

For the second experiment, suppose that initially everyone expected the money supply to increase at the constant rate μ forever but that at time T it becomes known that henceforth the money supply will increase at the rate 0 forever. In this case the inflation rate takes a sudden drop at time T, as shown by the path in Figure 3.N.2. Now since the inflation and the expected inflation rate experience a sudden drop at T in this case, it follows from equation (1) that real balances must increase at T. This will require a sudden once and for all *drop* in the price level at T.

This second example of a previously unexpected decrease in the inflation rate provides the material for an explanation of the growth of the money supplies after currency stabilization. In the face of a previously unexpected, sudden, and permanent drop in the rate of money creation, the only way to avoid a sudden drop in the price level would be to accompany the *decrease* in the rate of money creation with a once and for all *increase* in the money supply. In order to *stabilize* the price level in the face of a decreased rate of change of money, the level of the money supply must jump upward once and for all.

What actually occurred in the four countries studied here was not a once and for all jump but a gradual increase in the money supply over many months. This could be reconciled with the observations within the model (1) if people were assumed only gradually to catch on to the fact

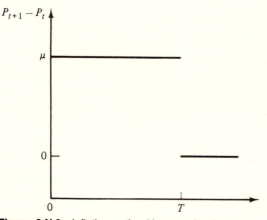

Figure 3.N.2 Inflation path with a previously unexpected decrease in money supply growth from μ to 0 at time T.

of stabilization and to decrease the rate of inflation that they expected as the currency stabilization continued to hold. I find this explanation hard to accept, but it is a possibility.

An alternative way to reconcile the preceding explanation with the gradual upward movement of "high-powered" money after the stabilizations is to add adjustment lags to the portfolio balance schedule (1). For example, consider replacing (1) with

$$(M_t - P_t) = \alpha(E_t P_{t+1} - P_t) + \lambda(M_{t-1} - P_{t-1}) \qquad \alpha < 0, 0 < \lambda < 1$$

In this case, an abrupt stabilization of expected inflation induces only a gradual adjustment of real balances upward at the rate of $1 - \lambda$ per period. My own preference at this point is for an explanation that stresses the distinction between backed and unbacked money.

19. Within a year and a half, these became a claim on gold as Britain returned to the gold standard.
20. Unlike Austria, Hungary, and Germany, Poland did not owe war reparations.
21. Keynes wrote: "A government can live for a long time, even the German government or the Russian government, by printing paper money . . . A government can live by this means when it can live by no other" (Keynes [10, p. 47]).
22. See Young [36, vol. 1, p. 402] and Bresciani-Turroni [3, p. 345].
23. After reading an earlier draft of this chapter, John Kennan directed me to the following passage in Constance Reid's biography of the mathematician Hilbert: "In 1923 the inflation ended abruptly through the creation of a new unit of currency called the Rentenmark. Although Hilbert remarked sceptically, 'One cannot solve a problem by changing the name

of the independent variable,' the stability of conditions was gradually restored'' (Reid [27, pp. 162–63]).

24. Theoretical models of money along the lines proposed by Samuelson [29] predict that too much capital will be accumulated when the government fiscal policy is so profligate that money becomes valueless. See Samuelson [29] and Wallace [35].

25. The frontiers were closed to prevent notes from Austria and Hungary from entering the country. The Treaty of St. Germain, signed 10 September 1919, provided that the successor states should stamp the Austro-Hungarian notes, signifying their assumption of the debt.

26. Of inflationary finance, Keynes wrote: "It is common to speak as though, when a government pays its way by inflation, the people of the country avoid taxation. We have seen this is not so. What is raised by printing notes is just as much taken from the public as is beer-duty or an income-tax. What a government spends the public pay for. There is no such thing as an uncovered deficit. But in some countries it seems possible to please and content the public, for a time at least, by giving them, in return for the taxes they pay, finely engraved acknowledgments on water-marked paper. The income tax receipts, which we in England receive from the surveyor, we throw into the wastepaper basket; in Germany they call them bank-notes and put them into their pocketbooks; in France they are termed Rentes and are locked up in the family safe" (Keynes [10, pp. 68–69]).

27. A deep objection to the interpretation in this paragraph can be constructed along the lines of Sargent and Wallace [30], who argue that for a single economy it is impossible to conceive of a rational expectations model in which there can occur a change in regime. In particular, the substantial changes in ways of formulating monetary and fiscal policy associated with the ends of the four inflations studied here can themselves be considered to have been caused by the economic events preceding them. On this interpretation, what we have interpreted as changes in the regime were really only the realization of events and human responses under a single, more complicated regime. This more complicated regime would have to be described in a considerably more involved and "state contingent" way than the simple regimes we have described. I believe that the data of this chapter could be described using this view, but that it would substantially complicate the language and require extensive qualifications without altering the main practical implications.

REFERENCES

1. Arrow, K. J., and M. Kurz. 1970. *Public Investment, the Rate of Return, and Optimal Fiscal Policy.* Baltimore and London: Johns Hopkins University Press.

2. Barro, R. J. 1974. Are government bonds net wealth? *Journal of Political Economy* 82 (November/December):1095–1117.
3. Bresciani-Turroni, C. 1937. *The Economics of Inflation*. London: George Allen & Unwin.
4. Cagan, P. 1956. The monetary dynamics of hyperinflation. In M. Friedman, ed., *Studies in the Quantity Theory of Money*. Chicago: University of Chicago Press.
5. de Bordes, J. v. W. 1924. *The Austrian Crown*. London: P. S. King & Son.
6. Fama, E. F. 1980. Banking in the theory of finance. *Journal of Monetary Economics* 6 (January):39–58.
7. Graham, F. D. 1930. *Exchange, Prices, and Production in Hyperinflation: Germany, 1920–23*. New York: Russel & Russell.
8. Kareken, J. H., and N. Wallace. 1980. *Models of Monetary Economies*. Minneapolis: Federal Reserve Bank of Minneapolis.
9. ———. 1980. Introduction to [8].
10. Keynes, J. M. 1924. *Monetary Reform*. New York: Harcourt Brace Jovanovich.
11. Keynes, J. M. 1925. The United States and gold. In Young [36, vol. 1, pp. 131–33].
12. Layton, W. T., and C. Rist. 1925. *The Economic Situation of Austria*. Report presented to the Council of the League of Nations, Geneva, 19 August.
13. League of Nations. 1946. *The Course and Control of Inflation*. Geneva.
14. ———. 1926. *The Financial Reconstruction of Austria*. General Survey and Principal Documents, Geneva.
15. ———. 1926. *The Financial Reconstruction of Hungary*. General Survey and Principal Documents. Geneva.
16. ———. 1926. *Memorandum on Currency and Central Banks, 1913–1925*, vol. 1. Geneva.
17. ———. 1927. *Memorandum on Public Finance (1922–1926)*. Geneva.
18. ———. 1925. *Memorandum on Currency and Central Banks, 1913–1924*, vol. 1. Geneva.
19. Lucas, R. E., Jr. 1976. Econometric policy evaluation: A critique. In K. Brunner and A. H. Meltzer, eds., *The Phillips Curve and Labor Markets*, pp. 19–46. Carnegie-Rochester Conference Series on Public Policy, vol. 1. Amsterdam: North-Holland.
20. ———. 1972. Econometric testing of the natural rate hypothesis. In O. Eckstein, ed., *The Econometrics of Price Determination*. Washington: Board of Governors, Federal Reserve System.
21. ———. 1980. Equilibrium in a pure currency economy. In Kareken and Wallace [8].
22. Lucas, R. E., Jr., and T. J. Sargent. 1979. After Keynesian economics.

Federal Reserve Bank of Minneapolis, *Quarterly Review,* 3 (Spring):1–16.

23. ———. 1981. Rational expectations and econometric practice. Introductory essay to R. E. Lucas, Jr., and T. J. Sargent, eds., *Rational Expectations and Econometric Practice.* Minneapolis: University of Minnesota Press.

24. Nichols, D. 1974. Some principles of inflationary finance. *Journal of Political Economy* 82, part 1 (March/April):423–30.

25. Pasvolsky, L. 1928. *Economic Nationalism of the Danubian States.* New York: Macmillan.

26. Paxton, R. O. 1975. *Europe in the Twentieth Century.* New York: Harcourt Brace Jovanovich.

27. Reid, C. 1979. *Hilbert.* New York: Springer-Verlag.

28. Salemi, M. K. 1976. Hyperinflation, exchange depreciation, and the demand for money in post World War I Germany. Ph.D. thesis, University of Minnesota.

29. Samuelson, P. A. 1958. An exact consumption-loan model of interest with or without the social contrivance of money. *Journal of Political Economy* 66 (December):467–82.

30. Sargent, T. J. 1980. Rational expectations and the reconstruction of macroeconomics. Federal Reserve Bank of Minneapolis, *Quarterly Review* 4 (Summer):15–19.

31. Sargent, T. J., and N. Wallace. 1975. Rational expectations, the optimal monetary instrument, and the optimal money supply rule. *Journal of Political Economy* 83 (April):241–54.

32. ———. 1976. Rational expectations and the theory of economic policy. *Journal of Monetary Economics* 2, no. 2 (April):169–83.

33. *Statistiches Jahrbuch für das Deutsche Reich.* 1924/25.

34. Townsend, R. M. 1980. Models of money with spatially separated agents. In Kareken and Wallace [8].

35. Wallace, N. 1980. The overlapping generations model of fiat money. In [8].

36. Young, J. P. 1925. *European Currency and Finance,* vols. 1 and 2. (Commission of Gold and Silver Inquiry, United States Senate, serial 9.) Washington: Government Printing Office.

chapter **4**

Stopping Moderate Inflations: The Methods of Poincaré and Thatcher

INTRODUCTION

In June 1979 Margaret Thatcher's administration began governing Great Britain. One of her primary goals was markedly to reduce the rate of inflation, an understandable goal in view of the experience of the past decade when Great Britain's rate of inflation had on average exceeded the rate of inflation in other industrial countries. Advocates of the two main groups of contemporary theories about inflation dynamics could have told Mrs. Thatcher that achieving that goal would be difficult, although each group would have characterized the nature of the difficulties quite differently. The first group consists of the "momentum" or "core inflation" theories (e.g., see Eckstein [14]). The second group comprises the rational expectations-equilibrium theories (e.g., see [3, 25, 29, 38]).

The first group of theories posits that there is some inherent momentum in the process of inflation itself, and that this momentum or persistence is neither superficial nor merely a reflection of slowly moving deeper forces that themselves cause inflation to behave as it does. Two distinct possible sources of sluggishness in inflation have been proposed. One is the notion of adaptive or autoregressive expectations. According to this doctrine, workers and firms form expectations about future rates of inflation by computing a moving average of current and lagged rates of inflation. The moving average makes expected inflation a simple function of current and past rates of inflation. Further, the weights in the moving average are assumed to be fixed numbers that are independent of the economic environment, including government monetary and fiscal policy, and are taken to characterize the psychology of expectations. Since firms and workers set current and future nominal wages and prices partly as functions of their expected rates of inflation, this model of inflationary expectations determines the actual rate of inflation partly as a long weighted average of past inflation rates. The other main determinant of inflation is the unemployment rate with which, by means of a Phillips curve mechanism, inflation varies inversely. According to this theory, the only way to eliminate inflation through conventional monetary and fiscal restraint is by moving along the short-run Phillips curve and suffering a period of high unemployment that is long enough to break the slowly moving inflationary expectations. In this model the momentum in the inflation process and the high cost in unemployment of ending inflation is caused by the irrational nature of agents' expectations. Reductions in inflation are costly because it takes agents a long time to understand that they are in a less inflationary environment. If they learned faster, reducing inflation would be less costly.

A second, more sophisticated mechanism that can lead to a notion of intrinsic momentum in inflation is the staggered wage contract model of John Taylor [42] and Phelps and Taylor [33]. Taylor posits rational expectations, so that agents in his model form expectations of inflation as functions of all of the variables relevant for forecasting future inflation. As a result of positing rationality, the particular function that agents optimally use to forecast inflation responds systematically and predictably to the economic environment, including the monetary policy and fiscal policy regimes, contrary to the fixed-function forecasts assumed under adaptive expectations. The source of momentum or persistence in Taylor's model comes from the overlapping structure of multiperiod wage contracts, and a particular nonstate contingent form that he imposes on contracts. In this class of models, in terms of unemployment it is costly to end inflation because firms and workers are now locked into long-term wage contracts that were negotiated on the basis of wage and price expectations that prevailed in the past. In Taylor's model, as in all rational expectations models, the observed momentum or serial correlation in the inflation process partly reflects the serial correlation in the "first causes" of inflation, such as monetary and fiscal variables. In addition, however, the wage-contracting mechanism contributes some momentum of its own to the process, so that the resulting sluggishness in inflation cannot be completely eliminated or overcome by appropriate changes in monetary and fiscal policies. The wage-contracting process gives rise to a nontrivial trade-off between the variance of inflation and the variance of unemployment.

Although they both embody a measure of momentum in wage and price dynamics, the adaptive expectations and Taylor wage contract models have substantially different implications about the unemployment costs of deflationary policies. The adaptive expectations or "core inflation" theory implies that inflation can be reduced only through a more or less extended period of higher unemployment. On the other hand, the wage-contracting models of Taylor and others imply the existence of a variety of alternative policy strategies, each of which could successfully deflate the economy with *no* costs in terms of higher unemployment. The classes of strategies that eliminate inflation without imposing unemployment costs are all characterized by a policy of gradual tightening of monetary and fiscal policy. How gradual to make this process depends precisely on the dynamics of the wage contracts. To avoid increases in unemployment, the deflationary actions must respect the persistence in nominal wages built in by the old wage contracts. Thus an inflation can be eliminated costlessly, but only if it is done gradually. For such a policy to work, it is necessary that the strategy of gradual tightening of aggregate demand be precommitted by the demand management authorities in a way that is sufficiently forceful and binding that it assures private agents' belief in the plan. Later in this chapter, I shall argue that there is a tension inherent in this kind of gradual policy, since promises to take strong contractionary actions in the more distant future in the face of only mild contractionary actions in the present and near future are open to skepticism. (Recall the campaign promises of Presidents Carter and Reagan to balance the federal budget in the last year of their respective administrations.) At this point it is sufficient to emphasize that adaptive expectations and Taylor-like contracting models with rational expectations have different practical implications about the feasibility of relatively painless disinflations. The reason for these important differences in implications resides in the difference between the assumptions of adaptive and rational expectations. The latter hypothesis has private agents' decision rules responding in a particular stabilizing way with respect to changes in the government's strategy for demand management, while the former does not.

We now turn to the second group of theories of inflation, which are the rational expectations, and equilibrium theories. These theories maintain that essentially all of the characteristics of the serial correlation of inflation are inherited from the random properties of the deeper causes of inflation, such as monetary and fiscal policy variables. These theories differ from Taylor's kind of theory in viewing wage and price contracts, whether implicit or explicit, as more state contingent, and contracting procedures as more responsive to the economic environment.[1] In order to explain observed Phillips curve trade-offs, these theories resort to the Phelps-Lucas device of information limitations and the temporary confusions that they cause. When measures of aggregate demand and/or variables that partially reflect them, such as prices and interest rates, are realized to differ from what they had previously been rationally expected to be, it sets in motion movements in real economic variables. On this view the first cause of business cycle fluctuations is uncertainty about the position of future and maybe even current relative prices and productivity disturbances.

Although differing among themselves in many important substantive details, members of the second group of theories are united by their assertion that under the proper hypothetical conditions a government could eliminate inflation very rapidly and with virtually no Phillips curve costs in terms of foregone real output or increased unemployment. The "measure" that would accomplish this would be a once-and-for-all, widely understood and widely agreed upon change in the monetary or fiscal policy regime. Here a regime is taken to be a function or rule for repeatedly selecting the economic policy variable or variables in question as a function of the state of the economy. Particular models within this class differ widely with respect to the particular policy variables (e.g., high-powered money, a wider monetary aggregate, or total government debt) that are focused upon. However, all the theories require that the change in the rule for the pertinent variable be widely understood and uncontroversial, and therefore unlikely to be reversed. These characteristics are essential in eliminating the costs in terms of foregone output that information limitations and confusions cause with the Phelps-Lucas version of the Phillips curve.

According to each of these two theories, Mrs. Thatcher has faced a formidable task. The momentum view obviously implies that she could use monetary and fiscal variables to depress inflation only at the cost of also depressing real economic activity. The rational expectations equilibrium view suggests that it is not in the power of a prime minister or even a united political party to create the circumstances required to bring about a quick and costless end to inflation. Whether or not the stage is set for successfully implementing a significant new policy regime is the result of intellectual and historical forces that individual political figures influence only marginally. Mrs. Thatcher came to power against the background of over 20 years of stop-go or reversible government policy actions.[2] Her economic policy actions are vigorously opposed both by members of the Labor Party and by a strong new party, the Social Democrats. Thus the economic spokesman for the Labor Party, Mr. Peter Shore, advocated an immediate 40 percent devaluation and a larger government deficit. Mrs. Thatcher's party now runs third in the political opinion polls. In addition, throughout her administration, speculation has waxed and waned about whether Mrs. Thatcher herself would be driven to implement a U-turn in macroeconomic policy actions, and whether her stringent monetary policy actions would be reversed by the Conservative Party itself, by choosing a new party leader. Furthermore there is widespread dissent from Thatcher's actions among British macroeconomic scholars, so that she cannot be regarded as implementing a widely agreed upon theory. For all of these reasons, it is difficult to interpret Thatcher's policy actions in terms of the kind of once-and-for-all, widely believed, uncontroversial, and irreversible regime change that rational expectations equilibrium theories assert can cure inflation at little or no cost in terms of real output.[3] This is not to render a negative judgment on Thatcher's goal or her methods, but only to indicate that the preconditions for the applicability of rational expectations "neutrality" or "policy irrelevance" theorems don't seem to exist in Margaret Thatcher's England. Where these conditions are not met, rational expectations equilibrium models imply that contractionary monetary and fiscal policy actions are likely to be costly in terms of real output and unemployment.

THE "POINCARÉ MIRACLE"

We have seen that extensive preconditions must obtain before rational expectations, equilibrium theories can be taken to imply that there is a costless cure to inflation, or equivalently, that the neutrality theorems of the theory can be expected closely to approximate reality. It has been argued by some that these preconditions are so stringent that they have rarely if ever been satisfied in practice, so that the example of Thatcher's England is the standard case. While this is a respectable argument, it is useful to point out that there are repeated historical episodes that seem to fit the rational expectations equilibrium model fairly well. I have described four such episodes, namely, the events surrounding the ends of hyperinflations in Poland, Germany, Austria, and Hungary from 1922 to 1924 [37]. Each of those countries successfully stopped drastic inflations dead in their tracks by interrelated fiscal and monetary policy changes that can be interpreted as abrupt changes in regime. The costs in foregone output were much smaller than would be suggested by modern estimates of Phillips curves and were in no sense proportional to the magnitudes of the inflations that were halted. Some readers' responses to those examples have been that because those inflations were so spectacular, between 5,000 and 1,000,000 percent per year, the procedures undertaken to end them have few implications about the problem of ending more moderate inflations like the ones faced by industrialized countries today. The argument seems to rest on an appeal to a model in the style of Taylor [43]. It asserts that the hyperinflations had proceeded to the point where long-term nominal contracts had ceased to operate, thereby destroying the dom-

Table 4.1   FRENCH WHOLESALE PRICE INDEX
           Base 1913 = 100, 1913 from 1901–1910 Index = 115.6

Year	January	February	March	April	May	June
1923	386.9	421.8	424.0	414.7	406.5	408.7
1924	494.0	543.7	499.3	450.0	458.5	465.3
1925	514.4	515.0	513.5	512.8	519.8	542.6
1926	633.5	635.6	631.8	650.1	687.9	738.4
1927	621.8	631.6	641.4	636.5	628.6	622.6

July	August	September	October	November	December
406.7	413.1	423.6	420.5	442.9	458.6
481.0	476.6	485.6	497.1	503.5	507.2
556.8	557.2	555.7	572.3	605.5	632.4
836.2	769.5	786.9	751.5	683.8	626.5
619.9	617.9	600.3	587.5		

Source: League of Nations Bulletin, Haig [21, p. 448].

inant source of momentum in the inflation process. The argument is then that for milder inflations, the existence of long-term nominal contracts still remains a source of momentum that will make it costly in terms of real output and unemployment to end inflation quickly by draconian changes in fiscal or monetary regime.[4]

However, in the 1920s other countries successfully used essentially the same monetary and fiscal reforms that worked in Austria, Poland, Germany, and Hungary to stabilize much milder currency depreciation.[5] One dramatic example was the stabilization of the French franc that was achieved by the government formed by Raymond Poincaré in July 1926.[6] (Tables 4.1 and 4.2 report the French wholesale price index and the dollar-franc exchange rate between 1923 and 1927.) Poincaré formed his government at a time when it was universally recognized that "the country was in trouble again, and all political parties except the Socialists and Communists gathered behind Poincaré. Five former premiers joined his government. There was a political truce," Shirer [41, p. 163]. For some time there had been broad consensus both about the principal economic factors that had

Table 4.2 DOLLAR EXCHANGE IN PARIS

	1923	1924	1925	1926	1927
January	15.57	21.74	18.49	26.77	25.32
February	16.45	25.57	19.38	27.49	25.55
March	15.23	18.32	19.06	28.65	25.54
April	14.84	15.45	19.20	30.15	25.53
May	15.15	18.80	19.83	30.60	25.53
June	16.32	18.88	21.56	34.93	25.54
July	16.84	19.86	21.11	41.15	25.56
August	17.65	18.48	21.30	35.12	25.51
September	16.15	18.96	21.12	35.66	25.48
October	17.19	19.13	23.92	32.52	25.47
November	18.51	18.82	26.09	28.11	25.43
December	19.59	18.56	26.90	25.25	25.40

Note: Averages of daily rates for final weeks of each month, francs per dollar.

caused the depreciation of the franc—persistent government deficits and the consequent pressure to monetize government debt—and the general features required to stabilize the franc—increased taxes and reduced government expenditures sufficient to balance the budget, together with firm limits on the amount of government debt monetized by the Bank of France. For several years a political struggle had been waged over *whose* taxes would be raised, with the monied interests in the country resisting efforts to raise taxes on them.[7] The accession to power of Poincaré in 1926 settled that issue in a fashion acceptable to the country's monied interests.

France financed its effort in World War I by borrowing at home and abroad, mainly in the United States. After the war France continued to run substantial government deficits. That it did so was partly rationalized by the expectation that "Germany will pay" for the French deficits. Under the Treaty of Versailles, Germany was obligated to pay massive reparations, which the French used partly to finance the reconstruction of territories devastated during the war. However, neither the total amount to be paid, nor the payment schedule was fixed by the treaty. Instead, these were to be determined by the Reparations Commission, and in the event were subject to continuous revision and renegotiation. The uncertain character of these claims complicated the public finances of both Germany and the countries that were owed reparations by Germany.[8] With the collapse of the German mark during 1923 and the relief from reparations provided Germany under the Dawes plan in 1924, it became clear that France could not continue to expect that German reparations would be sufficient to redeem the French government's debt. From that time on the franc depreciated, and the domestic price level rose, as Table 4.2 shows.[9] The big financial question for French governments was how much of its outstanding debt would be paid off or honored by channeling increased tax revenues to bondholders, and how much would be defaulted on through depreciation of the franc.

The period from 1924 through July 1926 was marked by political instability and a rapid succession of governments and finance ministers in "the waltz of the portfolios." There were repeated and unsuccessful attempts to deal with the increasing difficulties associated with refinancing the massive government debt as it gradually became due. The controversy was tainted by scandal as it was revealed that the government under Herriot had cooperated in an accounting subterfuge that concealed the fact that the Bank of France had exceeded the legal limit on the amount of its note issue that could be used to purchase government bonds. The period was also characterized by a massive flight of French capital abroad, partly an anxiety reaction to some of the tax proposals under discussion, such as a capital levy, and partly a reaction to the deteriorating prospects for the returns of franc-denominated assets.

Raymond Poincaré was a fiscal conservative, who had raised taxes while prime minister in 1924 and was known to advocate a balanced budget and France's return to gold. In 1926 he served as his own finance minister. As soon as he assumed control of the government, and even before his program was enacted by the legislature, the franc recovered, and inflation stopped. Under Poincaré, taxes were raised with an eye toward assuring persistent balanced or surplus government budgets. Some direct tax rates were actually reduced, including the highest rate for the general income tax, from 60 to 30 percent, and the rates of inheritance and estate taxes. However, indirect taxes were raised markedly. The government was authorized to raise all specific taxes up to six times their prewar rates, and decrees were issued implementing this authority [21, p. 163]. Customs duties were raised, and postal rates increased, as were taxes on passenger and freight rail service and on autos. The basic income tax rates were also raised, for example, from 12 to 18 percent on income from land and securities and from 7.2 to 12 percent on labor income. A once-and-for-all tax of 7 percent on the first sale of real estate or a business, a kind of capital levy, was also imposed.

There was also established an independent special fund to pay off outstanding government debt, administered by the Caisse d'Amortissement, a newly created agency independent of the treasury and with its own earmarked revenues from the tobacco monopoly, the total receipts from the inheritance and estate taxes, and the new 7 percent tax on first sale of real estate and businesses.

As the figures in Tables 4.1 and 4.2 show, these measures resulted in a sudden recovery of the franc and a cessation of inflation. The franc was permitted by the French authorities to appreciate from July until December, at which time France de facto returned to the gold standard. The appreciation of the franc was accompanied by open-market purchases of foreign assets by the French monetary authority as French citizens repatriated capital in response to Poincaré's policies. While Poincaré himself had wished to restore the franc to its prewar par, it was decided to halt the appreciation of the franc in December 1926 and de facto to return to gold at that rate. This amounted to an 80 percent depreciation of the franc from its prewar par. This magnitude indicates the substantial extent to which France had financed the war by issuing bonds to its citizens, on which it largely eventually defaulted. This is to be contrasted with the situation in England, which returned to the prewar par in 1925, thereby indicating an intention not to default on its long-term debt. However, the French did not default as thoroughly as did the Austrians or the Germans.[10]

The stabilization of the French franc was followed by several years of high prosperity. The French stabilization thus seems to fit the predictions of the rational expectations equilibrium approach. To the extent that it does fit, one reason is probably the high degree of political and intellectual consensus that prevailed at the time. It should be remembered that the French stabilization occurred after a variety of neighboring countries had successfully stabilized by resorting to the same budgetary principles that France eventually applied. At the time there was widespread professional consensus about the general budgetary situation that would have to prevail in order for the franc to be stabilized in the absence of exchange controls. Shirer indicates the degree of political consensus when he reports that "Frenchmen became obsessed with the idea that the 'Poincaré franc,' shrunk though it was, must never again be devalued lest they be ruined anew," Shirer [41, p. 166].

The French stabilized the franc by de facto returning to the gold standard. This amounted to standing ready to convert the debt of the French government into gold on specified terms, such as on demand for currency. In order to make a domestic currency freely convertible into gold, or into any foreign money for that matter, it is necessary that the government run a fiscal policy capable of supporting its promise to convert its debt. What backs the promise is not only the valuable stocks of gold, physical assets, and private claims that the government holds but also the intention to set future taxes high enough relative to government expenditures.

This method of stabilizing a currency remains available to a small country today, even though the world is no longer on the gold standard. One country, call it the domestic country, can obtain a domestic rate of inflation no greater than, and even less than, that of a large foreign country to whose currency it pegs its own currency.[11] To support this policy requires that the domestic country abstain from or at least much restrict the extent to which it resorts to inflationary finance. Indeed, the domestic government collects seigniorage only to the extent that it engages in clever devices such as holding its reserves of the foreign currency denominated assets in the form of interest-bearing assets, while at the same time adopting legal restrictions and fostering institutions that prompt its own residents to hold currency and other zero or low nominal interest assets. It is possible for a domestic government actually to experience a lower rate of inflation than the country to which it pegs its currency if it sets things up so that government and private institutions back their monetary liabilities with interest-bearing foreign-denominated assets and also pass the interest returns to their depositors. In so doing, the government completely abstains from using inflationary finance and provides domestic residents with a higher real rate of return on "money"—a lower rate of inflation than is experienced by residents of the foreign country who happen to be holding currency and other zero nominal rate of interest assets.[12]

As we turn our attention to Mrs. Thatcher's actions, it is useful to keep in mind a number of characteristics of the French financial crisis of 1926 and the subsequent salvation of the franc by Poincaré:

1. The extent to which the large interest-bearing French government debt created during the war and the reconstruction period became more and more difficult to refinance, thereby generating increasing pressures for its eventual monetization. This pressure eventually led to fraudulent accounting practices by the Bank of France and a scandal that brought down a government. The forces underlying these events are pertinent in Britain and elsewhere today in estimating the likely consequences and even the very feasibility of policies that propose to combat inflation with restrictive monetary policies alone, while at the same time permitting substantial government deficits to continue.

2. The manner in which France stabilized by pegging the franc to a foreign currency and adopting changes in tax and expenditure laws that delivered the prospective budget surpluses needed to support that peg without exchange controls. A similar course was available to Britain in 1979, but it did not choose to follow it.

3. The sense in which the preconditions for a successful and relatively costless stabilization along the rational expectations equilibrium model were met in France in 1926. Whether these preconditions are met is in large part a consequence of historical circumstance. However, it is also perhaps partly a function of the particular lines along which a stabilization is sought. For example, it is arguable that pegging to a foreign currency is a policy that is relatively easier to support and make credible by concrete actions, since it is possible to hook the domestic country's price expectations virtually instantaneously on to the presumably exogenous price expectations process in the foreign country.

4. The fact that France chose to stabilize at a value that was widely believed to undervalue the franc. To this the French prosperity

of the late 1920s has often been partly ascribed (e.g., see [1 or 44]). This is to be contrasted with the situation in England today, where contemporary monetary and fiscal policies have permitted a substantial appreciation of the pound, with consequent depressing influences on export industries.

THE BRITISH EXPERIENCE

Tables 4.3 through 4.12 report statistics that summarize the recent behavior of United Kingdom aggregates. Since Mrs. Thatcher took office in June 1979, much of the news has been bad. Real GNP has declined; industrial production, especially in manufacturing, has fallen precipitously; the unemployment rate has climbed from around 5 percent in June 1979 to over 10 percent in March 1981, to attain its highest level since the 1930s. Meanwhile, inflation in the retail price index accelerated for the first year of Thatcher's administration, though in the last nine months it has receded markedly so that the inflation rate in the United Kingdom during this more recent period was actually less than it was in the United States. The pound sterling rose vis-à-vis the U.S. dollar, from 2.11 \$/£ in June 1979 to 2.40 \$/£ in January 1981, while the balance of payments in current account swung toward surplus. Interest rates rose to very high levels.

Recent economic events in Britain have been well summarized in papers by Meltzer [30] and in the Morgan Guaranty Trust Survey [31]. I refer the reader to those sources for many interesting details and will devote most of my space to highlighting and interpreting a few of the facts from the viewpoint of rational expectations macro-economics.

MRS. THATCHER'S PLAN

A hallmark of Mrs. Thatcher's publicly announced economic strategy is gradualism. For the most part her government did not propose to execute any abrupt or discontinuous changes in aggregate government variables such as tax collections, government expenditures, or the money supply. Instead, the Conservatives proposed to carry out a

Table 4.3 GDP AT FACTOR COST AND FINAL EXPENDITURES ON GOODS AND SERVICES AT MARKET PRICES
£ Million, Current Prices

	(1) GDP at current prices based on expenditure data	(2) GDP at 1975 prices based on expenditure data	Implicit price deflator 1975 = 100 (column 1 divided by column 2 × 100)	GDP at market prices	Consumers' expenditure
1970	43,532	85,402	50.97	51,065	31,778
1971	49,442	87,572	56.46	57,291	35,599
1972	55,276	88,719	62.30	63,390	40,183
1973	64,258	95,506	67.28	72,936	47,759
1974	74,414	94,527	78.72	82,879	52,849
1975	93,954	93,954	100.00	104,413	64,424
1976	111,245	97,971	113.55	124,330	74,751
1977	126,111	98,993	127.39	143,064	85,474
1978	144,442	101,929	141.71	164,034	98,395
1979	163,647	102,563	159.56	189,702	114,805

General government final consumption	Gross domestic fixed capital formation	Value of physical increase in stocks and work in progress	Exports of goods and services	Imports of goods and services	Taxes on expenditure	Subsidies
8,991	9,470	421	11,551	11,146	8,417	884
10,250	10,517	158	12,960	12,193	8,788	939
11,675	11,606	44	13,653	13,771	9,627	1,153
13,380	14,238	1,448	17,124	19,013	10,121	1,443
16,609	16,867	1,304	22,985	27,375	11,469	3,004
23,074	20,417	1,534	27,011	28,979	14,162	3,703
26,779	23,599	864	35,211	36,874	16,553	3,468
26,209	25,739	1,860	43,352	42,570	20,252	3,299
32,934	26,695	1,070	47,442	45,502	23,253	3,661
38,316	33,646	2,760	54,676	54,501	30,361	4,306

Table 4.4 EXCHANGE, PRICE, AND BALANCE

| | | Current balance (million £) | Exchange rate ($/£) | Retail price (1975 = 100) | |
				Index	Percentage increase on one year earlier
1970		+779	2.396	54.2	6.4
1971		+1,076	2.444	59.3	9.4
1972		+189	2.502	63.6	7.1
1973		−1,056	2.453	69.4	9.2
1974		−3,380	2.340	80.5	16.1
1975		−1,674	2.220	100.0	24.2
1976		−1,060	1.805	116.5	16.5
1977		−206	1.746	135.0	15.8
1978		+707	1.920	146.2	8.3
1979		−1,630	2.122	165.8	13.4
1980		−2,737	2.328	195.6	18.0
1976	1	+106	1.998	110.9	22.5
	2	−352	1.805	114.9	16.0
	3	−436	1.766	117.6	13.7
	4	−378	1.651	123.0	15.0
1977	1	−362	1.714	129.2	16.5
	2	−431	1.719	134.9	17.4
	3	+307	1.735	137.0	16.5
	4	+280	1.813	139.0	13.0
1978	1	−194	1.928	141.4	9.5
	2	+417	1.835	145.3	7.6
	3	+87	1.932	147.8	7.9
	4	+397	1.984	150.3	8.1
1979	1	−692	2.016	155.0	9.6
	2	−192	2.081	160.7	10.6
	3	−189	2.234	171.4	16.0
	4	−557	2.157	176.2	17.3
1980	1	+70	2.254	184.6	19.1
	2	−88	2.286	195.3	21.5
	3	+870	2.382	199.4	16.4
	4	+1,885	2.387	203.2	15.3
1981	Jan.	+1,042	2.405	205.7	13.0
	Feb.	+614	2.294	207.6	12.5

Table 4.5 OUTPUT AND UNEMPLOYMENT

GDP (at 1975 factor cost, million £, seasonally adjusted)		Industrial production (1975 = 100, seasonally adjusted)		Unemployment rate
		All industries	Manufacturing	
1970	85,402	99.7	98.0	2.4
1971	87,572	99.8	97.5	3.1
1972	88,719	102.0	100.0	3.4
1973	95,506	109.5	108.4	2.4
1974	94,527	105.1	106.6	2.3
1975	93,954	100.0	100.0	3.6
1976	97,971	102.0	101.5	4.9
1977	98,993	105.9	103.0	5.2
1978	101,929	109.8	103.9	5.2
1979	102,973	112.6	104.2	5.0
1976 1	24,486	100.4	99.4	5.1
2	24,156	101.8	101.7	5.3
3	24,518	101.4	101.6	5.4
4	24,811	104.4	103.2	n.a.
1977 1	24,397	106.2	104.5	5.5
2	24,660	105.5	102.5	5.6
3	24,677	105.9	102.7	5.8
4	25,259	106.1	102.4	5.9
1978 1	25,156	107.6	102.9	5.8
2	25,602	110.6	104.5	5.8
3	25,507	111.0	104.9	5.7
4	25,664	110.0	103.1	5.4
1979 1	25,175	110.1	102.3	5.6
2	26,287	115.0	107.3	5.4
3	25,655	112.7	103.2	5.2
4	25,856	112.6	104.2	5.3
1980 1	25,596	110.0	100.0	5.7
2	25,445	106.6	96.8	6.2
3	24,991	102.9	93.3	7.0
4		100.2	89.1	8.4

Table 4.6 GROSS DOMESTIC FIXED CAPITAL FORMATION BY SECTOR

		Total	Private sector	General government	Public corporations
1969		18,954	10,390	5,385	3,201
1970		19,460	10,685	5,475	3,316
1971		19,743	11,099	5,297	3,334
1972		19,823	11,776	5,076	2,932
1973		21,195	12,267	5,793	3,135
1974		20,616	11,641	5,418	3,557
1975		20,417	11,530	4,974	3,913
1976		20,636	11,811	4,786	4,039
1977		20,089	12,438	3,964	3,687
1978		20,802	13,793	3,520	3,489
1979		20,506	13,761	3,352	3,393
1975	1	5,112	2,916	1,239	957
	2	5,086	2,846	1,306	934
	3	5,178	2,986	1,165	1,027
	4	5,041	2,782	1,264	995
1976	1	5,226	2,844	1,280	1,102
	2	5,158	2,920	1,226	1,012
	3	5,203	3,097	1,156	950
	4	5,049	2,950	1,124	975
1977	1	4,883	2,892	1,079	912
	2	5,065	3,149	988	928
	3	4,997	3,119	953	925
	4	5,144	3,278	944	922
1978	1	5,287	3,493	938	856
	2	5,282	3,499	899	894
	3	5,136	3,401	868	867
	4	5,097	3,400	825	872
1979	1	4,998	3,318	818	862
	2	5,052	3,401	820	831
	3	5,182	3,436	882	864
	4	5,274	3,606	832	836
1980	1	5,169	3,547	765	857
	2	5,058	3,429	741	888
	3	4,923	3,357	719	847
	4				

Table 4.7 MONEY SUPPLY IN THE UNITED KINGDOM

£ Million: Amounts Outstanding

At end period		M1 seasonally adjusted	Sterling M3 seasonally adjusted	M3 seasonally adjusted
1970	1	8,640	16,000	16,450
	2	8,920	16,460	16,980
	3	9,020	16,830	17,350
	4	9,420	17,300	17,810
1971	1	9,820	18,020	18,510
	2	9,900	18,270	18,780
	3	10,210	18,670	19,180
	4	10,310	19,530	19,960
1972	1	11,200	21,140	21,670
	2	11,680	22,480	23,090
	3	11,750	23,320	23,970
	4	12,240	24,720	25,520
1973	1	12,280	26,290	27,390
	2	13,130	27,650	28,720
	3	12,660	29,620	30,940
	4	13,040	31,450	32,880
1974	1	12,870	32,730	34,520
	2	13,370	32,810	34,940
	3	13,510	33,490	35,940
	4	14,330	34,610	37,100
1975	1	14,880	35,560	38,120
	2	16,080	35,840	38,100
	3	16,770	37,030	39,780
	4	17,070	36,920	40,010
1976	1	17,940	37,960	41,160
	2	18,530	33,790	42,210
	3	19,100	40,300	44,310
	4	18,980	40,380	44,470
1977	1	19,540	40,720	45,070
	2	20,530	41,740	46,220
	3	22,020	42,990	47,390
	4	23,180	44,540	48,950
1978	1	24,350	46,880	51,480
	2	25,090	48,230	53,260

(Continued)

127

Table 4.7 MONEY SUPPLY IN THE UNITED KINGDOM *(Continued)*
£ Million: Amounts Outstanding

At end period		M1 seasonally adjusted	Sterling M3 seasonally adjusted	M3 seasonally adjusted
	3	26,010	49,560	54,480
	4	27,020	51,310	56,350
1979	1	27,580	52,370	57,150
	2	28,250	54,380	59,290
	3	28,950	56,210	61,040
	4	29,460	57,830	63,270
1980	1	29,370	59,250	65,110
	2	30,110	62,570	68,140
	3	29,780	65,340	71,200
	4	30,520	68,350	74,870

preannounced and gradual tightening of monetary and fiscal policy over a five-year period. These intended goals were embodied in the "medium-term financial strategy" (MTFS) the new government announced in 1979. The plan included the following elements:

1. A gradual reduction in the rate of growth of the money supply over a five-year period. The monetary aggregate that was chosen as the monetary instrument variable was "sterling M3" or "£M3," which corresponds to currency plus sterling-denominated demand and time deposits of United Kingdom commercial banks. The initial plan called for £M3 to grow annually at a 9 percent rate in 1980–1981, with its rate of growth gradually to decline to 6 percent by 1983–1984.
2. A reduction in the real value of government spending within four years to a level 5 percent less than the level in 1979–1980.
3. A public sector borrowing requirement (PSBR) of £8.5 billion in 1979–1980, and £7 billion in 1980–1981, (both in 1978–1979 prices). Even these borrowing requirements, reduced though they were from those projected under the pre-

vious Labor Government's policies, represent deficits that as a ratio to GNP are several times those experienced in the United States.

Other elements of the government's plan were executed immediately. These included reductions in marginal income tax rates ranging from 33 to 30 percent for the lowest brackets to from 83 to 60 percent for the highest brackets, and substantial increases in the taxes on consumption, most notably a substantial increase in the Value-Added Tax (VAT). This change in tax structure was made with an eye toward increasing the rate of saving. In addition, in October 1979, exchange controls were removed, so that for the first time since World War II, residents of Britain were permitted freely to invest abroad. The government committed itself to flexible exchange rates with neither current nor capital account exchange controls, nor substantial government open-market operations in foreign assets designed to peg or influence the exchange rate. In line with the theme of deregulation, the government permitted the Special Depository Regulations, widely known as the "corset," to expire. These regulations had directly limited the extent to which the banks could increase their interest-bearing deposits. The corset represented an attempt to influence directly the £M3 aggregate and was widely and correctly believed to distort the interpretation of the £M3 figures, as depositors moved into close substitutes for £M3 in response to the restrictions.

In its conception, and even more so in its execution, the plan incorporates central aspects of monetarism. The key monetarist plank is embodied in the use of gradual reductions in a measure of the money supply, sterling M3, as the central vehicle for reducing the rate of inflation. These reductions in the money supply are recommended despite very large planned budget deficits, planned deficits that in the actual event have been overrun. A keystone of monetarist doctrine is that even in the face of persistent government deficits, by managing the money supply properly, the government can avoid inflation [18–20]. Referring to England's experience, Allan Meltzer put the case as follows: "Excess public spending, larger than expected budget deficits and the growth of money in excess of targets are related problems.

Table 4.8 GENERAL GOVERNMENT RECEIPTS AND EXPENDITURE

£ Million

		Receipts		Expenditure	
				Goods and services	
		Taxes national insurance, etc., contributions	Trading income, rent, interest, etc.	Final consumption	Gross domestic capital formation
1975		38,547	4,439	23,074	5,064
1976		44,724	5,223	26,779	5,483
1977		51,008	5,909	29,209	4,935
1978		56,704	6,488	32,934	4,741
1979		68,053	7,353	38,316	5,239
1977	1	12,700	1,527	7,040	1,565
	2	12,371	1,371	7,257	1,007
	3	12,822	1,697	7,368	1,171
	4	13,115	1,314	7,544	1,192
1978	1	14,116	1,720	7,972	1,483
	2	13,539	1,512	8,073	962
	3	13,897	1,702	8,252	1,145
	4	15,152	1,554	8,637	1,151
1979	1	16,032	1,917	8,875	1,500
	2	16,387	1,722	9,316	1,023
	3	17,250	1,962	9,896	1,356
	4	18,384	1,752	10,229	1,360
1980	1	20,845	2,045	10,872	1,700
	2	18,713	2,136	11,656	1,144
	3	21,811	2,157	12,386	1,415
	4			.	

Note: An article describing the new presentation of government income and expenditure was published in the March 1977 issue of *Economic Trends*.

[a]Net lending to public corporations, private sector and overseas; cash expenditure on company securities, etc. (net).

Table 4.8 GENERAL GOVERNMENT RECEIPTS AND EXPENDITURE *(Continued)*

Expenditure				
Current and capital transfers				
Current grants and subsidies	Capital transfers	Debt interest	Net lending, etc.[a]	Total
14,353	1,196	4,211	3,755	51,653
17,015	1,435	5,394	2,365	58,471
19,502	1,537	6,373	251	61,807
23,239	2,027	7,224	1,687	71,852
27,348	1,901	8,829	3,273	84,906
4,742	470	1,832	433	16,082
4,833	363	1,314	− 178	14,596
4,847	328	1,747	88	15,549
5,080	376	1,480	− 92	15,580
5,658	693	1,995	74	17,875
5,725	413	1,455	439	17,067
5,783	442	1,951	729	18,302
6,073	479	1,823	445	18,608
6,522	504	2,330	554	20,285
6,855	454	1,877	670	20,195
6,617	443	2,523	1,054	21,889
7,354	500	2,099	995	22,537
7,747	576	3,149	152	24,196
8,145	521	2,209	1,444	25,119
8,075	618	3,299	1,185	26,978

Table 4.9 FINANCIAL TRANSACTIONS OF THE PUBLIC SECTOR
£ Million

		Financial deficit		Net lending, etc., to private sector and overseas	
	Total	**General government**	**Public corporations**	**Total**	**Total**
1971	300	−786	1,086	620	920
1972	1,547	804	743	558	2,105
1973	2,764	1,997	767	880	3,644
1974	4,695	3,165	1,530	1,697	6,392
1975	7,705	4,912	2,793	1,833	9,538
1976	8,413	6,159	2,254	1,286	9,699
1977	5,868	4,639	1,229	126	5,994
1978	8,048	6,973	1,075	467	8,515
1979	8,344	6,227	2,117	432	8,776
1979 1	2,329	1,782	547	167	2,496
2	1,823	1,416	407	224	2,047
3	2,636	1,623	1,013	104	2,740
4	1,556	1,406	150	−63	1,493
1980 1	1,700	1,226	474	−128	1,572
2	3,543	2,646	897	490	4,033

Receipts

Public sector borrowing requirement

Financial transactions (net receipts)	Total	Contributions by central government	Contributions by local authorities	Contributions by public corporations	Seasonally adjusted total
−483	1,403	637	676	90	1,403
55	2,050	1,600	514	−64	2,050
−547	4,191	2,331	1,348	512	4,191
−41	6,433	3,523	2,161	749	6,433
−946	10,484	8,345	1,629	510	10,484
572	9,127	6,786	1,103	1,238	9,127
−1	5,995	4,469	183	1,343	5,995

		Receipts			

Public sector borrowing requirement

Financial transactions (net receipts)	Total	Contributions by central government	Contributions by local authorities	Contributions by public corporations	Seasonally adjusted total
184	8,331	8,371	659	−699	8,331
−3,788	12,564	10,396	1,732	436	12,564
1,031	1,465	247	1,003	215	2,117
−1,298	3,345	3,797	−267	−185	3,006
−1,085	3,825	2,842	666	317	3,893
−2,436	3,929	3,510	330	89	3,548
2,771	−1,199	−1,950	1,397	−646	131
−802	4,835	4,587	574	−326	4,122

The relation would disappear if the central bank changed its operating procedures and permitted market rates to fluctuate as much as is required to control money. The excess deficit would than be financed by domestic saving or by foreigners, but money growth and inflation would fall'' [30].

There are various possible interpretations of this argument, not all equally credible. In one rational expectations interpretation, by restricting itself now and forever to a binding ''k-percent growth rule''[13] for the monetary base, the government effectively limits the extent to which it will collect seigniorage by resorting to inflationary finance now and in the future. Under rational expectations, current government budget deficits—expenditures net of both explicit taxes and seigniorage—must be balanced by prospective government surpluses in the future. That is, additional government bonds will be valued according to the same principles that give bonds of private corporations value: their real prospective returns. Ultimately, these prospective returns are represented by the government's willingness to tax highly enough in

Table 4.10   NET PURCHASES (+) OR SALES (−)
OF GOVERNMENT DEBT, BY MATURITY

	Total stocks	Redemptions and conversions	Up to 1 year	Classification by maturity Over 1 and up to 5 years	Over 5 and up to 15 years	Over 15 years and undated
Financial years						
1975/76	+4159	−735	−1120	+2196	+1008	+2810
1976/77	+6290	−703	−1402	+2600	+817	+4978
1977/78	+6684	−672	−2259	+2931	+2826	+3858
1978/79	+6256	−404	+1098	+1994	+1441	+4323
1979/80	+8977	−1133	−2068	−2333	+2905	+6940
Quarter ended						
1978 Sept.	+793	−151	−364	+257	+154	+897
Dec.	+1288	−16	−57	+2	+802	+557
1979 Mar.	+2254	−234	−324	+824	+486	+1502
June	+2732	−1	−314	+358	+1159	+1530
Sept.	+2648	−403	−932	+1062	+496	+2425
Dec.	+2511	−431	−178	+159	+1317	+1644
1980 Mar.	+1086	−298	−644	+754	−67	+1341
June	+3377	−544	−574	+1358	+943	+2194
Sept.	+3186	−19	−136	−261	+3130	+472
Dec.	+3055	−263	−734	+1186	+1425	+1441

the future. On this view a k-percent rule for the monetary base plays a similar role as a gold standard rule, in the sense that it places a limit on the time path of real government deficits. Both the k-percent rule and the gold standard rule in effect require that if the government is to sell its debt, the expected present value of the current and prospective government surpluses must be positive. Each rule permits the government to run deficits, even a number of deficits in succession, but these deficits must be accompanied by prospects that eventually the government budget will turn to surplus in sufficient amount to outweigh the deficits. This interpretation of the k-percent rule is one that is compatible with the Barro-Ricardo result about the equivalence of bond and tax financing [6]. In this interpretation a k-percent rule is not

Table 4.11 CALCULATED REDEMPTION YIELDS
OF GOVERNMENT BONDS PERCENT PER ANNUM

		Short-dated (5 years)	Medium-dated (10 years)	Long-dated (20 years)
Last working days				
1980	Oct.	13.15	13.29	13.15
	Nov.	12.97	13.43	13.35
	Dec.	13.30	13.89	13.80
1981	Jan.	13.21	13.86	13.86
	Feb.	13.00	13.84	13.94
Mondays				
1980	Oct. 20	13.07	13.33	13.23
	Oct. 27	12.93	13.07	12.95
	Nov. 3	13.29	13.40	13.24
	Nov. 10	13.38	13.53	13.35
	Nov. 17	13.11	13.26	13.10
	Nov. 24	13.03	13.22	13.08
	Dec. 1	12.95	13.34	13.26
	Dec. 8	13.04	13.44	13.34
	Dec. 15	13.62	14.08	13.94
	Dec. 22	13.18	13.79	13.70
	Dec. 29	13.28	13.88	13.80
1981	Jan. 5	13.19	13.89	13.85
	Jan. 12	13.38	14.06	14.02
	Jan. 19	13.30	14.05	14.06
	Jan. 26	13.29	13.95	13.95
	Feb. 2	13.19	13.83	13.83
	Feb. 9	13.29	13.89	13.90
	Feb. 16	13.24	13.92	13.94
	Feb. 23	12.97	13.83	13.93
	Mar. 2	13.03	13.87	13.97
	Mar. 9	13.15	13.95	14.03
	Mar. 16	12.85	13.59	13.63

compatible with an everlasting government deficit but only with a deficit that is temporary in the appropriate sense.

In my view the preceding interpretation of the relationship of a *k*-percent rule to the budget deficit is the correct one. As with most

Table 4.12 INTEREST RATES, SECURITY PRICES, AND YIELDS
                PERCENTAGE RATE

	Last Friday		Last working day		Average of working days
	Bank of England's minimum lending rate to the market	Treasury bill yield	Eurodollar 3-month rate	Building Societies Association recommended rate on shares	British government securities: long-dated (20 years)
1969	8	7.80	10.07	5.00	9.05
1970	7	6.93	6.57	5.00	9.25
1971	5	4.46	5.75	5.00	8.90
1972	9	8.48	5.91	5.25	8.97
1973	13	12.82	10.19	7.50	10.78
1974	11.50	11.30	10.07	7.50	14.77
1975	11.25	10.93	5.88	7.00	14.39
1976	14.25	13.98	5.07	7.80	14.43
1977	7	6.39	7.19	6.00	12.73
1978	12.50	11.91	11.69	8.00	12.47
1979	17	16.49	14.50	10.50	12.99
1980	14	13.45	17.75	10.50	

rational expectations lines of thought, that interpretation emphasizes the dynamic or intertemporal features of the process, and the constraints that a k-percent rule requires on the future time path of the government deficit.

There is an alternative, and I believe defective, view that seems to assert that a k-percent rule is compatible with a more or less permanent deficit. This view is based on reasoning from standard Keynesian or monetarist models without rational expectations. Versions of those models exist in which the government can control inflation by sticking to a k-percent rule for the monetary base given an unrestricted path for the deficit.[14]

The preceding argument raises questions about the credibility of an announced plan to lower the monetary growth rate and to move to

a k-percent rule, while simultaneously projecting substantial government budget deficits for the several years in the immediate future. The
doubtful credibility of such a plan stems from the fact that a large
permanent real government deficit is simply incompatible with a k-
percent rule for the monetary base. A minimal requirement that a plan
be credible is that it be feasible in the first place. As we have argued,
a restrictive k-percent rule for the base and a permanent and large
government deficit just are not feasible. On this view, in order that the
current British plan be viewed as credible, it is necessary that the large
prospective government deficits over the next several years be coun-
terbalanced by prospective surpluses farther down the line. It is difficult to point to much either in current legislation or, equally important,
in the general British political climate that could objectively support
such an outlook. On this view, the large government deficits that have
accompanied the government's medium-term financial strategy raise
serious questions about whether the plan has the logical coherence that
is necessary for the plan to be credible to the public.

Samuel Brittan has drawn attention to a closely related issue. At
the same time that the government has touted its determination to
bring inflation permanently down through monetary restraint, the substantial government deficits have been financed by issuing large
amounts of nonindexed long-term government debt at nominal yields
to maturity ranging between 13 and 14 percent. Attention is directed
to Tables 4.10 and 4.11. Table 4.10 indicates the substantial extent to
which the government has been financing its deficit by selling additional long-term government debt. Thus in financial year 1979–1980
most of the additional government debt was over 15 years in maturity. Now if the government were actually to deliver on its hope
permanently to reduce the inflation rate, it would imply substantial
increases in the real value of the long-term government debt and the
real value of the interest payments on the debt. For example, investors
who purchased debt at nominal rates of 14 percent while expecting
average inflation of 12 percent and a real return of 2 percent would
experience ex post real yields higher than 2 percent, precisely to the
extent to which realized inflation falls short of the 12 percent inflation
rate that they had expected.[15] For the same reason, but in the other
direction, governments in the past have sometimes given way to the

temptation to default on part of their interest-bearing government debt by causing inflation to occur at a higher rate than was anticipated at the time that the debt was sold.[16] This same incentive confronts the government now and raises suspicions about the current and future governments' commitment permanently to lower the inflation rate. According to this argument, a government intent on eradicating inflation has a strong incentive to finance its deficit and refinance its outstanding debt by issuing indexed government bonds. This would isolate it from any increase in the real value of the burden of the debt once inflation is lowered. This the British government has not done to any significant extent.

For advocates of "Irving Fisher's effect," Table 4.11 contains an important piece of evidence about the public credibility of Mrs. Thatcher's plan for reducing inflation over the longer run. The term structure of interest rates on government bonds is high and fairly flat, suggesting that the market expects the continuation of high inflation rates on a sustained basis.

As emphasized earlier, in the rational expectations view, these matters of coherence and credibility are very important in determining the likely effects of a program on real variables such as output and employment. If a program is constructed in a fashion that makes private agents believe that its execution is uncertain, then, even if preannounced, restrictive monetary policy actions can easily produce substantial reductions in output and employment.

THE OUTCOME OF THE PLAN SO FAR

Having described the government's anti-inflation plan and some possible reservations about it, I shall now proceed briefly to describe how events have actually unfolded. First, sterling M3 has exceeded its target range, despite the fact of a restrictive minimum lending rate (MLR) and a basically tight open-market stance. For example, the fiscal year 1980–1981 target range for £M3 of 7 to 11 percent per year is to be compared with the annual rate of increase in £M3 of 21 percent between February 1980 and February 1981. During the same time period, sterling M1—currency plus demand deposits—increased by only 8 percent. Despite the overshooting of £M3, British interest rates

have been very high, making many commentators of Keynesian incli-
nation believe that monetary policy is very tight. Second, the public
sector borrowing requirement has overrun its target. The 1980–1981
PSBR had been forecast in the government's 1980 budget as £8.5
billion, or 4.5 percent of GDP, while it is now expected to be around
£13.5 billion, or 6 percent of GDP. I shall comment in turn on the
overshooting of each of these targets.

Overshooting the £M3 Target

There have been several reactions to the overshooting of the £M3 target.[17] One has been to argue that since the overshooting reflects
mainly a response to removal of the distorting effect of the corset, it
does not indicate a failure to pursue a tight monetary policy. As evidence in support of this position, the relatively slow growth of £M1 is
often cited. Another response has been to criticize the Bank of England's operating procedures for focusing too heavily on interest rates
as an intermediate instrument. Allan Meltzer [30] takes this line in
arguing that by pegging interest rates, the British monetary authority
necessarily gave up direct control over monetary aggregates and allowed them to be market determined.

The analytics of using monetary aggregates as opposed to interest rates as the monetary instrument have been characterized in Martin
Bailey's book [2] and in papers by William Poole [34] and John
Kareken [22]. The case for superiority of a particular monetary aggregate over a particular interest rate depends on the demand schedule for
that monetary aggregate being less uncertain than is the aggregate demand schedule expressed as a function of that particular interest rate.
Other things equal, factors that contribute to uncertainty about the demand for a given monetary aggregate diminish the relative merit of
using that aggregate as the monetary instrument.

This analytical argument is quite pertinent in evaluating the controversy about the overshooting of the £M3 target (and also about the
appropriate monetary instrument for the United States in 1981). The
removal of the corset and the dismantling of exchange controls at the
outset of Mrs. Thatcher's administration presumably shifted the demands for a whole host of assets in historically unprecedented and

uncertain ways. Regardless of the possible merits of the case for relaxing these controls, it seems clear that for some time after they are relaxed the interpretation of a variety of monetary aggregates becomes more uncertain and difficult than it had been. During such periods, the case for using an interest rate rather than a monetary aggregate as the monetary instrument becomes substantially strengthened. It is ironic that both in the United Kingdom and in the United States the accession of monetarists to a dominant influence over policy has coincided with substantial revisions in the structure of financial regulations that at least temporarily cloud the meaning of the particular monetary aggregates they favor controlling.[18] It seems to me that it is a defensible view that, despite their own problems of interpretation, the high nominal interest rates in Britain over the last year have more appropriately signaled the stance of monetary policy than any particular monetary aggregate.[19]

The Government Deficit

I now turn to discuss the behavior of the public sector borrowing requirement, which so far has exceeded the government's target by so much that the government has moved to correct the situation by raising taxes. The 1980–1981 PSBR which has been forecast by the government to be £8.5 billion or 4.5 percent of GDP, appears to be coming in at £13.5 billion or 6 percent of GDP. In the March 1981 budget the chancellor of the exchequer, Sir Geoffrey Howe, announced a number of tax increases designed to reduce the prospective PSBR for 1981–1982 to about £10.5 billion. Without those additional tax measures the government estimated that the 1981–1982 PSBR would have been about £14.5 billion. The new revenue-raising measures included increases in the excise taxes on drink, tobacco, gasoline, diesel road fuel, cigarette lighters, matches, and road vehicles. The extent to which income tax payments were indexed against inflation was reduced. A Supplementary Petroleum Duty on North Sea oil and gas was announced, which together with adjustments in the Petroleum Revenue Tax was expected to yield about £1 billion. The chancellor also announced a once-and-for-all tax on low-interest bank deposits that was expected to yield £4 billion in 1981–1982.[20] The government announced these tax increases because it became increasingly aware of the threat that a persistent and large government deficit sooner or later poses to an anti-inflation policy based on monetary restraint.

Before considering the nature of the British deficit in more detail, it helps to remember a few analytical principles about government finance. In interpreting reported figures on the government's budget deficit, it is useful to keep in mind the hypothetical distinction between current account and capital account budgets and their deficits. A pure current account expenditure is for a service or perfectly perishable good that gives rise to no government-owned asset that will produce things of value in the future. A pure capital account expenditure is a purchase of a durable asset that gives the government command of a prospective future stream of returns, collected, for example, through user charges, whose present value is greater than or equal to the present cost of acquiring the asset. A pure capital account budget would count as revenues the interest and other user charges collected on government-owned assets, while expenditures would be the purchases of capital assets. By these definitions government debt issued on capital account is self-liquidating and fully backed by the user charges that are earmarked to pay it off. Government debt issued to finance a pure capital account deficit is thus not a claim on the general tax revenues that the government collects through sales and income taxation. The principles of classical economic theory condone government deficits on capital account. The idea is that certain government capital projects are worthwhile on cost-benefit grounds and that it is reasonable to finance them by levying taxes on the people who receive the benefits throughout the time the benefits accrue. In short, so far as capital account deficits are concerned, a government is in a sense like a firm, it being wise to borrow to finance worthwhile long-lived projects with taxes and other user charges whose stream over time matches the time profile of the benefits.

A deficit on current account is very different because it is not self-liquidating. The classical economic doctrine was, first, that the current account budget should always be balanced and, second, on those extraordinary occasions such as wars when it could not be balanced, that a current account budget deficit should be financed by long-term debt and a plan to run current account surpluses in the future sufficiently large to retire the debt. Thus a current account deficit, should it be unavoidable, was to be financed by earmarking some future general tax revenues for the purpose of retiring the debt.

It is no coincidence that these classical doctrines about government finance were developed at a time when England and other leading economic powers were on the gold standard, each government promising to convert its currency and other government debt into gold on certain specified conditions. To make good on that promise, a government had to back its debt with sufficiently large and sufficiently probable prospective government surpluses denominated in gold. Deficits on capital account did not threaten a government's adherence to a gold standard, while deficits on current account did. The force of a gold standard was to cause the government to back its debt and to refrain from raising revenues from seigniorage.

Under contemporary monetary institutions in which currency is inconvertible or fiat, governments have access to seigniorage as an additional means of raising government revenues. (Whether the additional freedom this gives government is helpful is very controversial both among theorists and practical people.) When a government finances its long-term debt without indexing repayment to the price level, the freedom to expand government demand debt and longer-term debt without the limits imposed by adherence to the gold standard gives the government a wide range of options about if, when, and to what extent to default on its long-term debt by monetizing it and depreciating its real value.[21]

Under a fiat money regime the extent to which a current account deficit is inflationary depends on the extent to which private agents believe that the government will ultimately finance it by monetization. For example, the Ricardo-Barro doctrine about the irrelevance of the current taxation-debt-issuing choice assumes that the government refrains from monetizing the debt and in effect binds itself to a classical financial policy. Under that policy current real government deficits are not inflationary because they are accompanied by expectations of future government surpluses. The additional real government debt is backed by prospective real tax revenues. However, as Bryant and Wallace [9] have emphasized, in a policy regime where the current deficit is eventually monetized in some proportion, a current account deficit is inflationary. In some models it is more inflationary; the larger the proportion of it that is eventually monetized and the sooner the monetization occurs. In those models the precise dynamics by which the prospect of future monetization of the debt influences inflation rates depends on the detailed specification of the demand functions for assets, in particular, on how responsive they are to the expected rate of return on currency. It can readily happen, for example, as under a demand function for money like Phillip Cagan's [11], that *current* rates of inflation respond positively to the prospect of *future* increases in money brought about by eventual monetization of government debt; see Sargent and Wallace [43].

Although it seems not to have been something that Keynes himself would have advocated, the widespread adoption of Keynesian ideas about fiscal policy after World War II has been accompanied by abandonment of the classical public budgeting and accounting procedures at the level of national governments (although not at the level of state and local governments in the United States). For example, in the United Kingdom the nationalized industries do not float their own debt. Instead, they borrow from the National Loan Board, which in turn borrows by issuing government debt. This arrangement is one that departs from or at least obscures the earmarking of revenues from particular projects to back a given bond issue. Moreover the recent history of public finances in the United Kingdom displays little sensitivity to the distinction between capital and current account so, for example, as Table 4.6 and Figure 4.1 show, capital formation by the general government and nationalized industries has stagnated or actually fallen. Further, as Table 4.9 shows, while general government final consumption and current grants and subsidies have risen substantially in recent years, and have continued to rise under Mrs. Thatcher, capital expenditures have not. Under both Mrs. Thatcher's government and the previous Labor Government, belt tightening has fallen largely on public sector investment items. According to the classic canons of public finance that we alluded to earlier, this structure of expenditure cuts is perverse from the viewpoint of anti-inflationary policy.

The failure of Mrs. Thatcher's government to control public expenditures has been widely commented upon and will receive only brief mention here. Mrs. Thatcher has been criticized for a number of

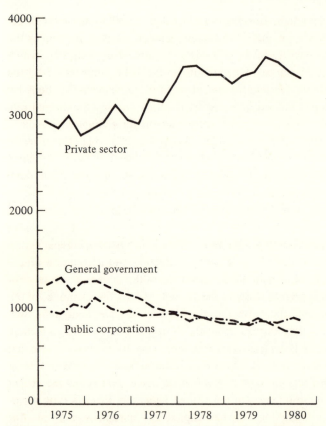

Figure 4.1 Gross domestic fixed capital formation (millions of pounds, 1975 prices seasonally adjusted).

what are essentially tactical errors, for example, in her stance toward pay for public employees. Her early decision to stand by the Conservative Party's campaign pledge to honor the recommendations of the Clegg Commission, which the Labor Government instituted to establish pay standards for civil servants comparable to those in the private sector, resulted in earnings increases for civil servants of 24.5 percent between 1979III and 1980III. Thatcher responded, albeit belatedly, to that criticism by eventually abolishing the Clegg Commission in the fall of 1980. Since that time, the government has announced the adoption of a cash limit system, which essentially creates a total wages fund with which the government intends to confront a given public sector union or collection of unions. The idea is to force the unions to take into account a trade-off between wage rates and the number of public sector employees. A problem is that such cash limits have been breached in the past and have already been breached by Thatcher in the coal miners' settlement.

NORTH SEA OIL AND THE POUND STERLING

In the late 1970s the magnitude of Britain's prospective revenues from North Sea oil became clearer and coincided with a simultaneous appreciation of the pound sterling from 1.65 U.S.$/£ in 1975IV to 2.39$/£ in 1980IV, and a swing of the current account balance of payments from a deficit toward surplus. The fact that Great Britain moved from being a net importer to being a net exporter of petroleum helped swing the current account into surplus. Some observers have attributed the strength of the pound to Britain's claim on North Sea oil and its contribution in swinging the current account toward surplus. However, few macroeconomic models imply that there is any direct connection between possessing oil and having a strong currency. There is an indirect connection, namely, that North Sea oil is heavily taxed and thus contributes to prospective government revenues, thereby tending to diminish the government deficit. Revenues from the taxation of North Sea oil are substantial and are expected to grow over time. The 1981 budget forecasts revenues from all taxes on oil (in 1979–1980 prices) of £3.25 billion in 1980–1981, £4.50 billion in 1981–1982, £4.75 billion in 1982–1983, and £5.25 billion in 1983–1984. These revenues are a substantial fraction of the current government deficit of £13.5 billion. However, most macroeconomic theories assert that only the total deficit and how it is financed influence inflation and the international value of the pound. So long as total prospective government deficits remain as large as they are, it is difficult to subscribe to the view that the United Kingdom's possession of oil strengthens the pound. As a scrap of empirical evidence supporting this judgment, it has been observed that Norway is in a similar situation to England vis-à-vis North Sea oil and that neither has its currency appreciated internationally nor has it experienced the severe depression of industry that England has. One explanation for the difference appears to be that Norway has embarked on a looser monetary policy than has England.

Another popular explanation for the strong pound is that OPEC countries have begun to diversify their overseas investments by holding assets denominated in a variety of foreign currencies and that this has resulted in an increased preference for pound-denominated assets. This factor is probably part of the explanation but is not the dominant force leading to a strong pound.

Probably the most plausible explanation for the emergence of a strong pound builds on the "overshooting" idea of Dornbusch and has the advantage that it simultaneously explains other aspects of the current situation including high British interest rates and depressed British output and employment.[22] Dornbusch modeled a small country under the following assumptions.

1. The domestic price level has some sort of stickiness. Either domestic prices are exogenous, as in one of Dornbusch's original formulations [12], or there is a Taylor-like long-term contracting mechanism, as in a later contribution by Dornbusch [13], or there are information discrepancies à la Lucas and Phelps that prevent domestic prices from adjusting instantaneously to certain classes of random events, as in the setup of Nasser Saidi [36]. Which of these devices is resorted to makes an important difference, as we shall see.

2. There is assumed to be perfect international capital mobility in high-yielding assets. This implies that the interest parity condition must hold. The interest parity condition states that the domestic interest rate must equal the foreign rate of interest minus the expected rate of appreciation of the domestic currency. Thus, letting r_{jt} be the domestic nominal interest rate on j-period bonds, r_{jt}^* be the foreign nominal interest rate on j-period bonds, e_t be the exchange rate or foreign price of domestic money, measured in foreign currency per unit of domestic currency, and $E_t \ln e_{t+j}$ be the logarithm of the exchange rate expected as of time t to prevail at time $t + j$, the interest parity condition is

$$r_{jt} = r_{jt}^* - \frac{1}{j} (E_t \ln e_{t+j} - \ln e_t)$$

The interest parity condition ensures that foreigners can attain the same nominal rate of return, in terms of their own currency, by investing in the domestic country as by investing elsewhere.

3. The market for domestic currency and other "money" is assumed to be isolated internationally in the sense that the real rate of return on domestic money is permitted to be strictly dominated by other assets, including domestic and foreign bonds and equities and maybe also foreign currencies. What is crucial for the results is that there be some restriction on the scope of international currency substitution, most formulations ruling out any currency substitution at all. Notice the asymmetry between the assumption of integrated world bond and equities markets but nationalistic markets for currencies. The demand for domestic real balances is assumed to vary inversely with the domestic nominal interest rate, and directly with domestic real output, in the standard way.

4. The demand for domestic real output depends, among other things, inversely on the domestic real rate of interest and on the "real exchange rate" or terms of trade. Thus, letting p be the domestic price level measured in pounds per British good, p^* the foreign price level measured in dollars per U.S. good, and e the exchange rate measured in dollars per pound, the "real exchange rate" is defined as ep/p^*. Thus, given p and p^*, an increase in e decreases the demand for British output, since it raises the relative price of British goods in terms of U.S. goods.

5. While the domestic price level is to some extent sticky, the exchange rate and domestic interest rate are perfectly flexible instantaneously.

6. The foreign price level and interest rate are exogenous to events in the domestic country, the operational meaning of the small-country assumption.

7. Expectations are rational.

Given these assumptions, consider a situation where the British monetary authority undertakes a restrictive monetary action. Because of price level stickiness, the initial effect is to drive the domestic interest rate upward. But the upward tendency in the domestic interest rate threatens to disturb the interest parity condition and to create a capital inflow. To maintain interest parity in the face of less than perfectly flexible prices, the entire expected exchange rate path must adjust to generate an expected path of subsequent depreciation of the pound sufficient to offset the higher British interest rate. For this to happen, the exchange rate e must first jump upward to a higher level than before the restrictive monetary action, from which higher level it gradually falls in order to generate the rational expectations of a depreciating pound needed to maintain interest parity. Thus the immediate effect of the restrictive monetary action is to cause the exchange rate initially to appreciate suddenly and subsequently to depreciate gradually. However, since the domestic price level is somewhat sticky, the initial effect of the appreciated pound is to raise the real exchange rate ep/p^*, and so to reduce the demand for British goods. This effect reinforces the effect on demand of the higher real domestic interest rate and leads to a recession along standard Keynesian lines of insufficient aggregate demand.

This sequence of events depends on there being some source of price stickiness that prevents the domestic labor market from clearing. Had domestic prices and wages been assumed perfectly flexible, the response to a downward movement in the domestic money supply would have been very different than that described here. In particular, under flexible prices equilibrium is restored by a drop in the domestic price p proportional to the drop in the money supply, together with an off-setting increase in the exchange rate just sufficient to leave the real exchange rate ep/p^* unaltered. No changes in the domestic interest rate or output are needed to restore equilibrium. A version of classic neutrality occurs in these models under flexible domestic prices.

Versions of the model such as Saidi's that rest on limited information and temporary confusion to provide price stickiness, or a Phillips curve, exhibit an interesting mixture of the responses under sticky prices and under perfectly flexible prices. In particular, with respect to monetary disturbances that were perfectly predictable given private agents' information and understanding in the past, the system responds exactly as if prices were perfectly flexible: There are no real effects, the domestic price level and the exchange rate adjusting just enough to off-set the disturbance while leaving domestic real output and employment unaltered. However, with respect to monetary disturbances that are not predictable, given agents' information and understanding, the system responds qualitatively in the same fashion as described when prices are sticky.

Each of these variants of the Dornbusch model works in explaining the broad features of recent British experience, including high nominal interest rates, a strong pound sterling, and depressed industry. However, the different versions of the model support different interpretations and perhaps also policy recommendations.[23] On the one hand, according to the models that rely on momentum or long-term contracts to generate domestic price inflexibility, the response to restrictive monetary actions will be qualitatively similar whether or not those actions were foreseen by private agents. Such versions of the model could explain events even on the interpretation that Mrs. Thatcher's restrictive actions represent execution of a once-and-for-all regime change that is widely believed and irreversible. On the other hand, according to versions of the model like Saidi's that rely solely on information limitations to induce a Phillips curve, the events must be interpreted as reflecting the perceived temporary and reversible nature of the restrictive monetary actions that the government has undertaken.

Explanations along Dornbusch's line seem to be the best ones available for simultaneously explaining the strong pound, depressed British industry, and persistent British inflation. However, the literature on currency substitution makes it clear that this argument is delicate in that it depends on a demand function for domestic currency that permits domestic currency to be dominated in rate of return by large and variable amounts by foreign currencies and other assets. As several researchers have emphasized, there are incentives for international currency substitution that threaten the temporal stability of the demand schedule for domestic currency and the durability of the preceding class of explanations.[24] The literature on currency substitution points toward a problem that may loom on the horizon for British policy. That literature predicts that a country that runs much larger persistent deficits than its neighbors and that monetizes a large fraction of them will require the imposition of international currency controls if it is to support its currency internationally [23]. The models analyzed in the currency substitution literature thus indicate that high and persistent government deficits are over the long haul incompatible with permanent abstention from exchange controls. While it might take some time for these forces to break through various frictions, they will acquire strength and create problems precisely to the extent that large budget deficits loom in the future. It is certainly arguable that only temporarily can a tight monetary policy delay the operation of these forces, à la Dornbusch, in the face of large, persistent government deficits.

CONCLUSION

The theoretical doctrines and the historical evidence described in this chapter provide little reason for being optimistic about the efficacy of a plan for gradual monetary restraint that is simultaneously soft on the government deficit. Gradualism invites speculation about future reversals, or U-turns, in policy. Large contemporary government deficits unaccompanied by concrete prospects for future government surpluses promote realistic doubts about whether monetary restraint must be abandoned sooner or later to help finance the deficit. Such doubts not only call into question the likelihood that the plan can succeed in reducing inflation permanently but also can induce high real costs in terms of depressed industry and lengthened unemployment in response to what may be viewed as only temporary downward movements in nominal aggregate demand due to the monetary restraint.

These considerations are pertinent in assessing the state of the United Kingdom's economy today and the situation facing the French in the 1920s. They are also pertinent in evaluating the wisdom of passing Kemp-Roth in the United States while simultaneously planning to implement a tight *k*-percent monetary rule.

If we are bent on reducing inflation, then by consulting both our theoretical imaginations and history, we can find methods that improve on gradualist money restraint in the face of large government deficits. That is why it behooves us to recall Poincaré and his contemporaries even as we think about Thatcher.[25]

NOTES

1. Robert Barro [5] has pointed out that after a change in policy regime, it can happen that it is in the interests of neither party to enforce some long-term contracts of the Taylor-Fischer variety that had been agreed upon before the regime change. Presumably such contracts would never be enforced.

2. Leland Yeager [44, p. 472] summarizes British postwar macroeconomic policy as follows: "The rapid reversibility of British policy . . . has been almost comical at times. Balance-of-payments troubles have brought a variety of *ad hoc* responses, including two devaluations and one abandonment of exchange rate pegging, the selective Employment Tax of 1966, the import surcharge of 1964, the import deposit scheme of 1968, the tightening and loosening of various exchange controls on current and capital transactions, and various attempts at wage and price control, as well as turnarounds in domestic financial policy. Reliance on such expedients creates chances of improper timing, of anticipatory private actions, of overshooting the mark, and of intensified instability as a result."

3. It goes without saying that the "credibility" that is essential under the rational expectations theory cannot be manipulated by promises or government announcements.

4. Rudiger Dornbusch made this argument in oral comments on my earlier paper [37].

5. The reader is referred to the accounts of post-World War I stabilizations in Brown [8] and Young [45]. For example, the Italian stabilization might as easily have served as our example as the French one. Brown [8, p. 431] quotes Count Volpi's account of the important aspects of the plan that the Italian government used to stabilize the lira:

   1. Balancing of the national budget.
   2. Consolidation of war debts.
   3. Unification of the note issue and its concentration in the hands of the Bank of Italy.
   4. Progressive and more efficient utilization of Italian resources and raw materials.
   5. Gradual deflation in currency and in credit.
   6. Consolidation of the floating debt and reorganization in the Treasury Department.
   7. Regulation of the influx of foreign capital into Italian industry.
   8. Reorganization in the whole field of production, and readjustment of taxes with a view to increased industrial efficiency.
   9. Gradual amortization of the domestic debt.
   10. Defense of the treasury surplus by the reduction of state expenditures.

   Count Volpi was the "architect of Italy's return to gold."

6. Interesting accounts of the "Poincaré miracle" appear in Shirer [41], Yeager [44], Alpert [1], Haig [21], and Rogers [35].

7. William Shirer [41] describes this struggle.

8. Another element of uncertainty was injected by the substantial war debts owed the United States, coupled with the French belief that the United States should not insist that these be repaid.

9. For accounts of the effects of war debts and reparations on the public finances and currencies in Europe after World War I, see Yeager [44] and Alpert [1].

10. The strength and endurance of French politicians' resolve not to repeat such a default was indicated by the fact that France was the last of the major countries to devalue its currency in terms of gold in the 1930s: France devalued in 1936, while England did so in 1931 and the United States in 1933.

11. Stanley Fischer [17] provides a more complete discussion of this issue and the other issues described in this paragraph. Bryant and Wallace [9] discuss optimal seigniorage from the viewpoint of price discrimination. They describe setups in which a government can find it worthwhile to issue an array of debt with differing yields, tailored to segments of the market with differing interest elasticities of demand for government debt. Applying their idea to the issue in the present discussion, setups can be imagined where the domestic country arranges to hold high-yielding foreign government debt and where it is in the interests of both the foreign and the domestic country to permit the domestic country to back its monetary liabilities by the higher-yielding foreign government debt rather than the lower-yielding debt.

12. Bilson [7] describes a scheme of this sort that can lead to a positive real return on government-issued or privately issued "currency" through a process of deflation.

13. Presumably, a rule in which k is a small number.

14. In the literature it has been pointed out that such a k-percent rule implies an explosive path for the government interest-bearing debt. As Bennett McCallum [28] has pointed out, depending on the precise specification of the model, that fact may or may not imply that other variables in the model that are of interest are unstable.

15. The recent issue of indexed bonds in England sold at a real rate of interest of about 2 percent.

16. This issue was central to the struggle for the post-World War I stabilizations.

17. From the technical viewpoint of controlling monetary aggregates, the banking and financial intermediary systems in the United Kingdom differ in important respects from those in the United States. First, in the United Kingdom banking is more concentrated, there being five main "Clearing Banks." Second, in the British assets eligible to meet the 12.5 percent reserve requirement include all of the following interest-bearing assets: money at call from discount houses, treasury bills and other short-term government securities, local authority paper, corporate tax anticipation certificates, and bills of exchange. Notice that some of these assets are evidences of government indebtedness, while others are private debts. Since demand deposits do not bear interest in the United Kingdom, vis-

à-vis the U.S. system, this system of reserve requirements tends to increase the banking system's share of seigniorage revenues relative to that of the government. On the other side of this issue, currency is a higher proportion of £M1 in the United Kingdom than in the United States. Third, the building societies (the analogue of savings and loan institutions in the United States) have long issued mortgages with variable maturities and variable rates of interest both linked to the general level of market interest rates. Therefore in the United Kingdom high interest rates do not produce the disintermediation from saving institutions that is so troublesome for the conduct of monetary policy in the United States. Fourth, partly as a result of the third feature, there is no analogue of Regulation Q in the United Kingdom, and small savers have access to a variety of instruments yielding close to market rates, as for example, Building Society shares. This fact also explains the absence of money market funds in the United Kingdom. Fifth, the Bank of England does not lend directly to the clearing banks but instead operates a discount window for the discount houses that make markets and hold portfolios of short-term government and private securities. The minimum lending rate, formerly known as the bank rate, applies to the Bank of England's loans to the discount houses.

18. I have in mind the Monetary Control Act.
19. As in the United States, in the United Kingdom there is a bewildering variety of monetary aggregates. The main ones are £M1, £M3, PSL 1 (Public Sector Liquidity number 1), and PSL 2. The variety of aggregates is spawned by the vagueness of "means of payments" as a category setting off one class of assets as "money." See Sargent and Wallace [40].
20. Recall the remarks in note 17 about the way in which seigniorage is allocated between the banks and the government under the British system of reserve requirements.
21. This was the choice that French politicians consciously faced and struggled with from 1919 to 1926 and that politicians also face today, although perhaps less consciously.
22. See Dornbusch [12, 13]. Buiter and Miller [10] argue that Dornbusch's idea explains contemporary observations in the United Kingdom.
23. One popular policy recommendation stemming from the momentum version of the model is to impose inward capital controls, for example, an interest equalization tax on the yields of British securities held by foreigners. Such a tax is presumed to weaken the pound and stimulate aggregate demand and real domestic output. See Buiter and Miller [10].
24. Kareken and Wallace [24] propound a model with an extreme amount of currency substitution.
25. Economists have begun devoting more attention to devising ways of reducing the costs of winding down inflation. For example, Jeffrey Shaefer and Axel Leijonhufvud have recently described a kind of dynamic cur-

rency reform scheme that aims to eradicate the costs of eliminating inflation that are due to long-term contracts. To illustrate their scheme, suppose that up to date t, the monetary and fiscal policy regime and the other random processes that influence inflation have been such as to make it rational for private agents to expect that future prices will follow some given path $\hat{p}(t + j)$, $j \geq 0$, where the expected price level $\hat{p}(t + j)$ is measured as usual in units of green dollars at time $t + j$ per good at time $(t + j)$. For example, if a constant rate of inflation of π is expected, then $\hat{p}(t + j) = (1 + \pi)^j p(t)$, where $p(t)$ is the actual price level at t. If these price expectations are built into long-term contracts that have been entered into t and earlier, and so form a legacy that influences actual prices and quantities at times $t + j$, then the act of bringing inflation to a sudden halt will cause substantial redistributions across traders. To the extent that actual prices turn out to be less than those expected at the time that the contracts were negotiated, real output and unemployment will be adversely affected.

The idea of Shaefer and Leijonhufvud is to circumvent these costs by carrying out an imaginative kind of currency reform. The government passes a law at date t that states that all contracts that call for payment of y dollars at date $t + j$ can be discharged by paying only $yp(t)/\hat{p}(t + j)$ dollars. Thus, in the constant expected inflation case, dollars due at $t + j$ are paid off at only $1/(1 + \pi)^j$ on the dollar. More important, the government successfully commits itself to run a fiscal and monetary policy that implies a stable price level so that the actual price $p(t + j) = p(t)$ for all $j \geq 1$. With a constant actual price path of $p(t + j) = p(t)$, and the new debt conversion law, both sides of all contracts end up being just as well off as if the debt conversion law had not been enacted and prices had risen as expected, $p(t + j) = \hat{p}(t + j)$. Thus the debt conversion law is crafted to neutralize the real effects of the monetary and fiscal policies needed to support a zero inflation price path. It is as if the government announces that it is calling in all the green-colored currency and issuing new blue-colored currency on the following terms: green dollars will be converted into blue dollars at par at time t, and subsequently the green dollar price of a blue dollar is $\hat{p}(t + j)/p(t)$.

REFERENCES

1. Alpert, Paul. 1951. *Twentieth Century Economic History of Europe*. New York: Henry Schuman.
2. Bailey, Martin. 1971. *National Income and the Price Level*. 2nd ed. New York: McGraw-Hill. 175–186.
3. Barro, Robert J. 1976. Rational expectations and the role of monetary policy. *Journal of Monetary Economics* 2 (January):1–32.

4. ———. 1977. Unanticipated money growth and unemployment in the United States. *American Economic Review* 67 (March):101–115.

5. ———. 1977. Long term contracting, sticky prices, and monetary policy. *Journal of Monetary Economics* 3 (July):305–16.

6. ———. 1974. Are government bonds net wealth? *Journal of Political Economy* 82 (November/December):1095–1118.

7. Bilson, John. 1980. A Proposal for Monetary Reform. Working paper no. 80–07, Domestic Studies Program, Hoover Institution.

8. Brown, William Adams, Jr. 1940. *The International Gold Standard Reinterpreted, 1914–1934*. Vol. 1. New York: National Bureau of Economic Research.

9. Bryant, John, and Neil Wallace. 1980. A suggestion for further simplifying the theory of money. Staff Report no. 62, Federal Reserve Bank of Minneapolis.

10. Buiter, Willem, and Marcus Miller. 1981. Monetary policy and international competitiveness. Oxford Economic Papers 33 (supp):143–75.

11. Cagan, Phillip. 1956. The monetary dynamics of hyperinflation. In M. Friedman, ed., *Studies in the Quantity Theory of Money*. Chicago: University of Chicago Press.

12. Dornbusch, Rudiger. 1976. Expectations and exchange rate dynamics, *Journal of Political Economy* 84:1161–1176.

13. Dornbusch, Rudiger. 1980. *Open Economy Macroeconomics*. New York: Basic Books. Chapter 9.

14. Eckstein, Otto. 1981. *Core Inflation*. Englewood Cliffs, N.J.: Prentice-Hall.

15. *Economic Progress Report,* no. 131, March, 1981. "The 1981 Budget." Published by the Treasury of U.K.

16. *Economic Trends.* 1981. Central Statistical Office, Her Majesty's Stationary Office.

17. Fischer, Stanley. 1981. Seigniorage and the case for a national money. Unpublished manuscript. Cambridge: Massachusetts Institute of Technology.

18. Friedman, Milton. 1970. A theoretical framework for monetary analysis. *Journal of Political Economy* 78 (March/April):193–238.

19. ———. 1971. A monetary theory of nominal income. *Journal of Political Economy* 79 (March/April):323–337.

20. ———. 1972. Comments on the critics. *Journal of Political Economy* 80 (September/October):906–950.

21. Haig, Robert Murray. 1929. *The Public Finances of Post-War France*. New York: Columbia University Press.

22. Kareken, John H. 1970. The optimim monetary instrument variable. *Journal of Money, Credit, and Banking* 2 (August):385–390.

23. Kareken, John H., and Neil Wallace. 1978. Samuelson's consumption

loan model with country-specific fiat monies. Staff Report no. 24, Federal Reserve Bank of Minneapolis, July.

24. ———. 1981. On the indeterminacy of equilibrium exchange rates. *Quarterly Journal of Economics* 96 (May):207–222.

25. Lucas, Robert E., Jr. 1972. Expectations and the neutrality of money. *Journal of Economic Theory* 4 (April):103–124.

26. ———. 1973. Some international evidence on output-inflation tradeoffs, *American Economic Review* 63 (June):326–34.

27. ———. 1975. An equilibrium model of the business cycle, *Journal of Political Economy* 83 (December):1113–1144.

28. McCallum, Bennett T. 1978. On macroeconomic instability from a monetarist policy rule, *Economics Letters* 1:121–124.

29. ———. 1979. The current state of the policy-ineffectiveness debate. *American Economic Review* 69 (May):240–45.

30. Meltzer, Allan. 1981. Tests of inflation theories from the British laboratory. Unpublished manuscript. Carnegie-Mellon University, February.

31. Morgan Guaranty Trust Company. February 1981. Thatcherism: A Mid-Term Review.

32. Phelps, Edmund S. 1970. The new microeconomics in employment and inflation theory. In *Microeconomic Foundations of Employment and Inflation Theory* New York:Norton.

33. Phelps, Edmund S., and John B. Taylor. 1977. Stabilizing powers of monetary policy under rational expectations. *Journal of Political Economy* 85 (February):163–190.

34. Poole, William. 1970. Optimal choice of monetary policy instruments in a simple stochastic marco model. *Quarterly Journal of Economics* (May):197–216.

35. Rogers, James Harvey. 1929. *The Process of Inflation in France, 1914–1927*. New York: Columbia University Press.

36. Saidi, Nasser H. 1980. Fluctuating exchange rates and the international transmission of economic disturbances. *Journal of Money, Credit, and Banking* 12 (November, part 1):575–91.

37. Sargent, Thomas J. 1983. The ends of four big inflations. In R. E. Hall, ed., *Inflation*. Chicago: University of Chicago Press.

38. Sargent, Thomas J., and Neil Wallace. 1976. Rational expectations and the theory of economic policy. *Journal of Monetary Economics* 2 (April):169–183.

39. ———. 1981. The limits of contemporary monetary policy. Unpublished manuscript.

40. ———. 1982. The real bills doctrine vs. the quantity theory: A reconsideration. *Journal of Political Economy* 90 (December):1212–1236.

41. Shirer, William L. 1969. *The Collapse of the Third Republic: An Inquiry into the Fall of France in 1940*. New York: Simon & Schuster.

42. Taylor, John B. 1979. Staggered wage setting in a macro model. *American Economic Review* 69 (May):108–13.
43. ———. 1979. Estimation and control of a macroeconomic model with rational expectations. *Econometrica* 47 (September):1267–1286.
44. Yeager, Leland B. 1976. *International Monetary Relations: Theory, History, and Policy.* 2nd ed. New York: Harper & Row.
45. Young, John Parke. 1925. *European Currency and Finance.* Vols. 1 and 2. Printed for the use of the Senate Commission of Gold and Silver Inquiry. Government Printing Office, Washington, D.C.

chapter 5

Some Unpleasant Monetarist Arithmetic

Written with Neil Wallace

This chapter is a variation on the theme that monetary and fiscal policies are interrelated and must necessarily be coordinated. They must be coordinated because the monetary authority controls the rate of seigniorage from money creation, which is a revenue source in the government's budget. The issue of coordination arises when one seeks to answer the following question: Is it possible for monetary policy permanently to influence an economy's inflation rate? The answer to this question hinges on how monetary and fiscal policies are imagined to be coordinated. On the one hand, one can imagine a monetary authority sufficiently powerful vis-à-vis the fiscal authority that by the imposition of slower rates of growth of base money, both now and into the indefinite future, it can successfully constrain fiscal policy by telling the fiscal authority how much seigniorage it can expect now and in the future. In this setting, monetary and fiscal policies are coordinated by having the monetary authority discipline the fiscal authority. Under this coordination scheme, the decisions of the monetary authority about the stream of seigniorage it will supply to the fiscal authority can permanently influence the inflation rate. On the other hand, one can imagine that the monetary authority is not in a position to influence the government's deficit path but is limited simply to managing the debt that is implied by the deficit path chosen by the fiscal authorities. Under this second coordination scheme, the monetary authority is much less powerful than under the first scheme. Under the second coordination scheme, it is the monetary authority that is constrained by the fiscal authority by having ultimately to deliver a seigniorage stream sufficient to finance the deficit stream that is chosen by the fiscal authority.

This chapter characterizes some of the dimensions of the limits of the monetary authority and discloses some of the choices open to it under the second coordination scheme. We analyze that scheme partly because we suspect that over the last decade the second coordination scheme has more nearly been the one in place in the United States and other major industrial countries; but even apart from that empirical judgment, we believe that analyzing some of the implications of the second scheme is a useful vehicle for directing attention to the issue of coordinating monetary and fiscal policies.

Our attention was attracted to this issue by the high pretax real rates of return on government securities that prevailed in the United States during the first half of 1981. The prevalence of before-tax rates of return on government securities that exceed the economy's rate of growth confronts the monetary authority with a difficult choice about inflation. With the government budget persistently in deficit and real rates of interest exceeding the economy's growth rate, the Fed must choose between fighting present inflation with "tight" monetary policy now or fighting future inflation with "easy" monetary policy now. Put differently, without help from the fiscal authorities, fighting current inflation with tight monetary policy must eventually lead to higher future inflation.[1]

That a real rate of return on government securities in excess of the economy's growth rate n puts the monetary authority in this bind is a consequence of a simple accounting identity. If the real rate of interest on government securities exceeds n, then simply to "roll over" a fixed amount of interest-bearing government debt in private hands requires raising revenue from other sources to pay the interest on the debt. In particular, the government must either levy taxes or reduce purchases or print currency to pay the interest. Another seeming alternative is to issue additional interest-bearing debt to pay the interest on the existing debt. However, this last alternative implies a growing stock of real government interest-bearing debt per capita. While such growth can occur for a while, it surely cannot go on forever. A limit to such growth would certainly be encountered when real interest-bearing government debt per capita equaled total savings per capita, and probably far before then. Thus, eventually either taxes must be levied or currency must be issued to service the debt. Moreover, the larger is the value at which the real interest-bearing debt per capita is ultimately stabilized, the larger the amount of revenue that eventually has to be raised either via tighter fiscal policy or via greater monetary expansion.

In the United States today, the responsibility for determining fiscal policy (the level of federal government expenditures and explicit taxes) rests with Congress and the executive branch. Subject to congressional oversight, the responsibility for determining the division of total government debt between interest-bearing debt and non-interest-bearing debt (base money) rests with the Federal Reserve Board. Given the growth in the total debt implied by fiscal policy, the Federal Reserve uses open-market exchanges of interest-bearing government bonds for base money to determine how fast base money and interest-bearing debt grow. If the federal budget is in deficit, then for example, the Fed can make the base money component grow more slowly than the growth rate of total debt implied by the deficit only by making the growth rate of the interest-bearing component exceed the growth of the total government debt. However, once the limit on the federal debt per capita that can be marketed with the public has been reached, the Fed has no choice: It must increase base money. That is, it must "monetize" all of the additional government borrowing by purchasing all real additions to the stock of interest-bearing debt that the treasury issues. More generally, given the time path of fiscal policy and given that government interest-bearing debt can be sold only at a real interest rate exceeding the growth rate n, the tighter is current monetary policy, the higher must the inflation rate be eventually.

This chapter describes the choices open to the monetary authority within a model that is extremely monetarist. The model goes as far as anyone would go in assigning monetary policy influence over the time path of the price level. It is also monetarist in imputing to monetary policy influence over almost no real variables.

In his 1968 presidential address to the American Economic Association [6], Milton Friedman warned not to expect too much from monetary policy. In particular, Friedman argued that monetary policy could not permanently influence the levels of real output, unemployment, and real rates of return on securities. However, Friedman did assert that the monetary authority could exert substantial control over the inflation rate, especially in the long run. The purpose of this chapter is to argue that if monetary policy is interpreted as open-market operations of the Federal Reserve under our second coordination scheme, then Friedman's list of the limits of monetary policy needs to be expanded to include severe limits on the ability of monetary policy to affect inflation permanently.

The results in the monetarist model occur because, given our specifications about fiscal policy and the real rate of return on government securities, tighter money now necessarily implies looser money later. This explains why in the monetarist model tighter money today attains a lower inflation rate today at the cost of enduring a higher inflation rate in the future. Next we produce an example of an economy in which there are even more severe limits on the ability of tight money to fight inflation. By amending the monetarist model to include a more sophisticated and dynamic description of the demand for base money, we describe an example in which tighter money today leads to a higher inflation rate and price level not only eventually but starting *today*. This example is spectacular because it describes a situation in which tighter money today lacks even the temporary ability to fight inflation. While the example is an extreme one, and probably overstates the limits on the achievements of tight money in the real world, it also has the virtue of isolating a force limiting the ability of tight money to fight inflation that is omitted in the monetarist model and that is probably present in the real world.

A SIMPLE MONETARIST MODEL

We describe a simple model that embodies unadulterated monetarism. The model incorporates the following features: (1) a common constant growth rate of n for real income and population, (2) a constant real return on government securities that exceeds n, and (3) a quantity theory demand schedule for base or high-powered money, one that exhibits constant income velocity.[2] A model with these features exhibits the two limitations on monetary policy stressed by Milton Friedman in his AEA presidential address. First, there is a natural, or equilibrium, rate of real income that monetary policy is powerless to affect. Second, the real rate of interest on government bonds is beyond the influence of monetary policy.

Our purpose in focusing on this very simple model is to describe yet one more serious limitation on the power of monetary policy, a limitation on its ability to influence the economy's inflation rate, over which Friedman and monetarists have asserted that monetary policy exerts considerable influence. In particular, we shall show how in this most monetarist of models, monetary policy by itself is only capable of postponing inflation. We have purposefully chosen to argue this proposition in the context of a model that embraces as unqualified a set of monetarist assumptions as we can imagine. We do this to show that the argument about the limitations of monetary policy is not based on abandoning any of the key assumptions that have been made by those monetarists who have stressed the potency of monetary policy for controlling inflation. Instead, the argument hinges entirely on taking into account the future budgetary consequences of alternative current monetary policies when the real rate of return on government bonds exceeds n.

We describe fiscal policy by a time path or sequence $D(1)$, $D(2)$, . . ., $D(t)$, . . ., where $D(t)$ is measured in real terms (time t goods) and is defined as real expenditures minus real tax collections net of all transfers except interest on the government debt and where, for convenience, we label the current date $t = 1$. We describe monetary policy by a time path $H(1)$, $H(2)$, . . ., $H(t)$, . . ., where $H(t)$ is the stock of base or high-powered money at time t. If, for simplicity, we assume that the entire government debt consists of one-period debt, then we can write the consolidated government budget constraint (consolidating the treasury and the Federal Reserve) as[3]

$$D(t) = \frac{H(t) - H(t - 1)}{p(t)} + B(t) - B(t - 1)[1 + R(t - 1)]$$

$$t = 1, 2, . . . \tag{5.1}$$

We are letting $p(t)$ be the price level at time t, while $R(t - 1)$ is the real rate of interest on one-period government bonds between time t

$- 1$ and time t; $B(t - 1)[1 + R(t - 1)]$ is the real par value of one-period government bonds that were issued at time $t - 1$ and fall due in period t, where $B(t - 1)$ is measured in units of time $t - 1$ goods and $1 + R(t - 1)$ is measured in time t goods per unit of time $t - 1$ goods. In equation 5.1 $B(t)$ is government borrowing between periods t and $t + 1$, measured in units of time t goods. Equation 5.1 states that the excess of government expenditures over tax receipts must be financed by some combination of issuing additional currency and interest-bearing debt. Finally, we let $N(t)$ be the population at time t. We assume that $N(t)$ obeys the difference equation

$$N(t + 1) = (1 + n)N(t) \qquad t = 1, 2, \ldots \qquad (5.2)$$

with $N(1) > 0$ being given and n a constant exceeding -1.

Dividing both sides of equation 5.1 by $N(t)$ and rearranging gives the following form of the government's budget constraint:

$$\frac{B(t)}{N(t)} = \left(\frac{1 + R(t - 1)}{1 + n} \right) \frac{B(t - 1)}{N(t - 1)} \\ + \left[\frac{D(t)}{N(t)} - \left(\frac{H(t) - H(t - 1)}{N(t)p(t)} \right) \right] \qquad (5.3)$$

We shall now use equation 5.3 and our monetarist model—assumptions (1)–(3)—to illustrate a version of the following proposition: If fiscal policy in the form of the $D(t)$ sequence is taken as given, then tighter current monetary policy implies higher inflation in the future.

To illustrate tighter current monetary policy, we specify alternative time paths for monetary policy in the following way. We take $H(1)$ as predetermined and let alternative monetary policies be alternative constant growth rates of $H(t)$ for $t = 2, 3, \ldots, T$ where T is some date greater than or equal to 2. For $t > T$, we suppose that the path of $H(t)$ is determined by the condition that the outstanding stock of interest-bearing real government debt per capita be held constant at whatever level it attains at $t = T$. The restriction on monetary policy from time T onward is one way of taking into account that the real debt per capita cannot grow without limit.[4] Thus, with $H(1)$ taken as given, we suppose that

$$H(t) = (1 + \theta)H(t - 1) \qquad t = 2, 3, \ldots, T \qquad (5.4)$$

and examine the consequence of various choices of θ and T.

Notice that we have written equation 5.1 in terms of real debt and real rates of return. If we want to apply this to a setting in which government bonds are not indexed, which is the situation in the United States today, then we must ensure that anticipated inflation is the same as actual inflation. We impose that condition, in part, by supposing that both the path of fiscal policy, the $D(t)$ sequence, and the path of monetary policy, θ and T, are announced at $t = 1$ and known by private agents. Once we assume that, it does not matter whether nominal or indexed debt is issued from $t = 1$ onward.

Now, to proceed, note that assumptions (1) and (3) imply that the price level at any time t is proportional to the time t stock of base money per capita, $H(t)/N(t)$, namely,

$$p(t) = \frac{1}{h} \frac{H(t)}{N(t)} \qquad (5.5)$$

for some positive constant h.

From equation 5.5 it follows that for $t = 2, \ldots, T$ one plus the inflation rate is given by $p(t)/p(t - 1) = (1 + \theta)/(1 + n)$. Thus, when we specify monetary policy, a θ and a T, we are simultaneously choosing the inflation rate for periods $t = 2, 3, \ldots, T$. We are interested in determining how the inflation rate for periods subsequent to T depends on the inflation rate chosen for the periods prior to T.

We do this in two simple steps. We first determine how the inflation rate subsequent to T depends on the stock of real government debt per capita attained at T and to be held constant thereafter. We denote that per capita stock by $b_\theta(T)$. We then show how $b_\theta(T)$ depends on θ.

To find the dependence of the inflation rate for $t > T$ on $b_\theta(T)$, we use equation 5.3 for any date $t > T$, substituting into it $B(t/N(t)) = B(t - 1)/N(t - 1) = b_\theta(T)$ and $H(t) = hN(t)p(t)$ as implied by equation 5.5. The result can be written:

$$1 - \left(\frac{1}{1 + n}\right)\frac{p(t - 1)}{p(t)} = \frac{\left[\dfrac{D(t)}{N(t)} + \left(\dfrac{R(t - 1) - n}{1 + n}\right)b_\theta(T)\right]}{h} \qquad (5.6)$$

In order that equation 5.6 be satisfied by positive price levels $p(t)$ and

$p(t - 1)$, it is necessary that the right-hand side be less than unity. This is one condition that limits the size of the stock of real interest-bearing government debt per capita.

If $R(t - 1) - n$ is a positive constant, as stated by assumption (2), then the right-hand side of equation 5.6 is higher the higher is $b_\theta(T)$. This in turn implies that the inflation rate is higher the higher is $b_\theta(T)$, a conclusion that holds for all $t > T$.

To complete the argument that a tighter monetary policy now implies higher future inflation, we must show that the smaller is θ, the higher is $b_\theta(T)$. To find $b_\theta(T)$ and its dependence on θ, we first find $B(1)/N(1) \equiv b(1)$ and then show how to find the entire path $b(1)$, $b_\theta(2)$, $b_\theta(3)$, . . ., $b_\theta(T)$.

We solve for $b(1)$ from the $t = 1$ version of equation 5.3, namely

$$b(1) = \frac{\bar{B}(0)}{p(1)N(1)} + \frac{D(1)}{N(1)} - \frac{H(1) - H(0)}{N(1)p(1)} \quad (5.7)$$

Here, in place of $B(0)[1 + R(0)]/(1 + n)$ we have inserted $\bar{B}(0)/p(1)N(1)$, $\bar{B}(0)$ being the nominal par value of the debt issued at $t = 0$. By making this substitution, we avoid assuming anything about the relationship between actual inflation between time $t = 0$ and $t = 1$ and what it had been anticipated to be. In conjunction with equation 5.5, equation 5.7 permits us to solve for $b(1)$ in terms of $D(1)$, $N(1)$, $H(1)$, $H(0)$, and $\bar{B}(0)$. Note that $b(1)$ does not depend on θ.

We now proceed to find $b_\theta(2)$, $b_\theta(3)$, . . ., $b_\theta(T)$. Using equations 5.4 and 5.5 and the definition $b(t) = B(t)/N(t)$, we can write equation 5.3 as

$$b(t) = \left(\frac{1 + R(t - 1)}{1 + n}\right)b(t - 1) + \frac{D(t)}{N(t)}$$
$$- h\left(\frac{\theta}{1 + \theta}\right) \quad t = 2, 3, . . ., T \quad (5.8)$$

By repeated substitution it follows for any $t > 2$ and $t \leq T$ that

$$b_\theta(t) = \phi(t, 1)b(1) + \sum_{s=2}^{t} \frac{\phi(t, s)D(s)}{N(s)} - \frac{h\theta}{1 + \theta} \sum_{s=2}^{t} \phi(t, s) \quad (5.9)$$

where

$$\phi(t, s) = \frac{[1 + R(s)][1 + R(s + 1)] \cdots [1 + R(t - 1)]}{(1 + n)^{t-s}} \qquad t > s$$

It follows from equation 5.9 that $b_\theta(T)$ is larger the smaller is θ.

This completes our demonstration of a version of the proposition that less inflation now achieved through monetary policy on its own implies higher future inflation. It is crucial for such a result that the real rate of return on government securities exceeds n from T onward (see equation 5.6) and that the path of fiscal policy given by $D(1)$, $D(2), \ldots, D(t) \ldots$ does not depend on θ.

THE CAGAN–BRESCIANI-TURRONI EFFECT

In the analysis of the preceding section, circumstances have been delineated in which tighter monetary policy lowers the current rate of inflation, but at the cost of increasing inflation in the future. Our having assumed a demand schedule for money of the simplest quantity theory form (equation 5.5) not only much simplified the analysis but had the substantive aspect of ignoring any dependence of the demand for base money on the expected rate of inflation. This dependence is widely believed to be important and acts to complicate the dynamics of the influence of monetary policy on the price level. Bresciani-Turroni [1] and Cagan [3] adduced substantial evidence for the existence of this effect by studying countries that had undergone rapid inflation. If the demand for money depends on the expected rate of inflation, then it turns out (see Sargent and Wallace [13]) that the current price level depends on current and all anticipated future levels of the money supply. This sets up a force whereby high rates of money creation anticipated in the future tend to raise the *current* rate of inflation. As we shall show, this force can limit the power of tighter monetary policy to deliver even a temporarily lower inflation rate.

We maintain all of the assumptions of the monetarist model except that we replace equation 5.5 by[4]

$$\frac{H(t)}{p(t)N(t)} = \frac{\gamma_1}{2} - \frac{\gamma_2}{2}\frac{p(t + 1)}{p(t)} \qquad t \geq 1, \gamma_1 > \gamma_2 > 0 \quad (5.10)$$

Equation 5.10 is a version of the demand schedule for money that Phillip Cagan used in studying hyperinflations. The equation is shown in Appendix 2 to imply the following equation for the price level at t:

$$p(t) = \frac{2}{\gamma_1} \sum_{j=0}^{\infty} \left(\frac{\gamma_2}{\gamma_1}\right)^j \frac{H(t + j)}{N(t + j)}$$

This equation expresses the current price level in terms of current and all future values of the per capita supply of base money. Thus, the current price level and inflation rate depend not only on how tight money is today but also on how tight it is for all "tomorrows." If the situation is, as in the monetarist model, that tighter money now causes looser money in the future, then this equation for $p(t)$ suggests the possibility that tighter money today might fail to bring about a lower inflation rate and price level even today. We shall now discuss an example in which this possibility in fact obtains.

As above, policy consists of a deficit sequence $D(t)$, a date T at which monetary policy from then on is determined by the condition that the real per capita interest-bearing government debt be held constant, and θ, the growth rate of the monetary base for periods prior to T. In the model of this section, the path of the price level prior to T depends on all of these aspects of policy, and not just on θ as was the case for the monetarist model.

Appendix 2 describes a way of solving for the paths of the endogenous variables. Here we simply present an example in which a tighter monetary policy in the form of a lower θ implies a uniformly higher price level and inflation rate.

The economy of the example is characterized by $\gamma_1 = 3.0$, $\gamma_2 = 2.50$, $R = 0.05$, and $n = 0.02$. The common features of policy are a per capita deficit sequence $d(t)$ with $d(t) = 0.05$ for $t = 1, 2, \ldots, 10$ and $d(t) = 0$ for $t > 10$, $T = 10$, and $[H(0) + \bar{B}(0)]/H(1) = 200/164.65$. Two different θ's are studied: $\theta = 0.106$ and $\theta = 0.120$. It turns out that the price level at $t = 1$ is 1.04 percent *higher* in the economy with the *smaller* θ. Tables 5.1 and 5.2 compare the inflation rates, price levels, per capita bond holdings, and per capita real money balances for the two economies. Figure 5.1 graphs the price levels.

This example is spectacular in that the easier monetary policy is uniformly better than the tighter policy. (In terms of the model of

Table 5.1

	Price level		Inflation rate	
Date	$\theta = 0.106$	$\theta = 0.120$	$\theta = 0.106$	$\theta = 0.120$
1	1.13695	1.12105	1.08415	1.08250
2	1.23262	1.21354	1.08413	1.08082
3	1.33632	1.31161	1.08411	1.07892
4	1.44871	1.41512	1.08409	1.07677
5	1.57053	1.52376	1.08406	1.07434
6	1.70255	1.63703	1.08404	1.07156
7	1.84562	1.75418	1.08401	1.06839
8	2.00067	1.87416	1.08397	1.06474
9	2.16867	1.99549	1.08394	1.06051
$t \geq 10$	$p(10)\pi(10)^{t-10}$		1.08390	1.05557

Appendix 1, the equilibrium for the easier monetary policy is Pareto superior to that for the tighter monetary policy.) In this example, the tighter current monetary policy fails to buy even a temporary improvement in inflation vis-à-vis the looser current policy.[5]

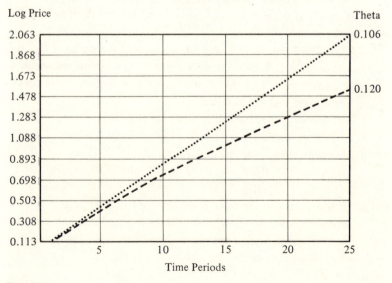

Figure 5.1

Table 5.1 *(Continued)*

Per capita bond holdings		Per capita real balances	
θ = 0.106	θ = 0.120	θ = 0.106	θ = 0.120
0.08109	0.08153	0.12023	0.14687
0.11960	0.11797	0.14484	0.14898
0.15923	0.15522	0.14486	0.15136
0.20003	0.19328	0.14489	0.15404
0.24202	0.23214	0.14492	0.15708
0.28525	0.27177	0.14496	0.16055
0.32974	0.31213	0.14499	0.16405
0.37554	0.35320	0.14504	0.16907
0.42268	0.39490	0.14508	0.17436
0.47120	0.43718	0.14513	0.18053

CONCLUSIONS, QUALIFICATIONS, AND EXTENSIONS

It bears emphasizing that our argument uses the assumption of a rational expectations equilibrium, which in this case is equivalent with perfect foresight because there is no randomness in the model. Thus, our statements involve comparing alternative paths for monetary and fiscal variables that are known in advance. The authorities are assumed to stick with the plans that they announce, and not to default, in real terms, on the interest-bearing debt issued from time 1 onward, so that it is as if all interest-bearing debt were indexed. We believe that such an assumption is appropriate for analyzing the available options with regard to choosing time sequences or strategies for monetary policy variables. We would be prepared to argue for the appropriateness of this assumption despite historical examples in which governments have defaulted on substantial fractions of their interest-bearing debt by inflating it away. Our reason is that such a default option is not available as a recurrent policy to which the government can persistently plan to resort.

We should also note that our argument is actually a version of a line of reasoning that exists in the literature on the macroeconomics of the government budget constraint, which is discussed, for example, by McCallum [9, 10] and Scarth [14]. Various authors have pointed out that in the presence of real rates of interest exceeding the growth rate of the economy, the government budget constraint can be interpreted as an unstable difference equation in real debt and that it implies an explosive path for real government debt per capita under some "k-percent" rules for monetary growth. What we have done in this chapter is simply to point out the implications for anti-inflation policy and that it is not feasible to follow such explosive paths forever.

We have made two crucial assumptions to obtain our conclusions. The first is that the real rate of interest exceeds the growth rate of the economy. We have used that assumption because it seems to be maintained by many of those who argue for a low rate of growth of money no matter what is the current deficit. If we were to replace that assumption, we would instead assume that the public's demand for government bonds is an increasing function of their real rate of return, with an initial range over which that demand is positive at rates of return that are negative or less than the growth rate of the economy. But to induce larger demands for government bonds, we would assume that their real rate of return would have to exceed the rate of growth of the economy. We would also continue to assume that there is an upper bound on the quantity of bonds demanded per capita. Such a demand function for government bonds would imply that monetary policy helps determine the real rate of interest on government bonds, and that for some monetary policies entailing low enough bond supplies, seigniorage can be earned on bonds as well as on base money. However, an analysis that includes such a demand schedule for bonds would share with ours the implication that a sufficiently tight monetary policy can imply growth in government interest-bearing indebtedness so rapid that inflation in the future results in being higher than it would be with an easier current monetary policy.

The second crucial assumption that we have made is that the path of $D(t)$ is given and does not depend on current or future monetary policies. This assumption is not about the preferences, opportunities, or behavior of private agents, as is our first crucial assumption, but is about the behavior of the monetary and fiscal authorities and the "game" that they are playing. Since the monetary authorities affect the extent to which seigniorage is exploited as a revenue source, monetary and fiscal policies simply have to be coordinated. The question is which authority "moves first"—the monetary authority or the fiscal authority—or to put it differently, who imposes discipline on whom? The assumption made in this chapter is that the fiscal authorities move first, their "move" consisting of an entire $D(t)$ sequence. Given that sequence, monetary policy is to be determined in a way consistent with that $D(t)$ sequence, if that is possible [as we have seen, it may not be possible if the $D(t)$ sequence is "too big" for "too long"]. Given this assumption about the game played by the authorities, and given our first crucial assumption, the monetary authorities can make money tighter now only by making it looser later.

One can interpret the call for monetary restraint differently than we have in this chapter, and as a call to let the monetary authority move first and thereby impose discipline on the fiscal authority. On this interpretation, the monetary authority moves first by announcing a fixed θ rule like equation 5.4 not just for $t = 2, 3, \ldots, T$ but for *all* $t \geq 1$. By doing this in a binding way, the monetary authority forces the fiscal authority to choose a $D(t)$ sequence consistent with the announced monetary policy. This form of permanent monetary restraint is a mechanism that effectively imposes fiscal discipline. Alternative monetary mechanisms that impose fiscal discipline that have been suggested are fixed exchange rates or a commodity money standard. It is evident that nothing in our analysis denies the possibility that monetary policies can permanently affect the inflation rate under such a monetary regime that effectively permanently disciplines the fiscal authority.

We wrote this chapter not because we think that our assumption about the game played by the monetary and fiscal authorities describes the way monetary and fiscal policies should be coordinated but out of a fear that it may describe the way the game is now being played.

APPENDIX 1

This appendix describes a simple formal model that implies the assumptions used in the text. It is a version of Paul Samuelson's [12] model of overlapping generations in which people use money to smooth out their consumption streams over time.

We describe the evolution of the economy from time $t = 1$ onward. The economy is populated by two-period lived agents. At each date $t \geq 1$ there are born $N_1(t)$ identical poor people who are endowed after taxes with α_1 units of the single good when young and α_2 units when old. At each date $t \geq 1$ there are also born $N_2(t)$ identical rich people who are endowed after taxes with β of the good when young and zero when old. We assume that $N_1(t) = (1 + n)N_1(t - 1)$, $N_2(t) = (1 + n)N_2(t - 1)$ for $t \geq 1$, with $N_1(0)$ and $N_2(0)$ given and $n > -1$. The total population is $N(t) = N_1(t) + N_2(t)$.

There is available a physical technology for converting time t goods into time $t + 1$ goods. In particular, if $k(t) \geq k$ goods are stored at time $t \geq 1$, then $(1 + R)k(t)$ goods become available at time $t + 1$. This is a constant returns-to-scale technology with a constant real rate of return on investment of $R > 0$. We assume that there is a minimum scale of k at which this investment can be undertaken and that $\beta/2 > k > \alpha_1$, the first period endowment of the poor. We also assume that a legal restriction on intermediation prevents two or more of the poor from sharing investments, thereby preventing the poor from holding the real investment.

The government issues currency, which does not bear interest, and interest-bearing bonds. The currency is held by the poor because government bonds are issued in such large denominations that only the rich can hold them. Again, a legal restriction on intermediation is relied on to prevent two or more people from sharing a government bond. There is no uncertainty in the model, so that the rich will hold government bonds only if the real interest rate on bonds at least equals that on private investment, which must be at least as large as the yield on currency.

As in the text, the government finances a real deficit $D(t)$ via some combination of currency creation and bond creation. The government's budget constraint is

$$D(t) = \frac{H(t) - H(t - 1)}{p(t)} + B(t) - B(t - 1)(1 + R) \qquad t \geq 1 \quad (5.11)$$

where $H(t)$ is measured in dollars, $p(t)$ in dollars per time t goods, $D(t)$ in time t goods, and $B(t)$ in time t goods.

In addition, at time $t = 1$ there are $N_1(0) + N_2(0)$ old poor and rich people, respectively, who hold $H(0)$ units of currency and maturing bonds of par nominal value $\tilde{B}(0)$. The old people alive at time $t = 1$ simply offer all of their currency inelastically in exchange for goods to those who are young at time 1.

The young of each generation $t \geq 1$ are assumed to maximize the utility function $c_t^h(t)c_t^h(t + 1)$ where $c_t^h(s)$ is consumption of an agent of type h of the s-period good of an agent born at time t. Letting $w_t^h(s)$ be the endowment of agent type h of the s-period good of an agent born at t and assuming that each agent faces a single rate of return R^h, a young agent h at generation t

chooses a lifetime consumption bundle to maximize utility subject to the present value constraint:

$$c_t^h(t) + \frac{c_t^h(t + 1)}{1 + R^h} = w_t^h(t) + \frac{w_t^h(t + 1)}{1 + R^h}$$

The solution to this problem is the saving function:

$$w_t^h(t) - c_t^h(t) = \frac{w_t^h(t) - w_t^h(t + 1)/(1 + R^h)}{2} \tag{5.12}$$

Since all saving of poor people is in the form of currency, if h is poor, $1 + R^h = p(t)/p(t + 1)$. Moreover, in the range where $p(t)/p(t + 1) < 1 + R$, only the poor hold currency. Thus, in this range the money market equilibrium condition is that $H(t)/p(t)$ equals the total real saving of the poor, which by equation 5.12 is $N_1(t)[\alpha_1 - \alpha_2 p(t + 1)/p(t)]/2$. Dividing by $N(t)$, we can write this condition as

$$\frac{H(t)}{p(t)N(t)} = \frac{[\alpha_1 - \alpha_2 p(t + 1)/p(t)]N_1(t)}{2N(t)} \tag{5.13}$$

This is equation 5.10 if we let $\alpha_1/2 = \alpha_1 N_1(t)/2N(t)$ and $\alpha_2/2 = \alpha_2 N_1(t)/2N(t)$. We get equation 5.5 if $\alpha_2 = 0$.

According to equation 5.12, each rich person saves a constant amount $\beta/2$ per period. So long as government bonds bear the real rate of return R, each rich person is indifferent between holding government bonds or private capital. However, in the aggregate, the rich only wish to save $N_2(t)\beta/2$ per period. The number $\beta/2$ determines the upper bound on per capita holdings of interest-bearing government debt that was alluded to in the text. We let $K(t)$ denote the total amount of real investment ("storage"), measured in goods, undertaken by the young members of generation t, all of them rich. We then have

$$K(t) + B(t) = \frac{N_2(t)\beta}{2} = \overline{B}(t) \tag{5.14}$$

where $B(t)$ is the amount of loans to the government. Equation 5.14 expresses the result that additional government borrowing merely crowds out private investment on a one-for-one basis.

The national income identity can be written:

$$N_1(t)c_t^1(t) + N_2(t - 1)c_{t-1}^1(t) + N_2(t)c_t^2(t)$$
$$+ N_2(t - 1)c_{t-1}^2(t) + K(t) + G(t)$$
$$= N_1(t)\alpha_1 + N_1(t - 1)\alpha_2 + N_2(t)\beta + T(t) + (1 + R)K(t - 1) \tag{5.15}$$

Here $G(t)$ denotes government purchases and $T(t)$ denotes total direct taxes. The government deficit as defined in the text is related to $G(t)$ and $T(t)$ by $D(t) = G(t) - T(t)$.

Thus, so long as solutions satisfy $p(t)/p(t + 1) < 1 + R$ and total real bond supply is less than $\overline{B}(t)$, the model just described implies *all* the assumptions made in the text. This particular model also has implications for how different agents fare under different policies. It is evident from the present value budget constraint set out above that each poor person is better off the lower the inflation rate, that each rich person is unaffected by the inflation rate, and that those who at $t = 1$ are in the second period of their lives and who are holding currency or maturing bonds are better off the lower is the initial price level, $p(1)$. These observations lie behind our claim that for the Cagan–Bresciani-Turroni (CBT) example, the tight-money policy is Pareto inferior to the loose-money policy.[6]

APPENDIX 2

In this appendix, we analyze the CBT model that results from generalizing the analysis of the monetarist model by assuming a demand schedule for base money that depends on the expected rate of inflation. The particular demand schedule that we use resembles Phillip Cagan's [3] famous demand schedule and can be deduced formally from the model in Appendix 1 by assuming that the "poor" of each generation are endowed with $\gamma_1 N(0)/N_1(0) > 0$ units of the assumption good when young and $\gamma_2 N(0)/N_1(0) > 0$ units when they are old. (The monetarist model emerges when we set $\gamma_2 = 0$.) Except for this generalization, all other features of the model remain as discussed.

We now assume a demand schedule for base money of the form

$$\frac{H(t)}{p(t)N(t)} = \frac{\gamma_1}{2} - \frac{\gamma_2}{2}\frac{p(t + 1)}{p(t)} \qquad t \geq 1 \qquad (5.16)$$

where $\gamma_1 > \gamma_2 > 0$. Except for replacing equation 5.5 with 5.16, we retain all the other features of the monetarist model, including the budget restraint 5.1 and the law of motion of total population 5.2. We describe experiments similar to the monetarist model: We hold the per capita real government debt $b(t)$ constant for $t > T$ and examine the choice of alternative rates of growth of base money θ for $t = 2, . . ., T$. The step of replacing equation 5.5 with 5.16 substantially complicates the dynamics of the system, as we shall see.

We begin by examining the behavior of the system for $t > T$. For $t > T + 1$ we specify as before that monetary policy is determined so that $b(t) = b(t - 1) = b(T)$. Using the budget constraint (equation 5.1) together with this condition implies

$$\frac{H(t) - H(t - 1)}{N(t)p(t)} = \frac{R(t - 1) - n}{1 + n} b(T) + \frac{D(t)}{N(t)} \qquad t > T + 1 \qquad (5.17)$$

We now assume that

$$\frac{D(t)}{N(t)} = d \qquad t \geq T$$

where d is a constant, which is a computationally convenient assumption, although the general flavor of our results does not depend on making it.

We now define per capita real balances as $m(t) = H(t)/N(t)p(t)$ and the one-period gross inflation rate $\pi(t) = p(t)/p(t - 1)$. In terms of these variables, equations 5.16 and 5.17 become

$$m(t) = \frac{\gamma_1}{2} - \frac{\gamma_2}{2} \pi(t + 1) \qquad t \geq 1 \qquad (5.18)$$

$$m(t) - \frac{m(t - 1)}{\pi(t)(1 + n)} = \xi \qquad t \geq T + 1 \qquad (5.19)$$

where $\xi = [(R - n)/(1 + n)] b(T) + d$. The variable ξ has the interpretation of the per capita deficit that must be financed by seignorage from time $T + 1$ onward. Eliminating $m(t)$ and $m(t - 1)$ from these equations by substituting equation 5.18 into 5.19 leads to the following nonlinear difference equation in $\pi(t)$:

$$\pi(t + 1) = \frac{\gamma_1}{\gamma_2} + \frac{1}{1 + n} - \frac{2\xi}{\gamma_2} - \frac{\gamma_1}{\gamma_2}\left(\frac{1}{1 + n}\right)\frac{1}{\pi(t)} \qquad t \geq T + 1 \qquad (5.20)$$

This equation is graphed in Figure 5.2. It is readily verified that if

$$\left(\frac{\gamma_1}{\gamma_2} + \frac{1}{1 + n} - \frac{2\xi}{\gamma_2}\right)^2 - \frac{4\gamma_1}{\gamma_2(1 + n)} > 0 \qquad (5.21)$$

then equation 5.20 has two stationary points, their values given by

$$\pi_1 = \frac{1}{2}\left\{\frac{\gamma_1}{\gamma_2} + \frac{1}{1 + n} - \frac{2\xi}{\gamma_2} \right.$$
$$\left. - \left[\left(\frac{\gamma_1}{\gamma_2} + \frac{1}{1 + n} - \frac{2\xi}{\gamma_2}\right)^2 - \frac{4\gamma_1}{\gamma_2(1 + n)}\right]^{1/2}\right\} \qquad (5.22)$$

$$\pi_2 = \frac{1}{2}\left\{\frac{\gamma_1}{\gamma_2} + \frac{1}{1 + n} - \frac{2\xi}{\gamma_2} + \left[\left(\frac{\gamma_1}{\gamma_2} + \frac{1}{1 + n} - \frac{2\xi}{\gamma_2}\right)^2 - \frac{4\gamma_1}{\gamma_2(1 + n)}\right]^{1/2}\right\}$$

We let $\bar{\xi}$ be the value of ξ for which the left side of equation 5.21 equals zero. Evidently, $\bar{\xi}$ is a function of γ_1, γ_2, and n and represents the maximum stationary per capita deficit that can be financed by seignorage. From equation 5.21 it follows that if $\xi = 0$, then $\pi_1 = 1/(1 + n)$ and $\pi_2 = \gamma_1/\gamma_2$. From Figure 5.1 it immediately follows that for $\bar{\xi} > \xi > 0$, $\pi_1 > 1/(1 + n)$, $\pi_2 < \gamma_1/\gamma_2$, and that raising ξ causes π_1 to raise and π_2 to fall.

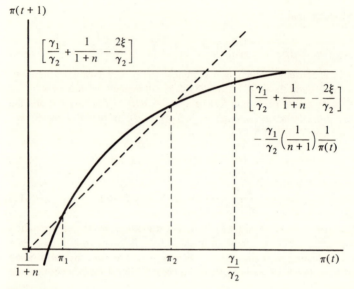

Figure 5.2

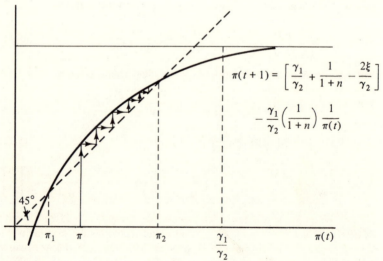

Figure 5.3

Inequality 5.21 is a necessary and sufficient condition for it to be possible to finance the per capita deficit ξ by seignorage. Assuming equation 5.21 is satisfied, there exists a multiplicity of inflation-real balance paths that finance the deficit. Any setting of $\pi(T)$ satisfying $\pi_1 < \pi(T) < \gamma_1/\gamma_2$, with $\pi(t)$ for $t > T + 1$ being given by equation 5.20, results in the deficit being financed. (Later we shall describe the money supply paths needed to accomplish these paths for inflation.) Figure 5.3 again graphs equation 5.20 and shows that for any $\pi(T) > \pi_1$, $\pi(t) \to \pi_2$ as $t \to \infty$. Thus, three classes of inflation paths finance the deficit: (a) the stationary path with $\pi(t) = \pi_1$, $t > T$; (b) the stationary path with $\pi(t) = \pi_2$, $t > T$; and (c) the class of nonstationary paths with $\gamma_1/\gamma_2 > \pi(T) > \pi_1$ and $\lim \pi(t) = \pi_2$ as $t \to \infty$.

We assume that the government selects the money supply path so that $\pi(T) = \pi_1$ and so that the deficit is financed by the uniformly lowest inflation rate path, and, therefore, in view of equation 5.18, the lowest price level path. This assumption is reasonable since this selection leaves the government with the same resources as any other selection, while leaving holders of money better off.

Having determined the inflation rate $p(t)/p(t - 1) = \pi_1$ for $t > T + 1$ from equation 5.21, we can determine the time T real balances and price level by setting $t = T$ in equation 5.18:

$$\frac{H(T)}{p(T)N(T)} = \frac{\gamma_1}{2} - \frac{\gamma_2}{2}\pi_1$$

or

$$p(T) = \frac{2}{\gamma_1}\left(\frac{1}{1 - (\gamma_2/\gamma_1)\pi_1}\right)\frac{H(T)}{N(T)} \tag{5.23}$$

Since $H(T)$ and $N(T)$ are given at T, this equation determines $p(T)$ as an inverse function of π_1. Also, since $\pi(t)$ is constant for $t > T + 1$, we have from equation 5.18 and the definition of $m(t) \equiv H(t)/N(t)p(t)$ that

$$\frac{H(t)}{N(t)} = \pi_1\frac{H(t - 1)}{N(t - 1)} \qquad t \geq T + 1$$

so that per capita nominal balances grow at the constant gross rate π_1, which is the rate of inflation for $t > T + 1$.

It is instructive briefly to describe the following alternative way to solve the system for $t > T + 1$ by obtaining a pair of linear difference equations. Define $h(t) = H(t)/N(t)$, and write the budget constraint (equation 5.17) as

$$h(t) = \left(\frac{1}{1 + n}\right)h(t - 1) + \xi p(t) \qquad t \geq T + 1$$

and the demand function for base money (equation 5.16) as

$$p(t) = \frac{\gamma_2}{\gamma_1}p(t + 1) + \frac{2}{\gamma_1}h(t) \qquad t \geq 1$$

Using the lag operator L, we write these two equations as

$$\left[1 - \left(\frac{1}{1 + n}\right)L\right]h(t) = \xi p(t) \qquad t \geq T + 1$$

$$\left(1 - \frac{\gamma_2}{\gamma_1}L^{-1}\right)p(t) = \frac{2}{\gamma_1}h(t) \qquad t \geq 1 \tag{5.24}$$

Solving the second equation in terms of $h(t)$ gives

$$p(t) = \frac{2}{\gamma_1}\left(1 - \frac{\gamma_2}{\gamma_1}L^{-1}\right)^{-1}h(t) + c\left(\frac{\gamma_1}{\gamma_2}\right)^t \tag{5.25}$$

or

$$p(t) = \frac{2}{\gamma_1}\sum_{j=0}^{\infty}\left(\frac{\gamma_2}{\gamma_1}\right)^j h(t + j) + c\left(\frac{\gamma_1}{\gamma_2}\right)^t \qquad t \geq 1 \tag{5.26}$$

where c is any nonnegative constant. Substituting equation 5.25 into 5.24 and operating on both sides of the result with $[1 - (\gamma_2/\gamma_1)L^{-1}]$ gives the following homogenous difference equation in $h(t)$:

$$L^{-1}\left\{-1 + \left(\frac{\gamma_1}{\gamma_2} + \frac{1}{1 + n} - \frac{2\xi}{\gamma_2}\right)L - \left(\frac{1}{1 + n}\right)\frac{\gamma_1}{\gamma_2}L^2\right\}h(t) = 0 \tag{5.27}$$

The characteristic polynomial in L can be factored in the usual way, so that

$$L^{-1}[(1 - \pi_1 L)(1 - \pi_2 L)]h(t) = 0 \tag{5.28}$$

where π_1 and π_2 are the same roots given in equation 5.22.

Since for $\xi > 0$ we have $\pi_1 < \pi_2 < \gamma_1/\gamma_2$, it follows that the geometric sum in current and future $h(t)$ that appears in equation 5.25 converges for any $h(t)$ paths that satisfy equation 5.28 or, equivalently,

$$h(t) = (\pi_1 + \pi_2)h(t - 1) - \pi_1\pi_2 h(t - 2)$$
$$t \geq T + 1, h(T) \text{ given}, h(T + 1) \text{ free} \tag{5.29}$$

To ensure that the deficit is financed each period, we have to add two side conditions to those listed under equation 5.29: It is necessary to set $c = 0$ in equation 5.25 and to set $h(T + 1)$ so that 5.25 implies that $\pi(T + 1) < \gamma_1/\gamma_2$. All of the price level paths with $c > 0$ have $\lim_{t\to\infty} \pi(t) = \gamma_1/\gamma_2$, which in view of equations 5.18 and 5.19 imply that $\lim m(t) = 0$ and that a positive deficit cannot be financed. Any path with $\pi(T) > \gamma_1/\gamma_2$ implies nonpositive real balances at T. Since we are assuming that the government selects $h(t) = \pi_1 h(t - 1)$, $t > T + 1$, $h(T)$ given, equation 5.26 with $t = T$ becomes equivalent to equation 5.23. We note that the admissible paths given by equation 5.29 with $h(T + 1) \neq \pi_1 h(T)$ have $\lim_{t \to \infty} h(t)/h(t - 1) = \pi_2$ and so constitute the per capita nominal money supply paths that correspond to the inflation paths with $\pi(T) > \pi_1$ in Figures 5.1 and 5.2.

In summary, we have that for $t > T$ the price level and the stock of base money per capita evolve according to

$$p(t) = \frac{2}{\gamma_1}\left(\frac{1}{1 - \gamma_2/\gamma_1\pi_1}\right)h(t) \qquad t > T \tag{5.30}$$

$$h(t + 1) = \pi_1 h(t) \tag{5.31}$$

subject to $h(T)$ given, where from equation 5.22 we have

$$\pi_1 = \frac{1}{2}\left\{\frac{\gamma_1}{\gamma_2} + \frac{1}{1 + n} - \frac{2\xi}{\gamma_2} - \left[\left(\frac{\gamma_1}{\gamma_2} + \frac{1}{1 + n} - \frac{2\xi}{\gamma_2}\right)^2 - \frac{4\gamma_1}{\gamma_2(1 + n)}\right]^{1/2}\right\}$$

and

$$\xi = \left(\frac{R - n}{1 + n}\right)b(T) + d$$

We now describe the behavior of the price level, supply of base money, and stock of real government debt per capita for $t < T$. As in the monetarist model, we assume a constant growth rate of base money,

$$H(t) = (1 + \theta)H(t - 1) \qquad t = 2, 3, \ldots, T \tag{5.32}$$

Equation 5.25 with $c = 0$ implies that for all $t > 1$,

$$p(t) = \frac{2}{\gamma_1}\sum_{j=0}^{\infty}\left(\frac{\gamma_2}{\gamma_1}\right)^j h(t + j) \tag{5.33}$$

Further, we know from equations 5.32 and 5.31 that

$$h(t) = \mu h(t - 1) \qquad t = 2, 3, \ldots, T \tag{5.34}$$

$$h(t) = \pi_1 h(t - 1) \qquad t = T + 1, T + 2, \ldots \tag{5.35}$$

where

$$\mu = \frac{1 + \theta}{1 + n} \tag{5.36}$$

Let us define the parameter ϕ by

$$\phi = \frac{\gamma_2}{\gamma_1} \tag{5.37}$$

and write 5.33 for $t < T$ as

$$p(t) = \frac{2}{\gamma_1}\sum_{j=0}^{T-t}\phi^j h(t + j) + \frac{2}{\gamma_1}\sum_{j=T-t+1}^{\infty}\phi^j h(t + j) \tag{5.38}$$

Table 5.2 BEHAVIOR OF THE SYSTEM BEFORE AND AFTER T

$$1 < t < T$$

$$h(t) = \mu h(t - 1) \qquad (t > 2) \tag{5.34}$$

$$\mu = \frac{1 + \theta}{1 + n} \tag{5.35}$$

$$p(t) = \frac{2}{\gamma_1} \frac{1 - \phi\pi_1 + (\pi_1 - \mu_1)\phi^{T-t+1}\mu^{T-t}}{(1 - \phi\pi_1)(1 - \phi\mu)} h(t) \tag{5.39}$$

$$b(t) = \left(\frac{1 + R}{1 + n}\right)b(t - 1) + d(t) - s(t) \qquad (t > 2) \tag{5.41}$$

$$b(1) = \frac{\bar{B}(0)}{p(1)N(1)} + d(1) - \frac{H(1) - H(0)}{N(1)p(1)} \tag{5.42}$$

$$s(t) = \frac{\theta}{1 + \theta} \frac{\gamma_1}{2} \frac{(1 - \phi\mu)(1 - \phi\pi_1)}{(1 - \phi\pi_1 + (\pi_1 - \mu)\phi^{T-t+1}\mu^{T-t})} \qquad (t \geq 2) \tag{5.40}$$

$$\xi = \left(\frac{R - n}{1 + n}\right)b(T) + d \qquad \phi = \frac{\gamma_2}{\gamma_1} \qquad \mu = \frac{1 + \theta}{1 + n}$$

$$h(t) \equiv \frac{H(t)}{N(t)} \qquad N(t) = (1 + n)N(t - 1)$$

$$\pi_1 = \frac{1}{2}\left\{\frac{\gamma_1}{\gamma_2} + \frac{1}{1 + n} - \frac{2\xi}{\gamma_2} - \right.$$
$$\left. \left[\left(\frac{\gamma_1}{\gamma_2} + \frac{1}{1 + n} - \frac{2\xi}{\gamma_2}\right)^2 - \frac{4\gamma_1}{\gamma_2(1 + n)}\right]^{1/2}\right\} \tag{5.22}$$

Substituting equations 5.34 and 5.35 into 5.38 and using some algebra implies

$$p(t) = \frac{2}{\gamma_1} \frac{1 - \phi\pi_1 + (\pi_1 - \mu)\phi^{T-t+1}\mu^{T-t}}{(1 - \phi\pi_1)(1 - \phi\mu)} h(t) \qquad t < T \tag{5.39}$$

Next, we define $s(t)$ as per capita seignorage,

$$s(t) \equiv \frac{H(t) - H(t - 1)}{p(t)N(t)}$$

$t > T$

$$h(t + 1) = \pi_1 h(t) \tag{5.31}$$

$$p(t) = \frac{2}{\gamma_1}\left[1 - \frac{\gamma_2}{\gamma_2}\pi_1\right]^{-1} h(t) \tag{5.30}$$

$$b(t) = b(T)$$

$$s(t) = \frac{\gamma_1}{2}\left[1 - \frac{1}{\pi_1(1 + n)}\right]\left(1 - \frac{\gamma_2}{\gamma_1}\pi_1\right)$$

$$d(t) = d$$

For $t < T$, we have that

$$s(t) = \frac{1}{p(t)} \frac{\theta}{1 + n} h(t - 1)$$

or

$$s(t) = \left(\frac{\theta}{1 + \theta}\right)\frac{h(t)}{p(t)}$$

Using equation 5.34 in the above equation gives

$$s(t) = \frac{\theta}{1 + \theta} \frac{\gamma_1}{2} \frac{(1 - \phi\mu)(1 - \phi\pi_1)}{1 - \phi\pi_1 + (\pi_1 - \mu)\phi^{T-t+1}\mu^{T-t}} \qquad t > 2 \tag{5.40}$$

Using (1), the definition of $s(t)$ and the definition $d(t) = D(t)/N(t)$, we have the law of motion for per capita real interest bearing government debt

$$b(t) = \left(\frac{1 + R}{1 + n}\right)b(t - 1) + d(t) - s(t) \qquad t > 2 \tag{5.41}$$

Finally, we repeat equation 5.7, the special version of equation 5.41 for $t = 1$,

$$b(1) = \frac{\bar{B}(0)}{p(1)} + d(1) - \frac{H(1) - H(0)}{N(1)p(1)} \tag{5.42}$$

where $\bar{B}(0)$ is the nominal par value of the one-period interest-bearing debt that was issued at time $t = 0$.

We have collected the equations describing the equilibrium before and after T in Table 5.2. Starting at $t = 1$, the system works as follows. We take

Table 5.3

Date	Price level		Inflation rate	
	$\theta = 0.106$	$\theta = 0.120$	$\theta = 0.106$	$\theta = 0.120$
1	1.13699	1.12300	1.08415	1.08240
2	1.23267	1.21553	1.08413	1.08070
3	1.33637	1.31362	1.08411	1.07878
4	1.44878	1.41710	1.08409	1.07662
5	1.57061	1.52568	1.08407	1.07416
6	1.70264	1.63883	1.08404	1.07136
7	1.84573	1.75578	1.08401	1.06816
8	2.00079	1.87546	1.08398	1.06447
9	2.16881	1.99637	1.08394	1.06020
$t \geq 10$	$p(10)\pi(10)^{t-10}$		1.08390	1.05521

as exogenous a time path of the per capita deficit net of interest payments, $\{d(t), t > 1\}$, with $d(t) = d$, $t > T$. We further take as exogenous $\bar{B}(0)$ and $H(0)$, which give the nominal par value of government debt inherited from the past. The date T is also taken as exogenous. The monetary authority chooses settings for $H(1)$ and θ. Then equations 5.34, 5.36, and 5.39 to 5.42 simultaneously determine $p(t)$, $b(t)$, $t = 1, \ldots, T$, while equation 5.30 determines $p(t)$ for $t > T$.

The equations of the model are linear in the endogenous variables, given a value for π_1. However, from equation 5.22 and the fact that $\xi = [(R - n)/(1 + n)] b(T) + d$, we see that π_1 is itself a function of $b(T)$, which in turn depends on the value of π_1 through its effect on the behavior of $p(t)$ and $s(t)$ for $1 < t < T$, via equation 5.39. Thus, determining the equilibrium of the system involves solving a nonlinear system of equations.

While the system can be solved in a variety of ways, we have found it convenient to use the following procedure based on backward recursions. We begin by taking θ as given, but *not* $H(1)$. We *choose* a value for $b(T)$ and solve equation 5.22 for π_1. Then we recursively solve equations 5.40 and 5.41 backward for values of $\{b(t), s(t + 1); t = T - 1, T - 2, \ldots, 1\}$. Also, from equation 5.39 we can determine per capita real balances $h(t)/p(t)$ for $t = 1, \ldots, T$. Finally, given the values of $b(1)$ and $h(1)/p(1)$ thus determined, we solve equation 5.42 for the value of $H(1)$ [or equivalently of $p(1)$]. This procedure produces a choice of $H(1)$ and θ, and associated sequences for $b(t)$, $p(t)$, $h(t)$, and $s(t)$ that solve the system.

By employing iterations on this procedure, it is possible to solve the model taking $b(1)$ as given. The method is simply to search over solutions of

Per capita bond holdings		Per capita real balances	
θ = 0.106	θ = 0.120	θ = 0.106	θ = 0.120
0.08109	0.08109	0.14481	0.14701
0.11959	0.11750	0.14483	0.14913
0.15923	0.15472	0.14486	0.15152
0.20002	0.19274	0.14489	0.15423
0.24202	0.23156	0.14492	0.15730
0.28524	0.27114	0.14495	0.16079
0.32974	0.31146	0.14499	0.16480
0.37554	0.35247	0.14503	0.16941
0.42268	0.39411	0.14507	0.17475
0.47120	0.43631	0.14512	0.18099

the type described in the previous paragraph, varying $b(T)$ until the specified initial value of $b(1)$ is found. In this way, a set of equilibria with different θ's can be calculated, each one of which starts from the same value of $b(1)$. In a similar fashion, it is possible to generate equilibria with different θ's, each one of which starts from the same value of $H(1)$ [of course $b(1)$ will then differ across the different θ's]. This last procedure was the one used to generate the examples in the text, each of which started with $H(1) = 164.65$.

We now describe the results of using this solution procedure to compute equilibria of economies with identical values of the parameters $\{\gamma_1, \gamma_2, N(0), d(t), \bar{B}(0), H(0), T, b(1)\}$ but different values of θ. Since their values of θ are different, the values of the endogenous variables $\{p(t), t \geq 1\}$ and $\{b(t), t \geq 2\}$ will in general be different.

Table 5.3 compares two economies, each with $\{\gamma_1 = 3, \gamma_2 = 2.5, N(0) = 1000, n = 0.02, d(t) = 0.05, 1 \leq t \leq T; d(t) = d = 0, t > T; \bar{B}(0) = 100, H(0) = 100, T = 10, b(1) = 0.08109, R = 0.05\}$. The tight-money economy has $\theta = 0.106$, while the loose-money economy has $\theta = 0.120$. As can be seen from Table 5.3, the $\theta = 0.120$ economy has a uniformly higher price level and inflation rate for all $t \geq 1$ than does the $\theta = 0.106$ economy. We note that as expected, the $\theta = 0.120$ economy is associated with a slower rate of bond creation from $t = 1$ to $t = 10$ and that therefore the looser-money $\theta = 0.120$ economy ends up permitting slower growth in base money T than does the alternative economy with tighter money initially. Thus, tighter money now eventually implies looser money later, as in the economy described in the monetarist model. In the present example, however, the effect of expected future rates of money creation on the current

Table 5.4

Date	Price level		Inflation rate	
	$\theta = 0.010$	$\theta = 0.030$	$\theta = 0.010$	$\theta = 0.030$
1	0.57675	0.59590	1.00431	1.01916
2	0.57924	0.60732	1.00893	1.02205
3	0.58441	0.62071	1.01495	1.02578
4	0.59315	0.63671	1.02272	1.03057
5	0.60662	0.65617	1.03259	1.03666
6	0.62640	0.68023	1.04494	1.04435
7	0.65455	0.71040	1.06005	1.05391
8	0.69386	0.74870	1.07806	1.06561
9	0.74802	0.79782	1.09887	1.07962
$t \geq 10$	$p(10)\pi(10)^{t-10}$		1.12205	1.09603

rate of inflation is sufficiently strong that the economy with tighter money initially is the one with higher inflation both *now* and in the future. This happens because, via equation 5.33, the higher eventual rate of money creation associated with the lower path more than offsets the downward effects on the initial inflation rates that are directly associated with the lower initial rate of money creation. Like the closely related example in the text, this comparison provides a spectacular example in which tighter money now fails to buy even a temporarily lower inflation than does looser money now.

Table 5.4 compares different θ's in an economy that provides an example intermediate between the economy of the monetarist model and the "spectacular" examples. Both economies of Table 5.4 have the parameters $\{\gamma_1 = 2, \gamma_2 = 1.5, N(0) = 1000, n = 0.02; d(t) = 0.05, 1 \leq t \leq T; d(t) = d = 0, t > T; \bar{B}(0) = 100, H(0) = 100, T = 10, b(1) = 1.4999, R = 0.05\}$. The tight-money economy has $\theta = 0.01$, while the loose-money economy has $\theta = 0.03$. The tight-money economy experiences a lower inflation rate for $1 \leq t \leq 5$ but a higher rate for $t \geq 5$. [Here the gross inflation rate at t is defined as the "right-hand" rate $p(t + 1)/p(t)$.] In this case the effect of the higher eventual rate of money creation that is associated with the initially tighter $\theta = 0.01$ economy causes inflation to be higher even before T when money actually becomes looser. But this effect is not strong enough to eliminate completely the temporary benefits of tight money on the current inflation. Notice, however, that as compared to the monetarist example, the effect of the initial tight money on the initial inflation rate is considerably weakened. For with all other parameters the same but $\gamma_2 = 0$ (the monetarist

Per capita bond holdings		Per capita real balances	
$\theta = 0.010$	$\theta = 0.030$	$\theta = 0.010$	$\theta = 0.030$
0.15000	0.15000	0.24678	0.23563
0.20200	0.19761	0.24330	0.23347
0.25558	0.24670	0.23879	0.23067
0.31079	0.29734	0.23296	0.22487
0.36770	0.34961	0.22556	0.22250
0.42637	0.40358	0.21629	0.21674
0.48688	0.45935	0.20295	0.20957
0.54930	0.51701	0.19145	0.20080
0.61372	0.57667	0.17585	0.19028
0.68020	0.63845	0.15846	0.17798

case), we would have had $p(t + 1)/p(t) = (1 + \theta)/(1 + n) = 0.9902$ for $1 \leq t \leq T$.

In the following appendix, Danny Quah establishes conditions on the parameters of the model that are sufficient to deliver the spectacular example of the Table 5.2 variety with $b(1)$ fixed across the economies.

APPENDIX 3 by Danny Quah

This appendix establishes sufficient conditions for the case where tighter monetary policy (lower θ) leads to uniformly higher price level and inflation for all $t \geq 1$. The method is by construction: A pair of inequalities will be reduced to a single relation by the correct choice of certain parameter values. We satisfy the inequalities by making the implicit discount rate $(1 - \gamma_2/\gamma_1)$ sufficiently low, while maintaining convergence of the relevant infinite sum.

Let $\theta_h > \theta_l$. Then we want[7]

$$\text{(a)} \quad p_t(\theta_l) > p_t(\theta_h)$$

$$\text{(b)} \quad \frac{p_{t+1}(\theta_l)}{p_t(\theta_l)} > \frac{p_{t+1}(\theta_h)}{p_t(\theta_h)}$$

for all t. By equations 5.30 and 5.31 in Table 5.1, for $t \geq T$, $p_{t+1}(\theta)/p_t(\theta) = \pi_1(\theta)$. For policy experiments that fix $b(1)$, it is clear that (over the relevant range) a lower θ leads to a higher $b(T)$ and hence to a higher ξ. This is exactly the statement that a tighter monetary policy now implies a higher deficit to be financed by seigniorage from time $T + 1$. From Figure 5.2 an increase in ξ increases the value of the root π_1. Therefore, $\pi_1(\theta_l) > \pi_1(\theta_h)$. Hence (b) is satisfied for $t \geq T$. Condition (a) follows, at most, T' periods after T (where T' is finite) given (b) for $t \geq T$.

Hence we restrict attention to $t < T$. It is clear that if (b) holds for $t < T$, $p_1(\theta_l) > p_1(\theta_h)$ implies (a) for $t < T$ and therefore for all t. From Equation 5.7

$$p_1(\theta) = \frac{[\bar{B}(0) + H(0)]/N(1)}{b(1) - d(1) + H_1(\theta)/N(1)p_1(\theta)}$$

But by equation 5.39

$$\frac{H_1(\theta)}{N(1)p_1(\theta)} = \frac{h_1(\theta)}{p_1(\theta)} = \frac{\gamma_1}{2} \frac{[1 - \phi\pi_1(\theta)][1 - \phi\mu(\theta)]}{1 - \phi\pi_1(\theta) + [\pi_1(\theta) - \mu(\theta)]\phi^T\mu(\theta)^{T-1}}$$

Calling this $m_1(\theta)$, $p_1(\theta) = k_1/[k_2 + m_1(\theta)]$ where $k_1 > 0$, $k_2 + m_1(\theta) > 0$. Then $p_1(\theta_l) > p_1(\theta_h) > p_1(\theta_h)$ if and only if $m_1(\theta_h) > m_1(\theta_l)$.

Define the function $\Gamma(\phi, \theta, t) = 1 - \phi\pi_1(\theta) + [\pi_1(\theta) - \mu(\theta)]\phi^{T-t+1}\mu(\theta)^{T-t}$. Then using equations 5.34, 5.36, and 5.39 to write out explicitly $p_{t+1}(\theta)/p_t(\theta)$ and the above characterization of the price level condition, (a) and (b) for $t < T$ are equivalent to

$$\text{(a')} \quad \frac{[1 - \phi\pi_1(\theta_h)][1 - \phi\mu(\theta_h)]}{\Gamma(\phi, \theta_h, 1)} > \frac{[1 - \phi\pi_1(\theta_l)][1 - \phi\mu(\theta_l)]}{\Gamma(\phi, \theta_l, 1)}$$

$$\text{(b')} \quad (1 + \theta_l)\frac{\Gamma(\phi, \theta_l, t + 1)}{\Gamma(\phi, \theta_l, t)} > (1 + \theta_h)\frac{\Gamma(\phi, \theta_h, t + 1)}{\Gamma(\phi, \theta_h, t)} \quad \text{for } t < T$$

We need to choose $\phi = \gamma_2/\gamma_1$, θ_l, θ_h that satisfy (a') and (b') and support positive values for nominal balances, prices and bond holdings, and real values for π_1 and π_2.

Recall that given $b(1)$, $b(T)$ can be found if π_1 is known. But π_1 is a function of $b(T)$. The only case where π_1 is determined independently of $b(T)$ is $\pi_1 = \pi_2 = [\phi(1 + n)]^{-1/2}$, as is easily seen by comparing equations 5.27 and 5.28. This occurs at the maximum value of ξ that yields real roots for the characteristic polynomial in equation 5.28. Using this, we pick a θ_l to simplify (a') and (b'). Conditions on parameter values that satisfy (a') and (b') will then become transparent.

Let θ_l solve $\mu(\theta_l) = \pi_1(\theta_l) = [\phi(1 + n)]^{-1/2}$. Since $\mu(\theta_l) = (1 + \theta_l)/(1 + n)$, this gives $\theta_l = (1 + n)^{1/2}\phi^{-1/2}$. Choosing $\pi_1 = \pi_2 = [\phi(1 + n)]^{-1/2}$ implies a value for ξ [and hence for $b(T)$] by comparing equations 5.27

and 5.28. Then fixing θ_l determines $b(1)$ by recursively solving equations 5.40 and 5.41 backward. This value of $b(1)$ is kept constant across policy experiments (different θ settings).

Choosing $\mu(\theta_l) = \pi_1(\theta_l)$ simplifies (a') and (b') to

$$\text{(a'')} \quad \frac{[1 - \phi\pi_1(\theta_h)][1 - \phi\mu(\theta_h)]}{\Gamma(\phi, \theta_h, 1)} > 1 - \phi\mu(\theta_l)$$

$$\text{(b'')} \quad (1 + \theta_l) > (1 + \theta_h)\frac{\Gamma(\phi, \theta_h, t + 1)}{\Gamma(\phi, \theta_h, t)} \qquad t \le T - 1$$

It will be shown below that we want to set $\phi \cong \pi_1(\theta_h)$. Then

$$\frac{\Gamma(\phi, \theta_h, t + 1)}{\Gamma(\phi, \theta_h, t)} \cong [\phi\mu(\theta_h)]^{-1}$$

so that the right-hand side of (b'') is approximately t independent. Therefore, consider (b'') for $t = 1$, and rewrite (a'').

$$\text{(a''')} \quad [1 - \phi\mu(\theta_l)]^{-1} > \frac{\Gamma(\phi, \theta_h, 1)}{[1 - \phi\pi_1(\theta_h)][1 - \phi\mu(\theta_h)]}$$

$$\text{(b''')} \quad (1 + \theta_l) > (1 + \theta_h)\frac{\Gamma(\phi, \theta_h, 2)}{\Gamma(\phi, \theta_h, 1)}$$

Maintain $(1 - \phi\mu(\theta_h)$ and $1 - \phi\pi_1(\theta_h)$ positive; multiply the left- and right-hand sides of (a''') and (b''') to get, after some manipulation,[8]

$$\text{(c)} \quad \left(\frac{1 + \theta_l}{1 + \theta_h}\frac{1 - \phi\mu(\theta_h)}{1 - \phi\mu(\theta_l)}\right) > \frac{\Gamma(\phi, \theta_h, 2)}{1 - \phi\pi_1(\theta_h)}$$

The left-hand side of (c) is the product of two terms, each of which is easily seen to be slightly less than unity for small $\theta_h - \theta_l > 0$. Therefore, the left-hand side of (c) is $1 - \epsilon$ for small $\epsilon > 0$.

Write the right-hand side as

$$1 + \frac{[\pi_1(\theta_h) - \mu(\theta_h)]\phi^{T-t+1}\mu(\theta_h)^{T-t}}{1 - \phi\pi_1(\theta_h)} = 1 + \delta$$

By the choice of θ_l, $\pi_1(\theta_l) = \mu(\theta_l)$. Therefore, $\theta_h > \theta_l$ implies $\pi_1(\theta_h) < \mu(\theta_h)$. Hence $\delta < 0$ and can be made arbitrarily large in magnitude when ϕ approaches arbitrarily close to $\pi_1(\theta_h)^{-1}$ from below. This will satisfy condition (c).

The condition for real and positive π_1 given $b(T)$ (for $d = 0$) is $b(T) \le \gamma_2/_2(1 + n)/(R - n)\{1/\phi + 1/(1 + n) - 2[\phi(1 + n)]^{-1}\}$. Values for $b(T)$ that are "too low" will imply negative b_1. To guarantee strictly positive $b(1)$, set $b(T)$ as high as desired by increasing both γ_2 and γ_1, keeping $\phi = \gamma_2/\gamma_1$ at the chosen value.

In recapitulation, the method involves carrying out the steps above in reverse order. Choose γ_2/γ_1 sufficiently close to 1; set γ_2 so that maximum $b(T)$ appears "high enough." Calculate θ_l and work backward from $b(T)$ to $b(1)$. Then, using this value of $b(1)$, set θ_h so that $\theta_h - \theta_l$ is small and positive.

NOTES

1. The messages of this chapter are very similar to those of Preston Miller [11] and Robert E. Lucas, Jr. [7, 8]. The papers of Bryant and Wallace [2], McCallum [9, 10] and Scarth [14] are also related to this chapter. McCallum and Scarth analyze some of the implications of an explosive difference equation in bond holdings like ours, while Bryant and Wallace discuss debt management as an optimal seigniorage problem.
2. In Appendix 1 we analyze a simple general equilibrium model that can be used to rationalize the demand relationships posited below in the text. The model of the appendix has the virtue that since individual agents are identified, policies can be compared in terms of the welfare of the individuals in the model.
3. The government collects income taxes on the interest payments on government debt, so that the after-tax real yield on short-term government debt might be negative in the United States today. However, the pretax yield is what belongs in equation 5.2, so long as private securities and government securities are taxed at a common rate. The reason is that any change in $B(t - 1)$ is offset by an equal change of $K(t - 1)$ in the opposite direction, where $K(t - 1)$ is private investment measured in time $t - 1$ goods. Therefore, the taxes collected by taxing interest on government bonds only just replace the taxes lost because of the private investment that is crowded out by a larger $B(t - 1)$. Thus, define $g(t)$ as government purchases minus all taxes except taxes on private and government securities, and let τ be the marginal tax rate. Then we have $D(t) = g(t) - \tau(1 + R)K(t - 1) - \tau(1 + R)B(t - 1)$, and equation 5.1 becomes

$$g(t) - \tau(1 + R)K(t - 1)$$
$$= \frac{H(t) - 1 + (t - 1)}{p(t)} + B(t) - B(t - 1)(1 + R)(1 - \tau) \quad (5.1')$$

which is the form of equation 5.1 in which the after-tax yield appears. We are assuming that complete crowding out occurs, which can be expressed as a constant level of total investment, $B(t - 1) + K(t - 1) = \bar{B}$. Substituting this equation into equation 5.1' gives

$$g(t) - (1 + R)\overline{B} = \frac{H(t) - H(t - 1)}{p(t)} + B(t) - B(t - 1)(1 + R)$$

This is equivalent with equation 5.1 in the text.

4. Note that equation 5.5 is a special case of equation 5.10 with $h = \gamma_1/2$, $\gamma_2 = 0$. See Appendix 1 for an underlying model that implies equation 5.10 and all of our other assumptions.

5. See Appendix 3 for a discussion of how to find parameter values that imply this "paradoxical" price level behavior.

6. By pursuing the CBT example and other examples comparing welfare of agents across stationary states, the model can be used to support Milton Friedman's 1948 prescription that the entire government deficit be financed by creating base money.

7. Where necessary, the time index is indicated by a subscript. This departs from the practice in the text but should cause no confusion.

8. This procedure almost always obtains the desired example. I say "almost" because strictly speaking (a''') and (b''') imply (c) but not conversely.

REFERENCES

1. Bresciani-Turroni, Constantino. 1937. *The Economics of Inflation*. London: Allen and Unwin.

2. Bryant, John, and Neil Wallace. 1980. A suggestion for further simplifying the theory of money. Staff Report no. 62, Federal Reserve Bank of Minneapolis.

3. Cagan, Phillip. 1956. The monetary dynamics of hyperinflation. In Milton Friedman, ed., *Studies in the Quantity Theory of Money*. Chicago: University of Chicago Press.

4. Friedman, Milton. 1948. A monetary and fiscal framework for economic stability. *American Economic Review* 38 (June):245–64.

5. ———. 1960. *A Program for Monetary Stability*. New York: Fordham University Press.

6. ———. 1968. The role of monetary policy. *American Economic Review* 58 (March):1–17.

7. Lucas, Robert E., Jr. 1981. Deficit finance and inflation. *New York Times,* Wednesday, August 26.

8. ———. 1981. Inconsistency in fiscal aims. *New York Times,* Friday, August 28.

9. McCallum, Bennett T. 1978. On macroeconomic instability from a monetarist policy rule. *Economics Letters* 1:121–4.

10. ———. 1981. Monetarist principles and the money stock growth rule. *American Economic Review* 71 (May):134–38.

11. Miller, Preston. 1981. Fiscal policy in a monetarist model. Staff Report no. 67, Federal Reserve Bank of Minneapolis.

12. Samuelson, Paul. 1958. An exact consumption-loan model of interest with or without the social contrivance of money. *Journal of Political Economy* 66 (December):467–82.

13. Sargent, Thomas J., and Neil Wallace. 1973. The stability of models of money and growth with perfect foresight. *Econometrica* 41 (November):1043–48.

14. Scarth, William M. 1980. Rational expectations and the instability of bond-financing. *Economic Letters* 6:321–27.

15. Wallace, Neil. 1980. The overlapping generations model of fiat money. In John Kareken and Neil Wallace, eds., *Models of Monetary Economies*. Federal Reserve Bank of Minneapolis.

chapter 6

Speculations about the Speculation against the Hong Kong Dollar

Written with David T. Beers and Neil Wallace

In this chapter, we attempt to explain the Hong Kong dollar's recent substantial depreciation, or its loss in value in terms of foreign exchange. This task is a challenge mainly because of the unusual monetary policy recently espoused by the government of Hong Kong. From 1974 until October 1983, the officially professed policy allowed both the quantity and the exchange value of Hong Kong currency to be determined by market forces (or to *float*). The subject is also interesting because current events in Hong Kong are so much affected by expectations, expectations about what will happen after 1997, the year that Britain's lease on most of the colony's territory expires.

The recent depreciation was indeed substantial. Between mid-1980 and October 1983, when the government announced a new policy, the U.S. dollar value of the Hong Kong dollar fell about 33 percent. During that period, there also occurred substantial declines (even in terms of local currency) in all the value of assets located in Hong Kong—Hong Kong real estate and common stock in Hong Kong companies. All of these declines coincided with a generally unfavorable reassessment of the prospects for maintaining the political status quo beyond 1997.

The unfavorable reassessment easily accounts for a decline in real estate and stock market values. Prospective events after 1997 can reasonably be expected to reduce the stream of returns flowing to the owners of real estate and shares in Hong Kong so that their value now would fall. The fall in the Hong Kong dollar has also been widely attributed to unfavorable speculation about 1997, apparently on the basis of a vague notion that the Hong Kong dollar is somehow a claim against the wealth of the current residents of Hong Kong. Closer scrutiny shows that movements in the value of the Hong Kong dollar are not directly linked with speculation about 1997. This is because the events of 1997 do not adversely affect interest-bearing foreign assets held as backing for the currency by the Hong Kong government. Thus, distinct lines of reasoning seem to be needed to account for the fall of Hong Kong real estate and stock prices, on the one hand, and the fall of the foreign exchange value of the Hong Kong dollar, on the other.

We explain the depreciation of the Hong Kong dollar as the result of a chain of influences involving the Hong Kong government and speculation about the events of 1997. The existence of this chain of influences is supported by indirect evidence that the Hong Kong government actually departed from its pre-October 1983 official float policy. In particular, we interpret the depreciation of the Hong Kong dollar as having been welcomed and supported by the government in order to help private financial intermediaries in Hong Kong face the substantial declines in the real value of Hong Kong real estate and other real assets.

Our case for this interpretation rests heavily on how we think the Hong Kong monetary system would have functioned if the government had actually adhered to its float policy. We argue that under that policy market fundamentals alone could not have determined an equilibrium exchange rate for the Hong Kong dollar and, in particular, did not propel that rate downward. Our circumstantial evidence supporting the case that the government departed from its official policy in order to promote the depreciation of the Hong Kong dollar is supported by an analysis of who stood to gain and who stood to lose from such a depreciation.[1]

Table 6.1   THE EXCHANGE FUND'S BALANCE SHEET

Branch	Assets	Liabilities
Monetary	Foreign exchange	Certificates of indebtedness
	Hong Kong bank deposits denominated in Hong Kong dollars	Debt certificates
Fiscal	Foreign exchange	Net worth
	Hong Kong bank deposits denominated in Hong Kong dollars	
	Debt certificates	

A LOOK AT HONG KONG'S MONETARY SYSTEM

Monetary and fiscal affairs in Hong Kong are now managed by a single institution, known as the *Exchange Fund*. (Though originally just Hong Kong's monetary institution, it took on most of the treasury's functions in 1977.)

The types of items on the Exchange Fund's balance sheet, divided into parts attributable to the monetary branch and the fiscal branch, are shown in Table 6.1. The certificates of indebtedness are non-interest-bearing instruments held by private banks as backing for currency. The debt certificates are an internal bookkeeping device between the monetary and fiscal branches of the Exchange Fund, which completely net out in the consolidated balance sheet. They seem to be a device for crediting the revenues accumulated from currency issue (the *seigniorage*) to the fiscal branch.

The Exchange Fund issues all of Hong Kong's coins, but two large private banks issue most of the paper currency, known as the *Hong Kong dollar* (HK$). These banks are the Hongkong and Shanghai Bank, which issues from 80 to 90 percent of the paper currency, and the Chartered Bank, which issues most of the rest.

These private banks issue the currency entirely at their own discretion, but they do not profit greatly from this privilege. Since the banks' names appear prominently on the notes, they get some prestige and free advertising from the privilege. However, as already noted, the government collects all of the seigniorage. It does this by requiring the banks to hold, behind all currency issues, 100 percent reserves of the non-interest-bearing certificates of indebtedness mentioned above as liabilities of the Exchange Fund.[2] The banks must buy these certificates of indebtedness from the Exchange Fund, which holds as assets behind these certificates a portfolio of interest-bearing assets denominated in foreign currencies and interest-bearing deposits in accounts in Hong Kong banks. These assets can thus be thought of as ultimately backing the Hong Kong dollar. The regulation governing certificates of indebtedness states that they are redeemable at the option of the financial secretary.

The asset effects of currency issues on the Exchange Fund and the banks are illustrated in Table 6.2.

Although only two banks issue notes, there is relatively free entry into other aspects of banking in Hong Kong. Furthermore, there are no reserve requirements against deposits and no government-supplied deposit insurance. There is a cartel, the Hong Kong Association of Banks, which sets interest rates.

The Official Float Policy

The system just described contains vestiges of Hong Kong's pre-1972 system, which was a British Currency Board System. In that system, the Exchange Fund pegged the Hong Kong dollar to the British pound. Behind certificates of indebtedness the Exchange Fund held 100 percent reserves in interest-bearing British pound instruments. After 1972, for about two years, the Hong Kong dollar was pegged to the U.S. dollar. Thereafter (until October 1983) it was allowed to float. During the float period, the Exchange Fund held a portfolio of interest-bearing instruments denominated in a variety of foreign currencies and

Table 6.2   BALANCE SHEET EFFECTS OF ISSUING HK$ 100

	Assets		Liabilities	
Exchange Fund	Foreign exchange	85	Certificates of indebtedness	100
	Hong Kong bank deposits denominated in Hong Kong dollars	15		
Private Hong Kong banks	Certificates of indebtedness	100	Hong Kong dollar notes	100

of interest-bearing deposits in Hong Kong banks. According to the official policy, the Exchange Fund passively supplied any amount of certificates of indebtedness that the private banks requested in exchange for foreign currencies at market rates of exchange. In effect, then, the Exchange Fund was willing to buy and sell Hong Kong dollars for foreign currencies at market rates of exchange.

During the float period, the Exchange Fund mostly kept secret its portfolio composition and its strategy for shifting the composition of the portfolio between foreign currencies and domestic deposits. (The exception is that the amount held in British pound sterling was revealed.) However, the guiding principle of the Exchange Fund's open-market strategy seems to have been to hold all or most of its portfolio in foreign currencies.[3] When the Hong Kong dollar was experiencing temporary weakness, the Exchange Fund might move temporarily into deposits denominated in Hong Kong dollars. Such moves were exceptional and temporary, though. The Exchange Fund professed no intention and acknowledged no ability to influence the basic direction of exchange rates. According to government officials, the exchange rate was determined by fundamental market forces that the Exchange Fund should not, and could not, oppose for long.

AN INDETERMINATE EXCHANGE RATE?

We strongly suspect that the Hong Kong government did not actually follow its official float policy. A major reason for this suspicion is that if the policy had been followed, then the exchange rate for the Hong Kong dollar would have been indeterminate. By *indeterminate,* we mean that there would have been a wide range of values of foreign exchange rates for the Hong Kong dollar that would have cleared markets. This indeterminacy is a consequence of the lack of any anchor in a system in which both the exchange rate and the quantity of Hong Kong dollars float. It results under any theory of the demand for Hong Kong dollars. The indeterminacy is a product of the responses required of the Exchange Fund under the official policy.

To establish that result, let us first examine the options available to the Hong Kong government if it were to have pegged the exchange rate for its currency to one or several foreign currencies. A government doing that simply announces that it is willing to buy and sell unlimited amounts of its currency at the chosen exchange rate. Then it must be prepared to cope with a run on its currency, or an attempt by holders of the domestic currency to convert their holdings into foreign currency. The government need not be concerned about high demands for its own currency, since it can always provide more if

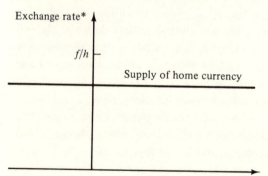

*Units of foreign currency per unit of home currency

Figure 6.1   The supply of Hong Kong currency under a fixed or floating rate policy.

needed. This asymmetry produces a range of values at which it is feasible to peg the exchange rate.

To simplify the exposition, suppose that there is only one foreign currency and that at some time a monetary authority has a balance sheet consisting of f units of foreign currency, which it possesses as assets, and h units of its own (home) currency outstanding, which are its liabilities. Starting in this situation, it is feasible for the authority to fix the exchange rate, the value of its own currency in terms of foreign currency, at any value between zero and the ratio f/h. That is because, with the exchange rate in this range, the foreign exchange value of its h units of home currency remains less than or equal to f [since $(h)(f/h) = f$]. In other words, with the rate in this range, no exchange that the authority could be called on to make would more than exhaust its holdings of foreign currency.[4] (Notice, by the way, that the net worth of the monetary authority [assets less liabilities] varies inversely with the exchange rate, being equal to f when the exchange rate is zero [$f - (h)(0) = f$] and being equal to zero when the exchange rate is f/h [$f - (h)(f/h) = 0$].)

Evidently, any such fixed-rate policy is effective in the sense that the market rate must be the fixed rate. Under the fixed-rate policy, the monetary authority would supply the market with any amount of home currency that is demanded at the fixed rate; in other words, at that rate, supply would be *perfectly elastic,* as shown in Figure 6.1. Regardless of the demand for home currency, then, the exchange rate would be the one announced.

Now consider matters under a strict version of Hong Kong's official float policy. Suppose again that the authority starts out holding f units of foreign currency with h units of home currency oustanding. The monetary authority's policy is now to buy and sell any amount of its currency at the exchange rate that the market determines. However, what rate would the market determine? Evidently, under this policy, it could be any rate between zero and f/h.

To establish that any such rate could be an equilibrium, we only need to verify that the home currency's supply and demand would be equal at that rate. Consider any particular rate in the interval $[0, f/h]$. Under the float policy, supply at that rate would look just like the perfectly elastic supply curve in Figure 6.1 because, according to the policy, the authority is willing to buy and sell unlimited amounts at the market rate. At the particular rate, then, regardless of the nature of the demand for home currency, demand would be satisfied. Therefore, the posited rate—any rate between zero and f/h—would be an equilibrium, or ruling, exchange rate under the official policy.

To demonstrate in this way that under Hong Kong's official float policy the exchange rate had to be indeterminate cannot be the end of things. For somehow the exchange rate was being determined. Therefore, our analysis is, at best, incomplete. In principle, our analysis could be regarded as defective either because we have mischaracterized how things are supposed to have worked under the official policy or else because the Exchange Fund actually pursued a policy different from the officially professed one. We favor the latter possibility.

We think that the Hong Kong dollar's exchange rate was determined throughout the float period by a series of discrete deviations from the official policy. In practice, the policy is likely to have more closely resembled a fixed-rate policy than a strict version of the official policy. In our view, the observed exchange rate was determined by signals given by the Exchange Fund, signals that in effect revealed the exchange rate at which the authority was willing to buy and sell Hong Kong dollars. This was feasible since the Exchange Fund was able to supply unlimited quantities of Hong Kong dollars and since it was continually engaging in transactions with the dealers who announced exchange rates.

A TIMELY DEPRECIATION

We have no direct evidence that the Exchange Fund ever actually deviated from its official float policy. Our evidence is circumstantial and consists partly of the fact that in practice the exchange rate was somehow tied down even though, under the official policy, it should not have been. Our view is also based on the fact that the recent depreciation in the Hong Kong dollar was quite timely for the Hong Kong government. It came, that is, just when the government would have welcomed it.

Seeing why that is so requires a look at who gains and who loses from the depreciation of this currency. Changes in the exchange rate of the Hong Kong dollar affect the distribution of wealth among issuers and holders of Hong Kong dollar–denominated liabilities. As mentioned above, since the Exchange Fund's portfolio consists primarily of assets denominated in foreign currency while its liabilities are in Hong Kong dollars, its net worth varies inversely with the exchange value of the Hong Kong dollar (the lower the exchange rate, the greater the government's net worth). Offsetting this, in terms of a consolidated balance sheet, everyone else has a net worth that varies directly with the exchange value of the Hong Kong dollar. However, the effects on any particular asset holder depend on the holder's portfolio composition, namely, on the extent to which the holder is unhedged (exposed to risk) with respect to the exchange rate and the direction in which the holder is unhedged. It is primarily in terms related to such effects that we will explain why the authority might have welcomed a depreciation of the Hong Kong dollar.

We will do this by examining the balance sheet of a hypothetical Hong Kong financial firm as it experiences what some real Hong Kong firms may actually have experienced: first a substantial decline in real asset prices and then that decline joined by a substantial decline in the value of the Hong Kong dollar. Our financial firm has some assets in the form of loans, denominated in Hong Kong dollars, that have as collateral real Hong Kong assets and some liabilities, denominated in Hong Kong dollars, in the form of deposits. We will assume, as seems plausible, that the value of the real assets in terms of foreign currency is determined in a world capital market. That is, their value measured in terms of foreign currencies does not depend on the exchange value of the Hong Kong dollar.

Our hypothetical financial institution begins with the balance sheet in the first column of Table 6.3. We measure all entries in foreign currency so that entries denominated in Hong Kong dollars will vary with the exchange rate but those denominated in foreign currency will not. Note that this institution has initial net worth equal to 10 percent of total assets and that it is unhedged with respect to the exchange rate in only a minor way. That is, an exchange rate depreciation would lower net worth in an amount proportional to the initial net worth denominated in Hong Kong dollars, namely, 10 percent of x.

Table 6.3 **HOW AN EXCHANGE RATE DEPRECIATION CAN HELP A FINANCIAL FIRM**
Balance Sheet Items Measured in Units of Foreign Currency

	Initially	After 50% decline in HK asset values	After asset value decline and 33⅓% depreciation
Assets			
Loans backed by HK assets denominated in HK\$	x	$(\frac{1}{2})(\frac{4}{3})x$	$(\frac{1}{2})(\frac{4}{3})x$
Foreign assets denominated in foreign currency	y	y	y
Total	$x + y$	$(\frac{2}{3})x + y$	$(\frac{2}{3})x + y$
Liabilities			
Deposits denominated in HK\$	$(\frac{9}{10})x$	$(\frac{9}{10})x$	$(\frac{2}{3})(\frac{9}{10})x$
Other liabilities denominated in foreign currency	$(\frac{9}{10})y$	$(\frac{9}{10})y$	$(\frac{9}{10})y$
Total	$(\frac{9}{10})(x + y)$	$(\frac{9}{10})(x + y)$	$(\frac{9}{10})[(\frac{2}{3})x + y]$
Net Worth			
Assets less liabilities	$(\frac{1}{10})(x + y)$ $=$ $(\frac{1}{10})x + (\frac{1}{10})y$	$[(\frac{2}{3}) - (\frac{9}{10})]x +$ $(\frac{1}{10})y =$ $(-\frac{7}{30})x + (\frac{1}{10})y$	$(\frac{1}{10})[(\frac{2}{3})x + y] =$ $(\frac{1}{15})x + (\frac{1}{10})y$

We now describe the effect on net worth of a substantial decline in the value, in terms of foreign currency, of the assets that serve as collateral for the loans denominated in Hong Kong dollars. We will assume for the sake of argument a 50 percent decline in the value of these assets, measured in terms of foreign currency, and we will assume that initially the value of the assets was equal to ⅘ of the loans.

(Put another way, the loans were equal to 75 percent of the value of the collateral.) In describing the firm's portfolio after the decline, we take the value of such loans to be the value of the collateral if the collateral is worth less than the initial value of the loans.

If the value of the collateral assets falls 50 percent and the exchange rate does not change, then these assumptions imply that loans backed by Hong Kong dollars are defaulted on and the firm's balance sheet changes to that in the second column of Table 6.3. A comparison of this column and the first shows that because of the asset price decline, net worth declines. In fact, it becomes negative, implying bankruptcy, if x is sufficiently larger than y.

If the value of the Hong Kong dollar falls at the same time as asset prices, however, the result is not as bad for the financial firm. Suppose that, along with the 50 percent decline in the value of real Hong Kong assets in terms of foreign currency, there occurs a decline of ⅓ in the exchange value of the Hong Kong dollar. (It takes 1½ times as many Hong Kong dollars to buy one unit of foreign currency as originally.) Then, per Hong Kong dollar of loans originally granted, there is collateral worth (⁴⁄₃)(½)(³⁄₂), or one Hong Kong dollar. Thus, there need be no default on the loans. As the new balance sheet, the last column of Table 6.3, indicates, the firm's net worth still declines somewhat from its initial value, but not as much as with just a decline in real asset values. When a depreciation accompanies the asset price decline, therefore, the firm can stay in business.

Individual depositors of the financial firm, of course, would not prefer this situation to the last, for a depreciation reduces the value of their deposits. At the same time, the value of assets in terms of foreign currency is the same whether or not a depreciation occurs. This is true in general. The extent of a depreciation of the Hong Kong dollar determines how the value of total assets is divided among categories of liabilities: the greater the depreciation of the Hong Kong dollar, the smaller the share that goes to deposits denominated in Hong Kong dollars.

Over the last two years, many Hong Kong financial institutions seem to have been in positions like the one depicted here. If they were, then the Exchange Fund could easily have viewed a depreciation of the Hong Kong dollar as a way to avoid the major disruption to the economy that numerous financial firm bankruptcies would cause. A depreciation could smooth the Hong Kong economy's adjustment to lower real property values in terms of foreign currency. The adjustment would be smoother not because financial firms' capital losses would be averted, but because they would be allocated partly to depositors, thereby helping to preserve existing financial institutions.

HONG KONG'S OTHER OPTIONS

With the exchange rate indeterminate under the official float policy, it is not surprising that the Hong Kong government should have departed from that policy in practice and reverted to an unofficial policy of pegging the exchange rate. It did, however, have other alternatives.

One feasible alternative is to make its unofficial policy official: to adopt a fixed-rate policy in which the Exchange Fund acts as a warehouse for foreign exchange. Then, if government budgets are balanced or in surplus (in a present value sense), it could not only peg but gradually appreciate the Hong Kong dollar. Appreciation could be engineered as a way of paying out all or part of the interest that is earned on the foreign securities that the Exchange Fund holds as reserves. (Singapore evidently manages its currency this way.) Such a policy would be feasible regardless of the fate of the wealth of Hong Kong, as determined by news about 1997 or other factors, as long as the government balanced its budget so that the portfolio available to back the Hong Kong dollar remained intact.[5]

Another alternative that has been suggested is for the Hong Kong government to fix the quantity rather than the exchange rate of Hong Kong dollars and allow the exchange rate to float [1]. However, this proposal is not complete without specific rules governing the asset side of the monetary authority's balance sheet. Whether the proposal would work depends on whether the foreign exchange backing of the currency stock is to be eliminated or maintained.

In one version of this proposal, fixing the quantity of Hong Kong dollars is viewed as a substitute for maintaining backing. Advocates of a fiat money (or unbacked paper money) regime seem to have this view. They see the ability to dispense with backing as a one-time dividend for the monetary authority to spend. The size of this dividend is sometimes said to be a measure of the inefficiency of a backed system compared to a fiat system.

This sort of fiat system would probably not work in Hong Kong. For a fixed-quantity, no-backing regime to determine the exchange rate, there must be a stable demand function for unbacked Hong Kong dollars; in other words, a preference among Hong Kong residents for Hong Kong dollars over other currencies. However, it is questionable that such a preference could exist for a fiat currency issued by the government of an economy as open to trade and capital transactions as is Hong Kong's economy. Foreign currencies circulate in Hong Kong now, and international transactions are not restricted. This suggests that extreme currency substitution potentially prevails in Hong Kong. If it does, then the exchange rate would not be determinate under a regime of a fixed quantity of unbacked Hong Kong dollars [2].

The other version of the proposal to fix the quantity of Hong Kong dollars would work, but it does not appear to be optimal. In this version, while the quantity of dollars is fixed, its backing is maintained, thus preventing Hong Kong dollars from becoming worthless. However, then there is no reason to fix the quantity. Indeed, when backing of the currency is maintained, it is desirable to allow the demand for Hong Kong dollars to determine their quantity for the same reason that it is desirable to let demand determine the quantities of other kinds of intermediary liabilities [4].

EPILOGUE

On October 15, 1983, the government abandoned the official float policy and announced a policy of pegging the Hong Kong dollar at 7.80 Hong Kong dollars per U.S. dollar. Short-term interest rates denominated in Hong Kong dollars reacted by climbing sharply, to as high as 40 percent per annum for overnight money. Such high nominal rates can be interpreted as reflecting the market's expectation that the government would not long maintain the current peg and that it would soon devalue. This widespread public pessimism is likely due to a variety of political forces currently operating in Hong Kong that are likely to affect and restrict the government's actual choices in ways we have so far abstracted from.

We have analyzed the valuation of the Hong Kong currency by viewing the monetary affairs branch of the Exchange Fund as though it were managing a mutual fund.[6] Given an initial stock, f, of assets that are potentially available to redeem Hong Kong currency in terms of foreign exchange, the managers of the mutual fund face a variety of feasible payout policies. The policy that is adopted determines the net worth left to the managers of the fund. For example, among fixed exchange rate policies, the lower is the value of Hong Kong currency, the higher is the net worth.

The Exchange Fund is likely to be managed by the British government until 1997 and by the Chinese government thereafter. In this situation, the Chinese government cares about how the Exchange Fund is administered before 1997, for this will influence the net worth of the fund at the time that the Chinese take over. To see this, suppose, for example, that the British managers of the Exchange Fund were to peg the Hong Kong dollar at the upper bound of the feasible range we have delineated, namely, f/h. Suppose further that holders of Hong Kong dollars (the fund's shareholders) were uncertain about how the new Chinese managers of the fund would manage it. Inevitably, a run on Hong Kong dollars would occur before 1997, a run the Exchange Fund could meet by drawing down to zero the foreign exchange backing, f. Then, the Hong Kong dollar would simply disappear too as the Exchange Fund paid out the backing to the owners of Hong Kong dollars. A fixed-rate policy such as this, that values the Hong Kong dollar at (or near) the upper bound f/h, could easily be viewed as unfriendly by the current Chinese government. Concern by the current government of Hong Kong to avoid such unfriendly acts could thus constrain the way the Exchange Fund is now managed.

Additional doubts about the likely management of the Exchange Fund between now and 1997 stem from what threaten to be new and growing departures from Hong Kong's traditionally conservative fiscal policy. These departures are partly induced by the fall in value of land and other assets in Hong Kong, the sale and taxing of which the government depends on for revenues.

During the 1970s, the Hong Kong government had budget surpluses totaling 8.6 billion Hong Kong dollars (usually expressed *HK$ 8.6 billion*). Government investment was financed largely by current revenues and the proceeds of public land sales. As a result, even now Hong Kong's public sector has large net claims on the domestic banking system and on the rest of the world. However, recent declines in government revenues have outpaced attempts to curb public expenditures, with the result that, in 1982–1983 and 1983–1984, the Hong Kong government had budget deficits for the first time in nearly a decade. These deficits are estimated at HK$ 3.9 billion and HK$ 3.2 billion, respectively.

By themselves, two consecutive annual deficits of such magnitude do not threaten responsible management of the Exchange Fund, because the government has accumulated substantial fiscal reserves. At the start of the 1983–1984 financial year, fiscal reserves amounted to HK$ 18.7 billion, of which HK$ 11.5 billion constituted *free reserves,* that is, reserves left after HK$ 7.2 billion were allocated to cover possible losses on capital projects. Deficits of the current magnitude would not wipe out these free reserves for about three years.

However, continued deficits—and devaluations—may be seen as the only politically feasible ways for the British government to deal with the government's capital losses resulting from the 1997 change in management. The 1997 situation creates special problems with regard to the pricing of services of long-lived, publicly owned capital—like the roads, the subway system, and the public housing. After 1997, the public capital of Hong Kong is likely to belong to the government of China, so that the tail of the stream of taxes and tolls from long-lived capital currently in place or under construction may not be available as backing for debt of the current government. To deal with this situation, the current government could increase charges on existing projects so that the revenue stream collected through 1997 would be sufficient to balance the budget in a present value sense, and it could undertake only those new public investment projects that would pay for themselves by 1997. Such policies would be drastic and amount to managing the economy as though it were going to end in 1997, a stance that could be expected to be opposed both by some current residents of Hong Kong and by the government of China. Such drastic policies could to some extent be avoided by accepting deficits and devaluations.

Finally, one other event raises questions about the Hong Kong government's commitment and ability to adhere to its tradition of conservative fiscal policy. As mentioned earlier, there is no government-supplied deposit insurance in Hong Kong. In the past, some banks have failed, but government intervention has been officially limited to a policy of accepting or encouraging the takeover or merger of threatened banks by or with stronger ones. However, on September 28, 1983, the Hong Kong government departed from this long-standing policy and took over the Hang Lung Bank. The financial secretary, Sir John Bremridge, explained this action by saying that the Hang Lung Bank's failure and the resulting losses to depositors were unacceptable to the government.

This departure from long-standing policy can be viewed as a threat to fiscal conservatism and a threat of further devaluations because it represents a major change in the categories of public and private liabilities that are potentially claims against the monetary and fiscal reserves of the government. Under the long-standing policy, only Hong Kong currency was a claim against the government's monetary reserves, while bank deposits represented (risky) claims backed by the (risky) loans and investment of the banks. If the government has instituted a new policy of protecting depositors against potential losses, the stream of implicit government obligations has increased substantially. Without tax increases, these extra obligations threaten to impair the funds available for backing the Hong Kong currency. While it might be desirable for other reasons, therefore, the takeover of the Hang Lung Bank is a signal that market participants could readily interpret as portending a weak Hong Kong dollar.

NOTES

1. Except for minor editorial changes, most of this chapter was written during the summer of 1983. The last section, an epilogue, was written after October 15, 1983, when the Hong Kong authorities announced and implemented a shift to a policy of pegging the value of the Hong Kong dollar to that of the U.S. dollar.
2. The government compensates the banks for the cost of issuing and maintaining the stock of currency.
3. Here and elsewhere in this chapter, our descriptions of the Hong Kong

government's strategy rely heavily on Sargent's discussions with various Hong Kong economists in June 1983.

4. In this pure system, the monetary authority can be regarded as acting as a warehouse for foreign currency, always having at least enough foreign-denominated assets to convert its total outstanding stock of notes. In practice, however, many countries' monetary authorities have managed to peg a rate of exchange of domestic currency for foreign currency while holding foreign exchange reserves that are smaller in value than the stock of outstanding domestic notes. Such a system can be administered if the monetary authority has a commitment from the fiscal authority to run prospective government surpluses sufficient to cover the obligations of the monetary authority in the event of a run. We assume that the Hong Kong system is a pure one, which is to say that the monetary branch of the Hong Kong Exchange Fund operates independently of the fiscal branch and cannot expect future government surpluses or deficits either to augment or to impair the funds available to back the currency.

5. This argument rests on the same considerations that led Keynes to write this of France in March 1924 [3, p. xvii]:

> It is often argued that the franc cannot fall in value because France is a wealthy, thrifty and industrious country, or because her balance of trade is *prima facie* satisfactory. This . . . springs from confusion as to the causes which ultimately govern the value of money. A very rich country can have a very bad currency, and a very poor country a very good one. The wealth of France and her balance of trade may render it easier for her authorities to pursue a sound monetary policy. But they are not the same thing. The value of a country's monetary unit is not a function of its wealth or even its trade balance.

6. Consider a mutual fund with h shares outstanding and with initial assets worth f invested in foreign exchange. There are at least two feasible ways that the mutual fund could operate. First, the mutual fund could close, with no new shares to be issued. On the understanding that shareholders are entitled to a pro rata share of the assets, the market could be permitted to determine a price of shares in the mutual fund. Abstracting from fees, the equilibrium price would be f/h. Here the mutual fund would be priced as though it were operating a warehouse for foreign securities. Second, the mutual fund could remain open by offering to sell new shares or redeem existing ones at any fixed price between zero and f/h. Thus, either the mutual fund could fix its supply of outstanding shares h and allow the market to price them or it could set a share price at which it would be willing to issue new shares and invest the proceeds. However, a policy of

offering to sell or redeem new shares at a price to be set by the market, with the proceeds to be invested and available for redeeming shares, would not pin down enough about the mutual fund's policy.

REFERENCES

1. Hong Kong's financial crisis: History, analysis, prescription. 1982. *Asian Monetary Monitor* 6 (November/December): 2–69.
2. Kareken, John, and Neil Wallace. 1981. On the indeterminacy of equilibrium exchange rates. *Quarterly Journal of Economics* 96 (May): 207–22.
3. Keynes, J. M. 1924. Preface to the French edition. In *A tract on monetary reform*. Reprint 1971. In vol. 4 of *The collected writings of John Maynard Keynes*, pp. xvi—xxii. London: Macmillan, St. Martin's Press, for the Royal Economic Society.
4. Sargent, Thomas J., and Neil Wallace. 1982. The real-bills doctrine versus the quantity theory: A reconsideration. *Journal of Political Economy* 90 (December): 1212–36.

Index